STUDIES IN UNITED STATES COMMERCIAL POLICY

STUDIES IN UNITED STATES
COMMERCIAL POLICY

Edited by William B. Kelly, Jr.

Directed by Harry C. Hawkins and John M. Leddy

Chapel Hill

THE UNIVERSITY OF NORTH CAROLINA PRESS

HF
1455
.K43

Preface

This volume is a compilation of studies in United States commercial policy. The studies, except for the last chapter, were selected from a series undertaken by The William L. Clayton Center for International Economic Affairs at The Fletcher School of Law and Diplomacy, Tufts University, with the aid of a grant from The Rockefeller Foundation. Their purpose is to fill a realized need for additional and more specific material in this field for graduate and specialized undergraduate courses.

The studies treat the historic, economic, and political-legal aspects of their subjects with varying emphasis. They assume that the long-run economic gains from freer trade far outweigh the short-run economic losses from adjustments caused by trade, and therefore, that a liberal trade policy is in the over-all national interest and is a desirable objective.

The original studies were not planned as parts of a comprehensive integrated history and analysis of United States commercial policy, but each was intended to stand independently. Consequently, the studies in this volume do not develop the subject in a completely orderly progression nor do they cover the same span of years. However, they are closely related, and with the aid of cross references, they present a useful discussion of the principal subjects of commercial policy. Also, the studies have been edited and updated to take account of recent developments. In this revision, care has been taken to preserve the ideas and treatment of the authors. In some instances, this objective has precluded the addition of, or extensive treatment of, new material.

The research and writing of the original studies were under the direction of Harry C. Hawkins, William L. Clayton Professor of International Economic Affairs Emeritus and former director of the Office of Economic Affairs, United States Department of State, and John M. Leddy, Assistant Secretary of the Treasury and, during the writing of these studies, Visiting Professor of International Economic Relations at The Fletcher School.

The authorship of the studies that comprise the chapters of this volume is as follows: Chapter I, "Antecedents of Present Commercial

Policy, 1922-1934," William B. Kelly, Jr.; Chapter II, "The Legislative Basis of United States Commercial Policy," Harry C. Hawkins and Janet L. Norwood; Chapter III, "The Escape Clause and Peril Points Under the Trade Agreements Program," John M. Leddy and Janet L. Norwood; Chapter IV, "United States Commercial Policy and the Domestic Farm Program," John M. Leddy; Chapter V, "The United Kingdom, the Commonwealth, the Common Market, and the United States," Don D. Humphrey.

Chapter V was not a part of the original project and is not so directly related to United States policy as the others. It replaces a study, "Anglo-American Relations and Imperial Preferences," by John M. Leddy, written before the negotiations relating to the possible accession of the United Kingdom to the European Economic Community. Other major studies that were part of the original project but that are not published here were: "Operation of the General Agreement on Tariffs and Trade," by Raymond Vernon; "United States Commercial Policy and European Economic Integration," by Miriam Camps; and "Buy American Policy," by Bernard Norwood. The Vernon study has been published in somewhat abbreviated form in *International Conciliation;* the essentials of the Camps study are contained in policy memoranda published by the Princeton University Center of International Studies and in papers published by *PEP*; the Norwood study is based on his doctoral dissertation, which is deposited in the Edwin Ginn Library at The Fletcher School.

Publication of this volume was made possible by grants administered by The Trustees of Tufts College, Tufts University, and The Fletcher School of Law and Diplomacy; and by the Ford Foundation under its program for assisting American university presses in the publication of works in the humanities and the social sciences.

WILLIAM B. KELLY, JR.

Washington, D.C.
September, 1962

Contents

STUDIES IN UNITED STATES COMMERCIAL POLICY

CHAPTER I

Antecedents of Present Commercial Policy, 1922-1934

Present United States commercial policy had its origins in the period from 1922 to 1934. During these years the principles upon which current policy is based were formulated and adopted. These principles are non-discrimination, opposition to quantitative restrictions, and negotiated tariff reductions. This chapter is concerned with this policy background and deals with (1) tariff policy in the 1920's and early 1930's; (2) adoption of the unconditional most-favored-nation (MFN) policy; (3) policy in regard to quantitative restrictions; and (4) the reversal of earlier tariff policy.

1. The High, the "Flexible," and the Non-Negotiable Tariff

THE HIGH TARIFF

Maintenance of a high tariff dominated United States commercial policy in the 1920's and early 1930's. This found its expression in the Fordney-McCumber Tariff Act of 1922 and the Hawley-Smoot Act of 1930, which marked a return to the upward movement in the level of the United States tariff since the Civil War.

Before 1860 the United States tariff was relatively moderate. Rates were increased during the Civil War, and they continued to rise during the latter part of the nineteenth and the early part of the twentieth centuries. The only significant deviation from this long-term upward movement was the Underwood-Simmons Act of 1913, in which the Wilson Administration attempted to reverse the direction of United States policy and return to a tariff for revenue only, the traditional position of the Democratic party. World War I and the consequent disruption of trade, however, made this legislation virtually inoperative. The war itself, by reducing or stopping completely the importation of many articles, had a protective effect for many industries that was greater than any previous tariff legislation.

After World War I there was less economic justification for high tariffs than at any time in the nation's history.[1] Almost overnight the

1. This is not to imply that pre-World War I tariff policy was wise. United States protective policy channeled many economic resources into relatively inefficient production.

United States had changed from a debtor to a creditor country. Before World War I and throughout its history, the United States had been a debtor nation, its international financial liabilities in terms of private and government loans and investments being greater than its assets in such terms. An excess of merchandise exports over imports in almost every year since 1874 had enabled it to make the necessary interest, amortization, and dividend payments required by this debtor position.[2] Around the turn of the century, United States loans and investments began to be made abroad, and the debtor position of the United States began to change correspondingly. This trend was greatly accelerated by World War I, when many foreign governments, in order to pay for the war, borrowed huge sums from the United States government, and many United States securities held abroad were liquidated. Between 1914 and 1919 the United States had changed from a net debtor of about $3 billion to a net creditor of around $14 billion.[3]

During the 1920's large private loans and investments were made abroad, enhancing the United States creditor position. Partly as a consequence of these loans and investments, merchandise exports continued to exceed imports. The net capital outflow of United States dollars enabled foreign countries to meet their financial and commercial obligations. The foreign exchange required to meet these obligations might have been earned from shipping services, tourist expenditures, and other invisibles, but such earnings by foreign countries in the 1920's were not large enough for this purpose. When United States loans and investments abroad were sharply curtailed during the stock-market boom of 1929 and when they declined further as the world depression became evident, defaults on foreign financial obligations to the United States resulted.

The changed position of the United States at the end of World War I from a debtor to a creditor suggested lower tariffs. Earnings from financial holdings in the United States, which other countries had used in prewar years to pay for the surplus of United States merchandise exports over imports, no longer existed. The new creditor position even required that interest, amortization, and dividend payments now be made to the United States. Lower United States tariffs should have

---

2. During most years prior to 1874, United States merchandise imports had been greater than exports. This excess of imports over exports was made possible largely by merchant-marine earnings and investments of European capital.

3. Adjustment of the war debts reduced this creditor position to approximately $10 billion. For details regarding the financial relations of the United States during the nineteenth and early twentieth centuries, see National Industrial Conference Board, *The International Financial Position of the United States* (New York: National Industrial Conference Board, Inc., 1929), Chaps. 1-3.

facilitated the payment of the commercial and financial obligations of other countries.[4]

This argument for lower tariffs does not imply that the United States creditor position necessitated a merchandise import surplus. A creditor country may continue with a merchandise export surplus as long as new capital exports exceed foreign interest, amortization, and dividend payments required by previously exported capital. Ultimately, however, when these payments exceed new capital invested abroad, the trade balance of a creditor country must change from an excess of merchandise exports to an excess of imports if these financial obligations are to be met, unless the required foreign exchange is obtained from other sources.[5] This consideration, coupled with the necessity of other countries to pay for the United States merchandise export surplus, suggested a lower tariff policy during the 1920's. Classical freer trade arguments had always been relevant to such a policy.

This discussion makes no attempt to judge the political and moral arguments advocating payment or cancellation of war debts owed the United States, which were a major factor in the United States creditor position. Insistence on payment of these debts, however, argued for the lowering of tariffs, although even under free-trade conditions the very large transfer of resources required by payment would have been most difficult to accomplish.[6]

Not only did the changed position of the United States from a debtor to a creditor suggest a change in tariff policy after World War I, but so did the changed composition of United States foreign trade. Before World War I the United States was primarily an exporter of agri-

4. Lower tariffs and increased United States imports could have produced income and price effects in the United States and abroad that would have worsened rather than improved foreign countries' payments positions vis-à-vis the United States. However, a more likely result would have been that such effects would merely have reduced somewhat the improved payments positions of foreign countries resulting from a reduction in United States tariffs.

This chapter does not discuss to any great extent the balance-of-payments, terms-of-trade, and other effects of tariffs, which are treated thoroughly in any good textbook in international economics. See, for example, Charles P. Kindleberger, *International Economics* (rev. ed.; Homewood, Ill.: Richard D. Irwin, Inc., 1958), Chap. 12.

5. The United States has continued since World War I as a creditor country with an excess of merchandise exports over imports. This was made possible in large part during the 1930's, because of gold shipments to the United States by foreign countries. The merchandise export surplus since World War II has been possible because of huge government grants and loans, and also, in recent years, because of military expenditures and private investments abroad.

6. For a discussion of the problem of the unilateral transfer of resources, see J. M. Keynes, "The German Transfer Problem," and Bertil Ohlin, "The Reparation Problem: A Discussion," republished in *Readings in The Theory of International Trade* (Philadelphia: The Blakiston Company, 1950), pp. 161-69 and 170-78.

cultural products and raw materials. After the war the United States found itself a large producer and exporter of manufactured goods. This change to an exporter of manufactures as well as of agricultural products and raw materials had been taking place gradually before the war, but by 1920 finished and semi-manufactures, other than food-stuffs, comprised half of United States exports compared to less than 30 per cent prior to 1900.[7] Many United States manufactured products were no longer consumed solely or primarily in the home market. Some segments of United States industry as well as of agriculture were now dependent on foreign sales. A lower United States tariff would have facilitated such sales by making it easier for foreigners to earn dollars that could be used to purchase United States exports.

Tariff policy in the 1920's, however, was not responsive to these considerations. As is frequently the case in government policies, there was a long interval between the need for a different policy and the recognition of this need and change in policy.

The following factors were largely responsible for the reversion to a high-tariff policy in the 1920's: (1) the return to power of the Republican party, (2) depressed agricultural prices, (3) fear of foreign competition resulting from depreciated currencies, (4) demand for protection of "war babies," (5) logrolling, and (6) nationalist and isolationist sentiment.

Traditionally the Republican party has been identified with a high tariff, the Democratic party with a low tariff. The line between them, however, has by no means been a sharp one.[8] The Democratic party has never advocated free trade; the Republican party has not favored the exclusion of imports. The tariff idea has been accepted generally by both parties. Controversy has centered around the height of duties and what goods should be dutiable.

In the election of 1920 the Republicans returned to power in the White House and increased further their Congressional majorities of 1918. Their fifty-eight senators and three hundred representatives gave them substantial control of both Houses. The party platform of 1920

7. U.S. Dept. of Commerce, Bureau of Foreign and Domestic Commerce, *Statistical Abstract of the United States*, 1922, p. 354.

8. It is most difficult to distinguish between the tariff positions of the two parties today. The swing toward more liberal trade policies by internationalists in the Republican party and the swing away from liberal trade policies by southern conservatives in the Democratic party have resulted in similar views on tariff matters. The 1956 and 1960 political plat-forms of the two parties, for example, had little to distinguish between them with regard to the parties' general positions on international trade. See Kirk H. Porter and Donald Bruce Johnson, *National Party Platforms*, 1840-1956 (Urbana, Ill.: The University of Illinois Press, 1956), pp. 527 and 557; *The Rights of Man*, The Democratic Platform, July 12, 1960, pp. 9-10; and *Building a Better America*, Republican Platform, 1960, July 27, 1960, p. 9.

had pledged "a revision of the tariff as soon as conditions shall make it necessary for the preservation of the home market for American labor, agriculture and industry."[9] Even though the tariff had not played a major part in the campaign, a return to traditional high-tariff policy, interrupted by the Wilson Administrations, was to be expected.

The conditions to make a revision of the tariff "necessary" soon developed. United States agricultural production during World War I, as in World War II, had been greatly expanded to take care of increased wartime demand. After the cessation of hostilities and the return of European agricultural output to prewar levels, world-wide overproduction of agricultural products resulted. In the postwar economic slump of 1920-1921, agricultural prices suffered more than others. During the war and postwar boom wholesale prices of farm products rose less than those of all commodities, but in the 1920-1921 depression they fell more than those of all commodities.[10] The average monthly farm price of wheat fell from a high of $2.58 to a low of $.93 per bushel; cotton from $.38 to $.09 per pound; and corn from $1.86 to $.41 per bushel.[11] Between 1919 and 1921 exports of agricultural products shrank by $1.9 billion or by almost 50 per cent.[12]

The farmer did not understand fully the reason for the drastic price declines. His representatives in Congress, eager to do something, turned to the tariff as a remedy. President Harding in a message to Congress on April 12, 1921, urged "instant tariff enactment, emergency in character and understood by our people that it is for the emergency only."[13] He said that "to-day American agriculture is menaced . . . through the influx of foreign farm products, because we offer, essentially unprotected, the best market in the world."[14]

The Emergency Tariff Act of 1921, imposing high duties upon about forty agricultural products, including wheat, apples, pork, and other export items, was passed quickly during a special session of Congress.[15] This measure was enacted for six months, but it was later extended indefinitely; and it remained in effect until 1922, when permanent legislation in the form of the Fordney-McCumber Act was passed.

A general tariff revision such as the Tariff Act of 1922 had not been

9. Porter and Johnson, *National Party Platforms*, p. 235.

10. Derived from Table No. 358, *Statistical Abstract*, 1921, p. 629.

11. *Statistical Abstract*, 1920 and 1921, pp. 582 and 634, respectively.

12. Derived from Table No. 502, *Statistical Abstract*, 1924, p. 584.

13. U.S. Dept. of State, *Papers Relating to the Foreign Relations of the United States*, 1921, Vol. I, p. ix.

14. *Ibid*.

15. Even before the new Administration took office, the Republican lame-duck Congress had passed an equivalent measure, which President Wilson vetoed on his last day in office.

contemplated by the Administration at this time. Currency instability and disrupted economic conditions in Europe and elsewhere made it seem desirable to postpone such a revision to a time when the effect of tariff rates on trade was more ascertainable. However, in January, 1921, before the Emergency Tariff Act was passed and even before the new Administration took office, tariff hearings on permanent legislation had begun in the House Ways and Means Committee.

Currency instability abroad, which in large part was the basis of the new Administration's desire to postpone further tariff legislation, caused many domestic producers to urge immediate legislation. They feared that depreciated foreign currencies would enable foreign producers to undersell them drastically in the United States market, and they wanted protection from such exchange dumping. Actually, in most cases there was little basis for this fear, because foreign prices tended to rise rapidly either before or shortly after exchange-rate depreciations. But this fear existed, nevertheless.

Demand also arose at this time for protection of "war babies," industries with war-stimulated production of goods that formerly had been imported. It was feared that once European production of these items was resumed, imports would replace domestic production unless tariff protection were provided. In many cases it was claimed that maintenance of domestic production was necessary for defense.

The Tariff Act of 1922 incorporated for the most part the high agricultural duties of the 1921 legislation and added manufactured goods to its scope of protection. Industrial rates were raised indiscriminately with little regard as to whether an industry was related to preparedness for war. For example, duties on painted chinaware went up to 70 per cent; costume jewelry to 80 per cent; and laces to 90 per cent. "The outcome was a tariff with rates higher than any in the long series of protective measures."[16] The average rate on free and dutiable products under the Tariff Act of 1922 was more than 50 per cent higher than that under the 1913 Underwood Tariff.[17]

16. F. W. Taussig, *The Tariff History of the United States* (8th ed.; New York: G. P. Putnam's Sons, 1931), p. 453. This chapter has benefited from this standard reference work on the history of United States tariff acts.

17. A common method of comparing tariff levels resulting from different legislative acts is by calculating the average of annual average rates of duty under these acts. This is done by dividing total duties collected by total valuation of all imports for each year that a tariff act remains in effect and then computing the average of these annual average rates of duty. This method can be very misleading. Changes in the prices of imports, which affect the ad valorem equivalent of specific rates of duty, and changes in the composition of imports distort such average-rate comparisons. Also, prohibitive tariffs have a zero average rate of duty, hardly reflecting their true incidence. Any average-rate comparison of the level of the Underwood Act is further complicated by the disruption of

Because of the logrolling process of Congressional tariff making, a general upward revision of industrial rates was almost sure to follow the raising of agricultural rates in the Emergency Tariff Act of 1921. In the 1921 legislation the representatives of the agricultural areas committed themselves to a policy of high protection, and the representatives of the manufacturing areas voted them virtually everything they asked. When the permanent legislation was considered, the farmer's representatives were no longer in a position to exert a moderating influence on the rates on manufactured goods as they had done in the past. The Democrats, the other political group traditionally opposed to higher tariffs, were not only hopelessly outnumbered but some had yielded to the agricultural pressure.

Underlying this upward revision of the tariff was a postwar wave of nationalist sentiment. It expressed itself in a desire for economic self-sufficiency—sometimes for reasons of defense, sometimes for insulation against the economic instability of other countries after the war, but frequently without any explicable reason.

Coupled with economic nationalism was a desire to return to the political isolation of the nineteenth century. Rejection of the Covenant of the League of Nations by the Senate reflected this attitude.[18] It is difficult to relate economic and political factors of this kind to the high tariff rates of the 1920's, but they clearly had a significant influence.

The purpose of the Emergency Tariff Act of 1921, as it has been indicated, was to help the farmer, since prices of agricultural products had fallen more sharply than others during the 1920-1921 depression. It was widely believed that a tariff could raise the prices of agricultural products. The Tariff Commission, reporting in 1922 on the effects of the Emergency Tariff Act of 1921, however, found no correlation between its enactment and price recovery. It noted that the price decline and recovery affected all agricultural products similarly whether they were on the emergency list or not. In practically no case did prices rise im-

trade during World War I. Nevertheless, it is safe to say that the level of the tariff under the Act of 1922 was very much higher than that of 1913, without attempting to say exactly how much higher.

For a discussion of the weakness of averages as an indication of tariff levels, see U.S. Tariff Commission, *The Tariff and Its History*, Misc. Ser., 1934, pp. 107-8.

For a discussion of even greater difficulties in comparing international tariff levels, see U.S. Congress, House Committee on Ways and Means, Subcommittee on Foreign Trade Policy, *Foreign Trade Policy*, Compendium of Papers on United States Foreign Trade Policy, 1957, pp. 225-29.

18. Isolationist sentiment was sometimes carried to ridiculous extremes. Mail from the League of Nations, for example, was not even opened by the Department of State during the first months of the Harding Administration.

mediately after the passage of the Act, and when recovery began in the fall of 1921, price response of a commodity was not related to its being dutiable.[19] On products of which the United States produces an export surplus, this lack of correlation between domestic prices and the imposition of a tariff could, of course, have been expected. The general effect of the tariff legislation of 1921-1922 as far as the farmer was concerned was to curtail his foreign markets and to increase the prices that he had to pay for both foreign and domestic products. During debate on the 1922 Act, Representative Hayden (D., Ariz.) clearly recognized the consequences of this legislation for the farmer. He said:

> An examination of the facts will demonstrate that the presence of many of the items in schedule 7 [agriculture] can be explained in no other way than that they represent an attempt to fool the farmers and swindle the stockmen into the belief that they will get enough benefit out of this bill to fully compensate them for the higher prices that they must pay for all the manufactured goods upon which high protective or even prohibitive duties are levied in this measure.
>
> *   *   *   *   *   *   *   *   *   *   *
>
> . . . time will soon disclose the utter futility of attempting by a tariff to boost the price of wheat or corn or short-staple cotton and the numerous other farm and range products where the importations are negligible and the surplus must be sold abroad.[20]

Agriculture remained in a relatively depressed state throughout the 1920's, and a net shift of hundreds of thousands of people from farm to city occurred.[21] At no time was the farmer's purchasing power comparable to the prewar period.

With some exceptions industry revived and flourished.[22] Prosperity was attributed to the tariff and the home market that it had created. President Coolidge stated the views of many when he said that "the towering stature of our industrial structure" was a complete vindication of the policy of conserving "to the American product first opportunity in the American market."[23] The protected home market was widely ac-

19. U.S. Tariff Commission, *Report on the Emergency Tariff Act of May 27, 1921,* rev. ed., 1922, p. 1. See also U.S. Tariff Commission, *Sixth Annual Report,* 1922, p. 30.

20. U.S. *Congressional Record,* 67th Cong., 1st Sess., Vol. LXI Pt. 4 (July 14, 1921), pp. 3835 and 3840.

21. This historical population movement away from the farm continues today, not only in percentage of farm population compared to total population but also, since 1916, in actual numbers of farm population. Domestic price supports, export subsidies, and other government measures designed to help the farmer have not reversed this long-run population movement.

22. Exceptions included textiles, shoes, shipbuilding, and coal.

23. Address before a group of textile manufacturers reported by *The New York Times,* September 13, 1925.

cepted as an adequate basis for United States prosperity by both manufacturers and farmers alike, even though important segments of United
States industry depended upon export markets and even though the
position of the farmer was anything but prosperous.

There was little recognition of the relationship between the United
States economy and economic conditions elsewhere. Exceptional was the
1929 Report of the President's Conference on Unemployment, which
noted that foreign conditions had not been too favorable to United States
business and had been eminently unfavorable to United States agriculture.
It said that important branches of industry had enjoyed a large increase in
foreign sales, "but had Europe been prosperous, American prosperity
would have been less 'spotty' and more intense."[24] General failure during
the 1920's to see any connection between national economies is one of
the reasons for the depression of the 1930's. Continued failure to see
this connection explains, in part at least, the prolonged period of this
depression.

The same conditions arguing for lower rather than higher tariffs at
the end of World War I continued to apply with increasing urgency
throughout the 1920's. The Tariff Act of 1930, however, brought no
change in United States tariff policy. It simply reaffirmed and reinforced
the high protective principle of the Tariff Act of 1922 by raising duties
even higher. In 1930, as in 1922, tariff policy did not reflect the needs
of the times. A more realistic tariff response to the changed position of
the United States after World War I was to be postponed for several
more years.

The Tariff Act of 1930 was not only as economically unjustifiable as
the Act of 1922 but it was less explicable. Many of the factors that
accounted for the Tariff Act of 1922 were absent in 1929, when Congress
began to consider tariff revision. The 1928 election had not produced
a political overturn as had occurred in 1920; the country, generally
speaking, was at the top of an economic boom instead of in a depression;
foreign currencies had been stabilized; the "war babies" were adequately
protected; and some of the extreme nationalist and isolationist sentiment
of the early 1920's had subsided.

The Act of 1930 even more than the Act of 1922 was largely a
consequence of logrolling. Its legislative history is similar to that of
its predecessor. The Republican party platform in the election of 1928
pledged, as it had in 1920, a revision of the tariff to preserve the home

24. National Bureau of Economic Research, *Recent Economic Changes in the United States,* Report of the Committee on Recent Economic Changes of the President's Conference on Unemployment (New York: McGraw-Hill Book Company, Inc., 1929), II, 883-84.

market.[25] President Hoover in 1929 called, as did President Harding in 1921, a special session of Congress to consider a limited revision of the tariff to help the farmer, whose position continued in a depressed state.[26] Congressional action on this "limited" revision took, as it had in the earlier "limited" revision, more than a year and a half. A general tariff revision, raising rates on agricultural and industrial products alike, again resulted.[27]

The Tariff Act of 1930 is a classic example of the logrolling process in Congressional tariff making and of the difficulty of a limited tariff revision by the Congress. Local pressures tend to preclude either objective or limited Congressional action on tariff rates.[28]

The Tariff Act of 1930 was not motivated by the onset of the great depression. Although this legislation did not become law until June of 1930, public hearings were announced by the House Ways and Means Committee as early as December, 1928, in anticipation of a general tariff revision. This was three months before President Hoover convened a special session of Congress to consider a "limited" revision. By the end of May, 1929, the original bill had been passed by the House of Representatives. At the time of the stock-market crash in October, Senate consideration was well under way. This legislation was initiated, and the scope and extent of the tariff revisions it was to make were evident long before the depression began.

In many instances the Tariff Act of 1930 had no effect on the domestic market because many of its increased rates were redundant. Higher rates on those agricultural products of which the United States produced an export surplus did not help the farmer any more than did the existing high rates of the Tariff Act of 1922. Similarly, many of the increased rates on manufactured goods were superfluous. In those import-competing industries amply protected by the 1922 legislation, little further displacement of imports could result from higher tariffs. The often-cited petition of a thousand economists, urging President Hoover to veto

25. The platform of 1920, however, envisaged a general tariff revision, while the platform of 1928 contemplated only a revision of schedules "where necessary." See Porter and Johnson, *National Party Platforms,* pp. 235 and 282.

26. President Hoover also included manufacturing industries that were severely depressed in his request for a limited revision.

27. Technically speaking, the Emergency Tariff Act of 1921 was a limited tariff revision because it raised rates only on agricultural products. Consideration and passage of this Act, however, is so involved with the comprehensive Tariff Act of 1922 (which incorporated most of the rates in the 1921 legislation) that these two acts should be considered together, as related steps in a general tariff revision, rather than as separate legislation.

28. For an account of the logrolling incident to the Tariff Act of 1930, see E. E. Schattschneider, *Politics, Pressures, and the Tariff* (New York: Prentice-Hall, Inc., 1935).

the Hawley-Smoot Act, pointed out that over 96 per cent of the manufactured goods consumed in the United States were already being supplied by domestic producers. However, higher duties may have increased monopolistic prices and profits. They may also have contributed to the improvement in the United States terms of trade that occurred after 1929; that is, Hawley-Smoot may have improved the relationship between United States export and import prices by causing the prices of imports (before duties) to be lower than otherwise.[29]

In its effect on exports, the Tariff Act of 1930 was more harmful to agriculture and industry than the Act of 1922. Foreign resentment of this measure was far greater than it had been of the 1922 legislation. The Act of 1922 had been passed in a period when prosperity was on the rise and when large loans and investments forthcoming from the United State cushioned the impact abroad of a high-tariff policy. At the time of the Tariff Act of 1930, however, capital movements out of the United States were curtailed, and many countries were already feeling the results of the developing world depression.

By August of 1929 communications had been received from twenty-four countries protesting the proposed tariff revision. After the Act was passed, retaliatory higher duties and, in many cases, discriminatory duties were levied against United States exports at a time when the depression made exports more essential than ever.[30] Furthermore, the Act encouraged the expansion of the British preferential system in the 1932 Ottawa Agreements, and it gave impetus to discriminatory bilateral trade balancing everywhere.[31]

The Tariff Act of 1930 probably deepened and prolonged the depression. It contributed to the drastic shrinkage of United States exports by inducing foreign retaliation and by continuing to limit foreign dollar earnings. Between 1929 and 1933 the value of United States exports fell by almost 70 per cent. Much of this decline in value was caused by prices that fell by nearly 40 per cent.[32] It is significant that the United

29. See Don D. Humphrey, *American Imports* (New York: The Twentieth Century Fund, 1955), p. 53.

30. For a study of the foreign reaction to the Hawley-Smoot Tariff Act, see Joseph M. Jones, Jr., *Tariff Retaliation: Repercussions of the Hawley-Smoot Bill* (Philadelphia: University of Pennsylvania Press, 1934).

31. This does not mean that there was a direct causal relationship between the Hawley-Smoot Tariff Act and foreign restrictive and discriminatory trade measures. Frequently these measures were imposed for other reasons, with Hawley-Smoot used as their justification. However, the importance of Hawley-Smoot in this connection should not be minimized.

32. These 1929 and 1933 export value and price statistics are derived from indexes published in *Statistical Abstract*, 1934, p. 404.

States share of world exports also fell—by about a third or from 16 per cent in 1929 to 11 per cent in 1933.[33]

Two years after the passage of the Hawley-Smoot Act United States high-tariff policy was reaffirmed again in the Revenue Act of 1932, which imposed excise taxes on imports of petroleum and petroleum products, coal, lumber, and copper and materials containing copper. Except in name these excise taxes on imports, which subsequently have been imposed on a few other products, are tariffs. They are levied, assessed, collected, and paid in the same manner as customs duties.

THE "FLEXIBLE" TARIFF

The principle upon which the high rates of the Tariff Acts of 1922 and 1930 were based was the equalization of foreign and domestic costs of production. This principle was stated in Section 315 of the Tariff Act of 1922, one of the so-called flexible provisions. Section 315 provided "that in order to regulate the foreign commerce of the United States and to put into force and effect the policy of the Congress by this Act intended," the President could raise or lower rates of duty prescribed in the Act by 50 per cent whenever he determined after investigation by the Tariff Commission that this was necessary to equalize differences in costs of production between the United States and the principal competing foreign country.[34]

A tariff to equalize production costs had been advocated by protectionists for many years. As early as 1904 the Republican party platform in advocating protection of industry stated that "the measure of protection should always at least equal the difference in the cost of production at home and abroad."[35] In the 1908 Republican platform the

33. Derived from U.S. Dept. of Commerce, Bureau of Foreign and Domestic Commerce, *Foreign Commerce Yearbook,* 1935, p. 373.

34. Sections 315, 316, and 317 are referred to as the flexible provisions of the Tariff Act of 1922.

Section 316 authorized the President to impose additional duties of from 10 per cent to 50 per cent ad valorem, or to exclude from entry into the United States products that he found were being imported under conditions of unfair competition. The purpose of Section 316 was to extend to import trade penalties against unfair methods of competition similar to those applied to interstate commerce by the Federal Trade Commission Act. Section 316 was to supplement the Antidumping Act of 1921, which was not considered comprehensive enough for this purpose.

Section 317 authorized the President to impose new or additional duties up to 50 per cent ad valorem or its equivalent, or under certain conditions to exclude from entry into the United States products from any country that he found was discriminating against United States exports. Section 317, although never applied, has significance in regard to the adoption by the United States in 1923 of an unconditional most-favored-nation policy. It will be discussed shortly in this connection.

35. Porter and Johnson, *National Party Platforms,* p. 138. Even earlier both parties'

equalization of production costs was said to be "the true principle of protection."[36] It was not until 1922, however, that this idea was embodied in United States legislation.

The idea of having a tariff commission make investigations of rates also was not new. Since 1865 various nonpermanent agencies had been created to investigate questions relating to the tariff.[37] In the elections of 1912 and 1916 many politicians favored the establishment of a permanent nonpartisan tariff commission to take the tariff out of politics and make it more scientific. Because of pressures from constituents and the extended periods of time involved, Congressional tariff making had become less and less popular among legislators. The present commission was established in 1916, but its authority was limited to the making of studies. It had no power to make recommendations on tariff rates such as that which was given the commission in the Tariff Act of 1922.

Section 315, therefore, combined the long-advocated and highly protectionist cost-equalization principle with Tariff Commission investigations that were supposed to make the tariff more scientific and less political. The circumstances that led to the inclusion of Section 315 in the 1922 legislation, however, were related only incidentally to either of these considerations.

Because of unstable world conditions in the immediate postwar period, the fixing of permanent tariff rates that would be neither inadequate nor excessive in relation to the principle of cost equalization was regarded as very difficult. The Tariff Act of 1921 was passed as a temporary emergency measure because no permanent legislation was favored by the Administration at that time. But when Congress also took up the matter of a general tariff revision in 1921, President Harding, prompted by continued world instability, sent a message to Congress on December 6, 1921, expressing the hope that "flexibility and elasticity" could be inserted into this revision, "so that rates may be adjusted to meet unusual and changing conditions which cannot be accurately anticipated."[38] He thought that the way to effect this flexibility was through

---

platforms had referred to the equalization of labor costs. In 1892 the Republican party platform stated that "on all imports coming into competition with the products of American labor, there should be levied duties equal to the difference between wages abroad and at home" (p. 93). The Democratic party's platforms of 1884 and 1888 contained, essentially, this same idea of equalizing foreign and domestic wages (pp. 66 and 78).

36. *Ibid.*, p. 158.

37. Nonpermanent agencies were created in 1865, 1866, 1882, 1888, 1909, and 1912. See U.S. Tariff Commission, *The Tariff and Its History*, pp. 97-99.

38. *Foreign Relations*, 1921, Vol. I, p. xxv.

"the extension of the powers of the Tariff Commission, so that it can adapt itself to a scientific and wholly just administration of the law."[39]

Flexibility was also favored by the Administration because of the fear of possible political consequences if the high rates of the Act of 1922 should prove to be excessive, i.e., if they should prove to be higher than necessary to equalize foreign and domestic production costs. Before the President's Message, William S. Culbertson, a member of the Tariff Commission and originator of Section 315 and the other flexible provisions, sent a memorandum, dated October 28, 1921, to President Harding urging flexibility in the new tariff law. He pointed out that "the tariff is notorious for causing political difficulties for parties in power" and that consideration should be given to how to "avoid in the pending tariff legislation the consequences which followed upon the enactment of the McKinley and Payne-Aldrich laws."[40]   Culbertson then suggested that "the economic and political difficulties which seem certain to follow" could be avoided "by introducing flexibility and elasticity into the new tariff law," so that rates could be adjusted to meet conditions that could not then be anticipated.[41]

Section 315 was a compromise measure introduced into the 1922 legislation as the result of disagreement between the Senate and the House over valuation provisions. The House originally passed the Fordney Bill with a provision for a change in the basis of assessing ad valorem duties from "foreign" to "American" valuation, i.e., from the wholesale price of goods in the country of export to the wholesale price of similar competitive goods produced in the United States. The uncertainty and variability of foreign prices were cited to support such a change, but its effect would have been to increase greatly the duties collected. Republican leaders became as concerned about the political effects of such a high valuation basis as they were about the high rates passed by the House. On November 28, 1921, at a White House meeting attended by the President, Secretary of Commerce Hoover, Senator Smoot (R., Ut.), and all the members of the Tariff Commission, possible substitute measures for the House valuation provision were discussed. Subsequently, Senator Smoot introduced Section 315 (along with the other flexible provisions) as an amendment to the Fordney Bill passed by the House.[42]   Section 315 met the objection of foreign price instability

39. *Ibid.*

40. U.S. Congress, Senate Select Committee on Investigation of the Tariff Commission, *Hearings,* 69th Cong., 1st Sess., 1926-1928, Pt. 5, p. 629.

41. *Ibid.*

42. Regarding this White House conference and the origins of Section 315, see the testimony of Tariff Commissioners Page, Costigan, and Culbertson, *ibid.*, Pt. 1, pp. 39-45; Pt. 3, pp. 257-59; and Pt. 5, pp. 628-32.

by allowing the President to adjust rates, "so that the rates may at all times conform to existing conditions."[43]

The flexibility of Section 315 did not make the tariff as scientific as some of its supporters had hoped. The principle of foreign and domestic cost equalization as a scientific basis for setting rates has both theoretical and practical weaknesses.

Many supporters of Section 315 did not understand that equalization of foreign and domestic production costs is the antithesis of international trade. Trade is based largely on cost differences. Tariffs designed to equalize costs would stop all trade except in those items where prestige value, special design, or some other feature is paramount irrespective of cost considerations. Senator Underwood (D., Ala.), whose name is associated with the 1913 tariff law, was one of the members of Congress who clearly recognized this connection between trade and cost differences. During the Senate debate on Section 315 he said that the equalization of production costs would "cut off all importations of commodities that the manufacturing interests of the United States are able to make in sufficient quantities to supply the demand of the home market."[44]

Unflinching application of cost equalization would encourage the domestic production of everything, no matter how costly such production might be. In *The Wealth of Nations* Adam Smith remarks that "by means of glasses, hotbeds, and hotwalls, very good grapes can be raised in Scotland, and very good wine too can be made of them at about thirty times the expence for which at least equally good can be brought from foreign countries."[45] Similarly, tropical products, now imported, could be grown in the United States if duties on these items were high enough.

Most protectionists do not advocate going this far, but in the Senate debate on Section 315 there was a real question as to where to draw the line. Senator Gooding (R., Id.) said that he would stop at tea, but Senator Stanfield (R., Ore.) said that he would stop only "when the

43. U.S. Congress, Senate Committee on Finance, *Report* to accompany H.R. 7456, 67th Cong., 2nd Sess., Rep. No. 595, April 10, 1922, p. 3; "American" valuation was discarded ultimately as the basis of customs valuation except for coal-tar products. If, however, under Section 315 the President should find that differences in foreign and domestic costs of production could not be equalized by raising or lowering duties within the 50 per cent limitation, then "American" valuation, or American selling price, as it was designated in the 1922 legislation, was to be used for valuation purposes.

44. U.S. *Congressional Record,* 67th Cong., 2nd Sess., Vol. LXII, Pt. 11 (August 11, 1922), p. 11207.

45. Adam Smith, *The Wealth of Nations,* Modern Library Edition (New York: Random House, Inc., 1937), p. 425.

rate is so high that it is not necessary to equalize the difference in the cost of production in this country and abroad."[46] Stanfield indicated that it would make no difference if this rate were as high as 5,000 per cent.[47] There is no logical stopping point once the principle of cost equalization is accepted.[48]

Even if Section 315 had been based on sound theory, its administration was not practicable. Between 1922 and 1929 more than six-hundred applications covering approximately 375 commodities were filed with the Tariff Commission. That only forty-seven investigations covering 55 commodities were completed is indicative of administrative difficulties.[49]

Problems such as joint costs in connection with by-products make computation of the cost of production for a particular product, even by a single producer, most difficult. Comparable cost information for producers in a domestic industry is still more difficult to calculate. It is virtually impossible to obtain comparable cost statistics abroad. Relatively uniform methods of accounting are practiced in the United States, but this is not usually the case in foreign countries. Not only do cost-accounting systems abroad differ among the various foreign countries but also among industries in the same country and among producers in the same industry.

Even if cost information were standardized, every producer would have different production costs for the same product. Which producer's costs should be used as the cost of production for a particular product? Should an average of producers' costs in an industry be taken? Should this average be weighted for large and small producers? How should differences in the articles produced be taken into account? Should transportation costs be included? If so, from what source of supply? To what market? Even if questions such as these were decided arbitrarily and a large staff of accountants and investigators finally arrived at some sort of representative statistics, would not such information be out of date by the time such a necessarily time-consuming investigation were

46. U.S. *Congressional Record*, 67th Cong., 2nd Sess., Vol. LXII, Pt. 11 (August 17, 1922), p. 11475.

47. *Ibid.*

48. Section 315 applied only to dutiable goods, so that the growing of such duty-free items as tropical fruits was not to be protected via cost equalization. Application of the cost-equalization principle to the production of dutiable manufactured products, however, was comparable to such protection, because in some cases industries that were to be protected were no more efficient, relatively, than would-be growers of tropical fruits.

49. U.S. Tariff Commission, *Thirteenth Annual Report*, 1929, p. 10. For an account by the Tariff Commission of administrative difficulties encountered in connection with Section 315, see the following *Annual Reports* of the Tariff Commission: *Eighth*, 1924, pp. 8-9; *Ninth*, 1925, pp. 16-18; *Tenth*, 1926, pp. 14-16; *Eleventh*, 1927, pp. 4-8; *Twelfth*, 1928, pp. 9-13; and *Thirteenth*, 1929, pp. 17-23.

completed? In 1910 President Taft in a public letter to the Chairman of the National Congressional Republican Committee wrote:

. . . The difficulty in fixing the proper tariff rates in accord with the principle [equalization of costs] stated in the Republican platform [of 1908], is in securing reliable evidence as to the difference between the cost of production at home and the cost of production abroad. . . . when we understand that the cost of production differs in one country abroad from that in another, and that it changes from year to year and from month to month, we must realize that the precise difference in cost of production sought for is not capable of definite ascertainment, and that all that even the most scientific person can do in his investigation is, after consideration of many facts which he learns, to exercise his best judgment in reaching a conclusion.[50]

Cost of production is a meaningful term only when it is applied to a specific producer at a particular time, and even then it may be difficult to calculate. It cannot be applied meaningfully in a general sense such as is required in the tariff acts.[51]

Furthermore, there is no reason to expect that foreign producers or their governments would give readily the type of co-operation required to carry out the kind of cost investigations necessary under Section 315. In fact, they were very reluctant to give this type of co-operation. Tariff Commission representatives sent abroad for this purpose had only limited success and caused much friction. Foreign data was obtained in only 49 of the 83 cost-of-production investigations conducted under Section 315.[52] The French in particular objected to foreign agents' requesting access to records from which French tax collectors themselves were barred. The attitude of French businessmen, reflecting that of other nationalities, was that these investigations were being conducted "in order that the American tariff can be adjusted in such a way that any advantage reaped by a foreign producer through cheaper labor, cheaper raw materials, or cheaper methods of manufacture may be counterbalanced by the tariff rate adopted in the United States."[53] It is not surprising that investigations based on such a predilection were resented.[54]

50. Quoted by the *Journal of Commerce and Commercial Bulletin* (New York), August 29, 1910. Reproduced in John Day Larkin, *The President's Control of the Tariff* (Cambridge, Mass.: Harvard University Press, 1936), p. 104.

51. For a short theoretical analysis illustrating the meaninglessness of cost equalization as a basis for tariff making, see Charles P. Kindleberger, *International Economics* (Homewood, Ill.: Richard D. Irwin, Inc., 1953), pp. 187-88.

52. U.S. Tariff Commission, *Thirteenth Annual Report*, 1929, p. 18.

53. *Foreign Relations*, 1925, Vol. I, p. 225.

54. Representatives of the U.S. Treasury Department met with similar opposition in conducting foreign market-value investigations required by the valuation provisions of the

F. W. Taussig, noted Harvard economist and first chairman of the Tariff Commission, in discussing the administrative practicability of Section 315, concluded by saying that "those who advocated this as a 'scientific' solution of the tariff question were obsessed by formula and surprisingly unable to face the realities."[55]

Also, the flexibility of Section 315 did not take the tariff out of politics. Assignment of the investigatory function of Section 315 to the Tariff Commission simply transferred some of the politics from the Congress to the commission.

The Tariff Commission, which is frequently referred to as a nonpartisan body, is actually bipartisan, and as such, it is necessarily subject to political influences. Throughout the commission's history, law has required that no more than three of its six members be of the same political party. In practice this has meant that its membership has been composed of three Democrats and three Republicans.

When the Tariff Commission was established in 1916, it was for the purpose of making the tariff less subject to political maneuvering. The commission was to make tariff studies and to publicize them. In this way it was hoped that a better tariff, a more scientific one, would be legislated by the Congress. In Section 315 an entirely new set of responsibilities, almost equivalent to the fixing of rates, was given to the commission. Although the President had the final authority in deciding upon rate adjustments under Section 315, it was assumed that his role would be a formality, that he would simply proclaim the rates scientifically determined and recommended by the commission. The commission itself was divided on the wisdom of its changed function, but President Harding advocated it.[56]

Of prime importance to the proper functioning of the Tariff Commission in its new role was that it be completely objective, recommending rate adjustments almost automatically on the basis of the cost information available to it. However, cost determination is so vague and imprecise that the tariff views of the individual commissioners were almost certain to emerge, and they did. Given the impossible "scientific" function imposed on the commission by Section 315, it would have been most dif-

---

Tariff Act of 1922. Despite the threat of exclusion from the United States of the products of producers who refused to allow inspection of their books, many producers declined to co-operate. An attempt in 1925 to obtain from foreign governments diplomatic recognition of Treasury representatives in order to facilitate their investigatory functions met with almost universal failure. See *Foreign Relations*, 1925, Vol. I, pp. 211-54.

55. Taussig, *Tariff History of the United States*, p. 481. Professor Taussig discusses the theoretical weaknesses of foreign and domestic cost equalization in *Free Trade, the Tariff and Reciprocity* (New York: The Macmillan Co., 1920), pp. 134-41.

56. See above, pp. 15-16.

ficult to have had an objective commission even if its membership had been nonpartisan.

Furthermore, appointments to the Tariff Commission after 1922 were based on the views of the appointee rather than on open-mindedness, ability, and training. Commissioners Burgess and Marvin, for example, were recognized high-tariff lobbyists at the time of their appointment. In addition, a conscious attempt was made to influence the holdover appointees of the Wilson Administration. President Coolidge, for example, subtly tried to impress upon Commissioner Culbertson the importance of devoting most of the commission's time to cases involving duty increases rather than reductions. The President put it this way: "If a man is drowning he needs immediate help, but if he merely needs a bath he can wait until Saturday night."[57] Culbertson, the driving force behind a nonpolitical, scientific tariff, was provided in 1925 with a graceful exit from the commission as minister to Rumania. Commissioner Lewis, holding similar views, was not handled with the same consideration. The President simply asked as a condition of his reappointment in 1924 that he sign an undated resignation that might be used at the President's discretion. He refused and received only a recess appointment, which expired six months later. Mr. Costigan, the remaining Wilson appointee, continued his opposition to many of the rate increases until 1928, when he resigned. By 1926 the commission that was to take the tariff out of politics had become so political that a Congressional investigation was held. The Senate investigating committee held "that the commission as a body was not functioning in an impartial or quasi judicial manner as we believe it was the intention of Congress that it should function."[58] The Tariff Act of 1930 abruptly cut off the terms of office of all the existing commissioners, and it empowered the President to set up an entirely new body, reappointing incumbents or not as he saw fit. Aside from this personnel reorganization, however, the function of the commission remained essentially the same.

Despite the extreme protective principle of cost equalization upon which rate changes under Section 315 were to be based, this provision, as has been indicated, was introduced for the purpose of lowering the high rates of the Tariff Act of 1922 that might prove excessive. It was clearly the intent of the framers of Section 315 that it would operate to reduce rather than to raise duties. Senator Smoot, who was closely associ-

57. Quoted from a letter of Culbertson to William Allen White, July 25, 1924, published in Select Committee on Investigation of the Tariff Commission, *Hearings*, Pt. 5, p. 721.

58. U.S. Congress, Senate Select Committee on Investigation of the United States Tariff Commission, *Report*, 70th Cong., 1st Sess., Rep. No. 1325, 1928, p. 4.

ated with the framing of this provision and who introduced it into the 1922 legislation, said in a speech on the Senate floor that he thought that there would be "many many more occasions" when the President would exercise his authority "in lowering rates than in increasing them," and if conditions became normal, he expected that the President would lower "the majority of rates."[59]   In the relatively few instances when action was taken, however, Presidents Harding and Coolidge used Section 315 to raise duties.   Between 1922 and 1929, thirty-three of the thirty-eight changes that were made were increases.   Only the duties on millfeeds, live quail, paintbrush handles, cresylic acid, and phenol were reduced.[60]

Section 315 of the Tariff Act of 1922 was retained without significant changes as Section 336 of the Tariff Act of 1930.[61]   Section 336 emphasizes the role of the Tariff Commission rather than that of the President, attempts to define more clearly what is meant by cost of production, and provides a formula for computing cost of production if it is not otherwise ascertainable, but it does not alter the theoretical and practical objections to the concept.   In 1930, unlike in 1922, protectionists rather than moderates supported this flexible-tariff idea.

President Hoover, who as Secretary of Commerce between 1921 and 1928 had been one of the most farsighted public officials in tariff matters, supported Section 336.   Despite the inconsequential use of Section 315 and the high-tariff principle on which it was based, Hoover justified his signature of the Hawley-Smoot Act on the grounds that authority granted him under Section 336 should make it possible "to secure prompt and scientific adjustment" of any "serious inequities and inequalities" contained in the Act.[62]   President Hoover said: "I do not assume that the rate structure in this or any other tariff bill is perfect. . . .   I believe that the flexible provisions can within reasonable time remedy inequalities; that this provision is a progressive advance and gives great hope of taking the tariff away from politics, lobbying, and logrolling."[63]

Relatively, Section 336 has been used even more sparingly than Section 315.   Between 1930 and 1962, four times as long as Section 315 remained

59. U.S. *Congressional Record*, 67th Cong., 2nd Sess., Vol. LXII, Pt. 11 (August 10, 1922), pp. 11192 and 11193.

60. U.S. Tariff Commission, *Thirteenth Annual Report*, 1929, pp. 10, 24, and 25.

61. Sections 316 and 317, the other flexible provisions of the Tariff Act of 1922, were also retained without significant changes as Sections 337 and 338 of the Tariff Act of 1930.   Penalties provided in both sections, however, were made somewhat more restrictive. Exclusion from entry into the United States of products found to be imported under conditions of unfair competition was the only action that could be taken under Section 337. Products imported in the vessels of a country discriminating against United States exports were also subject to new or additional duties or exclusion from entry under Section 338.

62. U.S. Dept. of State, *Press Releases*, Weekly Issue No. 38, June 21, 1930, p. 311.

63. *Ibid.*, p. 313.

in effect, only fifty-eight duty changes—twenty-seven increases, thirty decreases, and one involving an increase in the specific part and a decrease in the ad valorem part of a compound rate—have been made.[64]

The Trade Agreements Act of 1934, recognizing the conflict between cost equalization and tariff bargaining, exempted all articles included in trade agreements from the application of Section 336. This largely accounts for the relative paucity of duty changes. However, difficulties involved in applying the cost-equalization principle have been a contributing factor. Only 80 of the 121 investigations instituted during this period were completed, and only 42 of these resulted in duty changes.[65] Many completed investigations made no finding with respect to duty changes, because of the inability to make foreign and domestic cost comparisons. For the same reason many of the investigations that were instituted were not completed.[66]

Experience with Sections 315 and 336 of the Tariff Acts of 1922 and 1930 reflects some of the difficulties inherent in any attempt to assign tariff-making functions to an appointed body. Some success along these lines has been made in other fields, such as interstate commerce and public utilities, but no comparable success has been realized in regard to the tariff. Because of the tariff's more complicated and peculiarly sectional nature, it is probably too much to expect that any politically appointed body could scientifically determine proper rates even if the principle on which rates were based were more practicable than the equalization of foreign and domestic production costs.

Nevertheless, the idea of assigning to the Tariff Commission the task of scientific investigations and rate determinations still persists. It is the basis of legislation in regard to peril-point determinations and escape-clause investigations. In this legislation the principle governing the scientific determination of rates is the prevention of serious injury or threat of serious injury to domestic producers, but otherwise the function of the commission is very similar to that of Sections 315 and 336. A great many of the theoretical and practical objections to the principle of cost

64. Compiled from U.S. Tariff Commission, *Annual Reports, Fourteenth–Forty-fifth*, 1930-1961. The President has not yet acted on the Tariff Commission's recommendation in the investigation on brooms made of broomcorn. In this investigation, the commission recommended that the statutory 25 per cent rate of duty be applied to the American selling-price basis of valuation. An increase in the rate of duty to 37.5 per cent, the maximum permissible under Section 336, would not equalize foreign and domestic production costs. See U.S. Tariff Commission, *Brooms Made of Broomcorn*, Investigation No. 336-121, TC Publication 49, January, 1962.

65. *Ibid.*

66. For an account by the Tariff Commission of some of the difficulties encountered in cost-of-production determinations under Section 336, see U.S. Tariff Commission, *Seventeenth Annual Report*, 1933, pp. 7 and 8.

equalization also apply to the serious-injury concept as this is defined in legislation.[67]

Section 315 has additional significance for United States commercial policy because it serves as a precedent for the Congressional delegation of authority to the President to alter tariff rates. Under the Constitution, Congress is given the power "to lay and collect . . . Duties" and "to regulate Commerce with foreign Nations."[68]   It may not delegate this legislative function. In 1926 the constitutionality of Section 315 was challenged. The Supreme Court in *Hampton and Co. v. United States* held that Section 315 was not an unconstitutional delegation of legislative power, because it laid down an "intelligible principle" on which the President could base changes in rates.[69]   This principle was the equalization of foreign and domestic costs. Therefore, whenever the President proclaimed rate changes under Section 315, he was not exercising a legislative function but simply carrying out the will of Congress.[70]

The Trade Agreements Act of 1934, which is the statutory basis for the General Agreement on Tariffs and Trade (GATT) and the trade-agreements program, also delegates to the President authority to change duties. It also has been challenged as an unconstitutional delegation of legislative power. The "intelligible principle" upon which the President is to base modifications of duties and other import restrictions in foreign-trade agreements negotiated under the Trade Agreements Act is a finding that "existing duties or other import restrictions of the United States or any foreign country are unduly burdening and restricting the foreign trade of the United States" and that the exercise of his authority will promote the purpose of the legislation, i.e., "expanding foreign markets for the products of the United States." During debate on the Trade Agreements Act in 1934, Senator George (D., Ga.) declared that this was "as intelligible and practicable a principle within the rule announced in the Hampton case as that of equalizing the costs of production."[71]   The Supreme Court has never ruled on the constitutionality of the Trade Agreements Act, but in 1959 the Court of Customs and Patent Appeals upheld its constitutionality. In *Star-Kist Foods, Inc. v. United States,* the

67. See Chap. III.   68. Article I, Section 8.

69. *J. W. Hampton, Jr., and Co. v. United States,* 276 U.S. 394 (1928).

70. An earlier precedent concerning Congressional delegation of tariff-making authority to the President is *Field v. Clark,* 143 U.S. 649 (1892). In this case the Supreme Court upheld the constitutionality of a provision in the Tariff Act of 1890 that authorized the President to suspend the duty-free treatment on certain products imported from countries that he found to be imposing duties on United States products that were "reciprocally unequal and unreasonable."

71. U.S. *Congressional Record,* 73rd Cong., 2nd Sess., Vol. LXXVIII, Pt. 9 (May 31, 1934), p. 10077.

court referred to the Hampton case and expressly held that the delegation of authority to reduce duties in the Trade Agreements Act was constitutional.[72]

THE NON-NEGOTIABLE TARIFF

In addition to marking a return to high protection, the Tariff Acts of 1922 and 1930 mark a departure from the principle of tariff negotiability. Neither of the Acts contained any provision for reciprocity agreements,[73] nor was it a policy of the Executive during the 1920's to negotiate treaties for the reduction of tariff rates. The high rates of the Acts of 1922 and 1930 could be lowered under Section 315 in order to equalize foreign and domestic production costs, but during the 1920's the reduction of rates was not considered to be a subject for negotiation. The height of the United States tariff was regarded as a matter of strictly domestic concern.

The tariff had always been regarded as a domestic matter, but before 1922 the United States tariff had been negotiable. Negotiations, however, had been limited and in most cases unimportant.

Since 1844 several attempts had been made to negotiate reciprocity treaties. These efforts were largely unsuccessful because of the failure of these agreements to obtain the necessary advice and consent to ratification of the United States Senate. Only three such treaties—Canada in 1854, Hawaii in 1875, and Cuba in 1902—ever came into force.[74]

72. *Star-Kist Foods, Inc.* v. *United States,* 275 F. 2d 472 (1959). The court also cited other precedents, including *United States* v. *Curtiss-Wright Export Corp.,* 229 U.S. 304 (1936) in which the Supreme Court established the principle that the scope of permissible delegation of authority from Congress to the President is broader in the area of foreign than in the area of domestic affairs.

73. A reciprocity agreement as defined by the U.S. Tariff Commission and as used in this chapter is "a treaty or convention in which the contracting States grant to each other particular concessions in return for particular concessions without the intention or expectation that these concessions shall be generalized." U.S. Tariff Commission, *Reciprocity and Commercial Treaties,* 1919, p. 59.

74. The treaty with Canada was in force from 1855 to 1866, when it was terminated by the United States. The treaty with Hawaii was in force from 1876 to 1900, when, as the result of annexation, the islands became a customs district of the United States. The treaty with Cuba was in force from 1903 to 1934, when it was suspended by the 1934 trade agreement with Cuba.

In addition to these agreements, treaties containing incidental reciprocity provisions have also been concluded.

A claims treaty with France in 1831 provided for the lowering of United States duties on French wines for a period of ten years in exchange for abandonment by France of certain claims under the Treaty of Louisiana and the establishment of the same duty on United States long-staple cotton as on short-staple cottons.

The Treaty of Washington of 1871 with Great Britain, which provided for settlement of the "Alabama" claims and other matters also provided for the duty-free exchange of fish between the United States and Canada and Newfoundland. This provision was

The Tariff Acts of 1897 and 1913 contained provisions authorizing the President to enter into reciprocity treaties, but because these treaties were to be submitted to Congress for approval, this authorization added nothing to the treaty powers already held by the President under the Constitution. Nevertheless, inclusion of this authorization in legislation can be interpreted as reflecting Congressional approval of the principle of reciprocity. However, none of the eleven "Kasson" treaties[75] concluded under the authority of the Act of 1897 ever came to a vote in the Senate. No treaties were negotiated under the authority of the Act of 1913.

Reciprocity agreements not subject to Congressional approval were authorized in the Tariff Act of 1897. Under this authority the President could lower the duties on certain products to specified rates in return for equivalent concessions by other countries.[76] The so-called "argol" agreements, named after the first item on the list of United States concessions, were concluded with nine countries.[77] Authority to make these agreements was rescinded, and by provisions of the Tariff Act of 1909 the agreements themselves were to be terminated.

The treaties with Canada, Hawaii, and Cuba and the "argol" agreements are the only examples of negotiated tariff agreements made effective by the United States until after passage of the Trade Agreements Act in 1934.[78] The constitutional conflict between the power of the President to make treaties and the control of tariff matters by the Congress partly explains the very limited success of reciprocity prior to 1922. A more basic reason is that a high-tariff policy, such as that

terminated in 1885 by the United States in pursuance of an 1883 joint resolution of Congress.

75. These treaties are named after John A. Kasson, the special commissioner appointed by President McKinley to negotiate them.

76. The items on which duty reductions could be made were relatively insignificant. They were argols, or crude tartar, or wine lees, crude; brandies, or other spirits manufactured or distilled from grain or other materials; champagne and all other sparkling wines; still wines and vermouth; and paintings in oil or water colors, pastels, pen-and-ink drawings, and statuary.

77. Countries with which "argol" agreements were concluded were France, Portugal, Germany, Italy, Switzerland, Spain, Bulgaria, the United Kingdom, and the Netherlands.

78. The Tariff Acts of 1890, 1897, and 1909 contained provisions authorizing the President to impose penalty duties on imports from countries that accorded unequal and unreasonable or discriminatory treatment to United States exports. Negotiations and agreements concluded under these penalty provisions, however, are not examples of tariff negotiability as this term is usually understood. Such negotiations and agreements were concerned with the imposition of increased duties and did not contemplate the granting of concessions. Under these penalty provisions the tariff could be raised but not lowered. Similar penalty provisions were included in the Tariff Acts of 1922 and 1930. These provisions will be discussed in connection with United States adoption of the unconditional most-favored-nation principle.

maintained by the United States since the Civil War, almost precludes negotiated tariff reductions. Congressional approval of the three reciprocity treaties that were made effective was based on political and economic considerations other than a desire to lower trade barriers. The "argol" agreements were negotiated primarily to eliminate discrimination against United States exports by European countries; they also did not reflect any desire to reduce the protective level of the United States tariff.

The Fordney Bill, when it first passed the House in 1921, contained provisions similar to those in previous acts authorizing the President to enter into reciprocity agreements both with and without the approval of Congress. These provisions were struck out by the Senate Finance Committee when Section 315 and the other flexible provisions of the 1922 Act were added to the bill.

The elimination of the reciprocity provisions logically followed after Section 315, which based tariff rates on the principle of foreign and domestic cost equalization, was introduced. Negotiation of lower rates would have been inconsistent with such a principle. Negotiation would also have been impracticable. Theoretically, reductions in duties that might be made as the result of cost-of-production investigations under Section 315 could have been used as concessions in reciprocity negotiations with foreign countries, but it is improbable that worthwhile agreements could have been concluded, given the highly protectionist principle upon which lowered rates would have had to be based.[79]

The Senate Finance Committee, however, deleted reciprocity provisions from the House bill, primarily because previous United States reciprocity policy had been "without important results and not warranted in view of the international complications which result from it."[80] The committee substituted Section 317, one of the flexible provisions, for the House approved reciprocity provisions, thereby providing for a non-negotiable tariff with penalty provisions against the products of countries discriminating against United States exports.[81]

Before 1922, therefore, the United States tariff, although negotiable in principle, had not been very negotiable in fact. After 1922, even the principle of negotiability was discarded.

In 1932, Congress, with the Democrats in control, attempted to change

79. Negotiations on the basis of lowered rates resulting from Section 315 investigations were proposed by France in 1927. See below, pp. 50-51. Similar proposals were made by a few other countries during the 1920's, but nothing ever resulted from any of these overtures.

80. Senate Committee on Finance, *Report* to accompany H.R. 7456, p. 4.

81. Section 317 is discussed below, pp. 37-44.

United States tariff policy. It passed legislation known as the Collier Bill, which, however, was vetoed by President Hoover, and this veto was sustained. The principal features of this bill:

(1) Requested the President to initiate a movement for an international economic conference with a view to lowering excessive tariff duties and eliminating discriminatory and other trade barriers, any resulting international agreement to be approved by Congress.

(2) Requested the President to negotiate trade agreements for mutual tariff concessions, such agreements to be approved by Congress.

(3) Amended Section 336 of the Tariff Act of 1930, so that Congress, rather than the President, would act upon Tariff Commission recommendations in cost-equalization cases and so that the interests of other domestic industries and exporters would be taken into consideration in such cases.

(4) Created an office of Consumers' Counsel to represent consumer interests in any proceedings before the Tariff Commission.

(5) Authorized the President to suspend the duty on any article that the United States Customs Court should find not being produced or distributed competitively within the United States.[82]

Even though the Collier Bill failed to take into account the demonstrated difficulty of obtaining Congressional approval of international agreements dealing with tariff matters, it would have reversed the high, non-negotiable features of United States tariff policy and would have altered its "flexibility." It also would have recognized the interest in tariff matters of consumers, exporters, and domestic producers other than those seeking protection from foreign competition.

President Hoover's veto message on the Collier Bill reaffirmed United States tariff policy of the 1920's and early 1930's. In this message the President defended United States high-tariff policy as "essential to the welfare of the American people."[83] He said that because of the depreciation of foreign currencies and widespread domestic unemployment, "it is imperative that the American protective policy be maintained."[84] Any tariff rates believed to be too high could be adjusted under the "flexible" provisions of the Tariff Act of 1930. He defended the use of Section 336 and criticized the amendment to this provision requiring Congressional

82. For the text of the Collier Bill (H.R. 6662), see U.S. *Congressional Record,* 72nd Cong., 1st Sess., Vol. LXXV, Pt. 8 (April 28, 1932), pp. 9147-49.
83. *Press Releases,* Weekly Issue No. 137, May 14, 1932, p. 477.
84. *Ibid.,* p. 478.

action on Tariff Commission recommendations as practically destroying the "flexible" tariff. He said that the international conference referred to in the bill would "subject our tariffs to international agreement" and that one of our firm national policies since Washington's Administration was that "tariffs are solely a domestic question."[85] In regard to the negotiation of trade agreements for the mutual lowering of tariffs, he pointed to the futility of negotiating such agreements in view of the previous lack of success in obtaining Congressional approval of them. He also opposed the negotiation of such agreements, because he equated them with discriminatory treatment.

The devotion of the Republican Administration to an untouchable tariff policy was affirmed again in connection with the proposed World Monetary and Economic Conference, later held in London in 1933. The decision to hold the conference was made, and the preparatory work on it began while the Republicans were still in office. If any subject needed consideration at such a conference, it was the excessive use of tariff and other trade barriers that countries had imposed in the throes of the world depression. Yet Secretary of State Stimson informed the British that the United States would be unable to consider at such a conference "questions of tariff rates," which both Britain and the United States considered to be "purely domestic issues."[86]

Although under Republican Administrations during the 1920's and early 1930's United States tariff policy was high, "flexible," and non-negotiable, it was not discriminatory. As noted above, one of the reasons why President Hoover objected to the provision in the Collier Bill requesting the negotiation of agreements for the mutual lowering of tariff barriers was that he assumed (erroneously)[87] that such agreements must be preferential in nature and, therefore, in conflict with a policy of nondiscrimination, a basic principle of United States commercial policy.

2. THE UNCONDITIONAL MOST-FAVORED-NATION PRINCIPLE

In 1923 the United States adopted the policy of unconditional most-favored-nation (MFN) customs treatment. A major change in policy was effected, and one of the bases of present-day United States commercial policy was laid. Other than passage of the Trade Agreements Act in 1934, there is probably no development in United States commercial policy of greater importance.

85. *Ibid.*, p. 479.
86. *Foreign Relations,* 1932, Vol. I, p. 809. See also p. 817.
87. For a discussion of the compatibility of negotiated tariff reductions with a policy of nondiscrimination, see Chap. II, pp. 97-99.

CONDITIONAL MFN TREATMENT

Since 1778, when the United States concluded its first commercial treaty, it had adhered to a policy of conditional MFN treatment.[88] Article 2 of this treaty with France provided that: "The most Christian King, and the United States engage mutually not to grant any particular Favour to other Nations in respect of Commerce and Navigation, which shall not immediately become common to the other Party, *who shall enjoy the same Favour freely, if the Concession was freely made, or on allowing the same Compensation, if the Concession was Conditional.*"[89]

The first part of this provision was the customary MFN pledge mutually guaranteeing nondiscriminatory treatment of the goods (and vessels) of the contracting parties. This pledge, however, was qualified by the italicized phraseology. Instead of agreeing to extend unconditionally to France tariff and other benefits negotiated with third parties, the United States agreed to do so only if France paid the "same compensation" as had been paid by the party with which benefits had been negotiated. This provision in the treaty with France is the first example in international commercial treaties of a conditional MFN clause.

A MFN policy based on the conditional clause results in discrimination whenever agreements for the reduction of tariffs are concluded. Negotiated tariff reductions made effective between two countries and not extended to third countries are *ipso facto* discriminatory.

Under the conditional MFN clause, third countries can obtain the benefits of such agreements and thereby eliminate discrimination against their exports if they pay the "same" or, as this has been interpreted and provided for in later treaties, "equivalent" compensation. However, there are serious difficulties in this connection. Establishing exactly what is "equivalent" compensation is not easy and sometimes not possible. A country might contend, and properly so, that no matter what compensation a third party might be willing to pay, it could not be equivalent. Suppose, for example, two countries of great commercial importance to each other, such as the United States and the United Kingdom, were to conclude an agreement involving duty reductions on both sides. A third country of relatively minor commercial importance having a conditional MFN treaty with the United States might find it impossible to offer concessions that would be considered comparable to those given by the United Kingdom, and therefore it would be unable to obtain nondis-

88. The following discussion benefits from two articles on the MFN clause written by Jacob Viner and reproduced in his *International Economics* (Glencoe, Ill.: The Free Press, 1951).

89. Italics added. Hunter Miller, *Treaties and Other International Acts of the United States of America*, II, 5.

criminatory treatment of its exports to the United States.[90] Low-tariff countries, irrespective of the size and importance of their domestic market, might also be unable to offer equivalent compensation because they would have little in the way of tariff concessions to make.[91]

Not only is agreement on "equivalent" compensation difficult, if not impossible, but negotiations have to be carried on with every country having a trading interest in the products concerned if discrimination against third parties is to be prevented. This negotiating problem would be enormous, particularly if many countries adhered to the conditional MFN clause. If, for example, countries A and B concluded an agreement exchanging commercial benefits, both A and B would then be obliged to engage in equivalent-compensation negotiations with C, D, E, etc. The process would not end with these negotiations, however, because if A successfully concluded an equivalent-compensation agreement with C, C would then be obliged to negotiate with B, because what C offered A as equivalent compensation might not be deemed equivalent compensation by B for the concessions that B made to A in the original agreement. If in this compensation agreement with B, C were to grant B different equivalent concessions than it had already granted to A, which is likely, then negotiations would have to be reopened with A. Furthermore, C would also have to negotiate with D, E, etc. D, E, etc. would also face the same negotiating tasks with A and B and with each other as did C. Negotiation and renegotiation of compensation agreements that could result from just one reciprocity agreement could be endless, and while such negotiations continued, discrimination would result not only between the parties to the agreement and third parties but, as the result of subsequent compensation agreements, among the third parties themselves. Commercial policy based on conditional MFN treatment, for these reasons, inevitably results in discrimination, whether intentional or not.

Unconditional MFN treatment, on the other hand, by immediately and freely extending or generalizing negotiated tariff reductions to third parties avoids discrimination and any subsequent negotiating problem.

90. In 1878 the United States contended that nothing the United Kingdom and other countries might offer Hawaii could be considered as compensation for the concessions that the United States had granted Hawaii in the Treaty of 1875, and therefore, that these countries could not obtain the concessions that Hawaii granted to the United States in this treaty. See *Foreign Relations*, 1878, p. 404.

91. The United Kingdom experienced difficulty in obtaining for its exports the reduced rates negotiated by the United States in the "argol" agreements. Because of its free-trade policy, the United Kingdom had little to offer as compensation, and it was only partially successful in eliminating the discrimination resulting from these agreements. See U.S. Tariff Commission, *Reciprocity and Commercial Treaties*, 1919, p. 214.

Arguments favoring the conditional MFN clause contend that it is only equitable that third parties pay for tariff reductions extended to them by countries that themselves have exchanged concessions and that unconditional MFN treatment extends these negotiated tariff reductions to third parties without obtaining anything in return—in other words, unconditional MFN gives something for nothing.

This attitude, which regards tariff reductions as something given up, is unfortunate, for such reductions may be of great benefit to consumer, exporter, and other domestic interests.[92] Moreover, though it may appear that unconditional MFN gives something for nothing when looked at narrowly from the viewpoint of a single tariff-reducing agreement, this is an inaccurate interpretation. Under unconditional MFN, rates must be generalized only to those third countries with which unconditional MFN treaty obligations apply, i.e., those countries that are also willing to generalize reduced rates in agreements that they make. In other words, the *quid pro quo* for unconditional MFN is unconditional MFN. Concessions freely granted to third countries are "paid for" by these countries when they freely grant concessions that they have made in tariff agreements. Even if such third countries do not as a matter of policy engage in negotiations for tariff reductions, and consequently, no negotiated tariff reductions are received from them, an unconditional MFN pledge from such countries still is important. It assures nondiscriminatory treatment in the event that a change in negotiating policy should occur. Such assurance of nondiscrimination is of great value in stabilizing trade conditions and in expanding trade.[93]

Discriminatory tariff treatment can be as important an impediment in

92. The view that tariff reductions are something given up might be defensible if based upon the effect of tariff reductions on a country's terms of trade.

93. Another advantage of an unconditional MFN policy as opposed to a conditional policy is that tariff reductions generalized to all countries will normally benefit domestic consumers in the form of lower prices. Unless a country to which a nongeneralized tariff reduction is extended furnishes all or a very great part of the supply of a commodity, no price reduction to domestic consumers is likely to occur. The benefits of such a non-generalized tariff reduction will recur to the foreign producers of the favored country, who will not be inclined to lower the price of that part of the domestic market that they supply.

Illustrative of this lack of consumer benefit under a conditional MFN policy is the United States experience with the Hawaiian reciprocity treaty of 1875. This treaty admitted Hawaiian sugar duty-free, while sugar coming from other sources continued to pay a duty. After the remission of duty, Hawaiian sugar, which constituted only a small portion of total supply, continued to sell in the United States at the same price as other sugar paying duty. The duty-free treatment of Hawaiian sugar benefited Hawaiian producers (who in many instances were United States citizens) rather than United States consumers. If duty-free treatment of Hawaiian sugar had been generalized under an unconditional MFN policy to all sugar imports, a reduction in the price of sugar to United States consumers could have been expected.

international trade as high tariffs. High tariffs restrict trade and displace imports with less economical domestic production. Discriminatory tariffs divert trade and displace imports from some countries with imports from favored countries that are not necessarily the most economical producers. From the viewpoint of the handicapped exporter, interested in expanding foreign sales, or the economist, interested in the best allocation of resources, high tariffs and discriminatory tariffs can have the same restrictive effect.

UNITED STATES PRACTICE OF NONDISCRIMINATION

Even though the 1778 United States treaty with France introduced the conditional form of the MFN clause into international commercial usage[94] and the United States adhered to the conditional form or a conditional interpretation of the MFN clause prior to 1923,[95] the United States did not, generally speaking, practice a policy of discriminatory customs treatment. With a few exceptions the United States maintained a single-column tariff, so that *de facto,* if not *de jure,* United States policy, for the most part, amounted to one of nondiscrimination.

George Washington in his farewell address sounded the keynote for United States policy in regard to discrimination when he said that "our commercial policy should hold an equal and impartial hand, neither seeking nor granting exclusive favors or preferences."[96] United States practice has not deviated very much from Washington's views.

Adoption by the United States of the conditional MFN clause was not motivated by a desire to foster discriminatory trade relations. In the early days of United States history, foreign tariffs were of relatively minor importance in restricting United States exports as compared to navigation laws and colonial trade policies, which frequently prohibited United States trade or discriminated against United States vessels and goods that were allowed to trade. A bargaining policy based on conditional MFN treatment was looked upon as the only way to deal effectively with the great European powers in maritime and trade matters. Adherence to this conditional policy was never regarded as discriminatory because it offered countries equality of opportunity to negotiate and

94. It is questionable whether it was the United States or France that introduced the conditional MFN clause into the 1778 treaty. See Vernon Setser, "Did Americans Originate the Conditional Most-Favored-Nation Clause?" *The Journal of Modern History,* V (September, 1933), 319-23.

95. Since 1787 the United States has interpreted MFN clauses in United States treaties as conditional even though these clauses have not always been expressed in the conditional form. See U.S. Tariff Commission, *Reciprocity and Commercial Treaties,* 1919, pp. 404-12.

96. James D. Richardson, *A Compilation of the Messages and Papers of the Presidents* (Bureau of National Literature and Art, 1910), I, 215.

obtain for themselves all benefits that the United States might grant third countries. It was hoped that such a bargaining policy, through the process of negotiation, would eliminate all forms of discrimination against United States trade. In 1828 President John Quincy Adams expressed this early United States attitude as follows: "This system [of conditional MFN], first proclaimed to the world in the first commercial treaty ever concluded by the United States—that of 6th February, 1778, with France —has been invariably the cherished policy of our Union. . . . With this principle, our fathers extended the hand of friendship to every nation of the globe, and to this policy our country has ever since adhered. *Whatever of regulation in our laws has ever been adopted unfavorable to the interests of any foreign nation has been essentially defensive and counteracting to similar regulations of theirs operating against us.*"[97]

After the middle of the nineteenth century, when the old navigation laws and colonial prohibitions disappeared or were less important and tariffs became the dominant consideration in commercial relations, United States conditional policy was less defensible. This was particularly true after the conclusion of the famous Cobden Treaty of 1860, which established commercial relations between England and France on an unconditional MFN basis and which gave impetus to the adoption of the unconditional clause by most of the countries of Europe.

However, even though the United States retained the conditional MFN policy after the causes for its adoption disappeared, very little discrimination resulted from retention of this policy, because few reciprocity agreements were ever made effective. Only the tariff reductions made in the treaties with Canada, Hawaii, and Cuba and in the "argol" agreements were not generalized to third countries under United States conditional policy. Theoretically, third countries could obtain the benefits of these reductions by offering "equivalent" compensation, but these reductions were not always extended to third countries, even though compensation was offered.[98] Furthermore, the reciprocity treaty with Cuba was regarded as exclusive and not open to third countries under any condition.[99] It should be added, however, that the "argol" agreements, even though discriminatory in their effects on third countries, were negotiated primarily for the purpose of eliminating discrimination against United States exports by European countries, rather than for the purpose of obtaining or granting preferential treatment. Therefore, they

97. Italics added. *Ibid.*, II, 975.   98. See footnotes 90 and 91, above.

99. Preferential tariff arrangements with Cuba are still regarded as exclusive, and since 1923 they have been the principal exception to United States unconditional MFN policy. These tariff preferences have only academic interest as long as the United States embargo on virtually all trade with Castro Cuba remains in effect.

were in the tradition of early United States conditional policy. Also, the treaties with Canada, Hawaii, and Cuba were motivated primarily by political and economic considerations other than tariff preferences.

Because United States conditional MFN policy resulted in relatively little discrimination, the adoption of an unconditional MFN policy in 1923 would not be of such major significance had the United States tariff continued to be virtually non-negotiable. With the passage of the Trade Agreements Act of 1934, however, the United States tariff became negotiable, and the retention of the unconditional MFN policy adopted a decade earlier not only precluded negotiations concluded under the authority of this Act from discriminating against third countries but it determined the selective nature of the negotiating procedure for both the bilateral and multilateral phases of the trade-agreements program.[100]

A less excusable exception than conditional MFN to United States nondiscriminatory practice was the use of penalty duties provided for in the Tariff Acts of 1890 and 1897 to obtain preferential treatment for United States exports. The Tariff Act of 1890 authorized the President to impose penalty duties on otherwise duty-free coffee, tea, hides, sugar, and molasses whenever he deemed that countries exporting these items to the United States levied duties on United States products that were "reciprocally unequal and unreasonable." Under threat of use of this authority, executive agreements, which in many cases obtained preferential treatment for United States exports, were concluded with ten countries.[101] The Tariff Act of 1894 repealed the President's authority to impose such penalty duties, and by reimposing a duty on sugar, it terminated these agreements. The Tariff Act of 1897 again authorized the President to impose penalty duties on coffee and tea, but the substitution of tonka and vanilla beans, articles of very slight commercial importance, for hides, sugar, and molasses so greatly impaired his bargaining power that no agreements under this authority were ever concluded. Diplomatic pressure applied against Brazil, however, secured preferential treatment, beginning in 1904, for certain United States exports, the most important of which was wheat flour. No formal agreement providing for this unilateral preference was ever concluded, but it remained in effect until 1923.

The only other significant exception to United States nondiscriminatory practice before 1923 was the provisions for contingent duties,

100. See Chap. II.

101. Agreements were made with Brazil, Dominican Republic, Spain, Salvador, Germany, Great Britain, Nicaragua, Honduras, Guatemala, and Austria-Hungary. Colombia, Venezuela, and Haiti failed to make satisfactory agreements, and they were subjected to the penalty duties.

which were included in all United States tariff acts since 1890. These provisions made United States tariff treatment of certain products dependent upon foreign treatment of like or similar products. Provisos attached to tariff paragraphs changed the duty stipulated on articles imported from countries that granted less favorable, but not necessarily discriminatory, treatment on like or similar articles imported from the United States. If the paragraph in question were in the free list, the proviso required the imposition of a duty on articles coming from any country that levied a duty on like or similar products or that imposed an export duty or restriction on such products. If the paragraph were in the dutiable list, the proviso ordinarily required an increase in duty on articles imported from any country that levied a higher duty on like or similar products. A few provisos prescribed the removal of the duty on articles imported from a country that allowed like or similar products to enter duty-free. Because such contingent provisions result in discriminatory tariff treatment, they are recognized generally as inconsistent with both unconditional and conditional MFN obligations.[102]

Deviations from nondiscrimination, however, should not be overemphasized. The preferential agreements concluded under the Tariff Act of 1890, the preferential arrangement with Brazil, and the provisions for contingent duties are exceptions to traditional United States practice.

PENALTY DUTIES TO OBTAIN NONDISCRIMINATION

In granting for the most part nondiscriminatory tariff treatment to the exports of other countries, the United States had long sought similar treatment for its own exports. Various methods had been used: conditional MFN policy as a bargaining weapon was one; tariff reductions in the "argol" agreements was another. Imposition of penalty duties was a third, the use of which had significance in the 1923 MFN policy change.

Penalty duties that were authorized in the Tariff Acts of 1890 and 1897 largely to obtain preferential treatment for United States exports were authorized in the Tariff Act of 1909 to obtain nondiscriminatory treatment. Under the Tariff Act of 1909, maximum rates 25 per cent higher than the minimum were to apply to the goods of all countries unless

102. For a brief discussion of the incompatibility of contingent-duty provisions with MFN obligations, see Viner, *International Economics*, pp. 30, 31, and 38.

For a more lengthy discussion and a description of the various contingent-duty provisions in United States tariff acts, see Wallace McClure, *A New American Commercial Policy*, As Evidenced by Section 317 of the Tariff Act of 1922 (Vol. CXIV, No. 2, "Studies in History, Economics and Public Law," ed. by the Faculty of Columbia University [New York: Longmans Green & Co., 1924]), pp. 139-61. See also S. H. Nerlove, "Contingent Duty Provisions in American Tariff Legislation," *The Journal of Political Economy*, XXXIII (June, 1925), 318-39.

the President were satisfied that a country was not "unduly" discriminating against United States exports, in which case the minimum rates would apply. By this provision the United States for the first time in its history legislated a double-column tariff. This was a drastic measure, because penalty duties (the maximum schedule) were to apply to all the exports of an offending country. There was no way in which the President could graduate the penalty according to the degree of discrimination; either the full 25 per cent penalty duties or the minimum rates were applicable. This was a meat-cleaver application of the penalty method to obtain nondiscriminatory treatment of United States exports.

Despite the fact that negotiations threatening the imposition of the maximum rates were only partially successful in eliminating discrimination against United States exports, the penalty duties of the Tariff Act of 1909 were never applied. Before April 1, 1910, when the maximum rates were to be applicable, President Taft issued 134 proclamations applying the minimum rates to the products of as many countries or colonies.[103] This series of proclamations embraced the entire commercial world.

The maximum-minimum provision of the Act of 1909 was not flexible enough to be used to eliminate discrimination against United States exports. In a letter dated December 13, 1911, to Mr. Underwood, then chairman of the House Ways and Means Committee, Secretary of State Knox expressed the belief widely held in the Administration that it would be necessary to amend the Tariff Act of 1909, in order to provide for the imposition of penalty duties that could be varied in proportion to objectionable discriminations.[104] He pointed out that "the gravity of the offense should be met by a suitable remedy."[105] The removal of discrimination might demand in one instance that a few additional duties be imposed upon a few commodities, in another instance that all of a nation's exports be subjected to penalty rates, and in aggravated cases that all imports be prohibited from an offending country.[106] Secretary Knox enclosed with his letter a draft amendment to the Act of 1909 embodying the suggestions that he had made, but this was never submitted to the House.[107]

After the Republicans returned to power at the end of World War I, the penalty method of obtaining nondiscriminatory treatment for United States exports was again incorporated into legislation. The meat-cleaver

103. U.S. Tariff Commission, *Reciprocity and Commercial Treaties*, 1919, p. 274.
104. This letter is published in full in *The New York Herald*, December 15, 1911. The pertinent parts are reproduced in *ibid.*, pp. 274 and 275.
105. U.S. Tariff Commission, *Reciprocity and Commercial Treaties*, 1919, p. 275.
106. *Ibid.*
107. This amendment is reproduced in *ibid.*, pp. 275-76.

provision of the 1909 Act, however, was discarded in favor of a more flexible provision similar to that suggested by Secretary Knox. Section 317, one of the flexible provisions of the Tariff Act of 1922, authorized the President to impose penalty duties up to 50 per cent ad valorem on any or all products of any country discriminating against United States exports whenever he found that "the public interest will be served thereby." If the imposition of such penalties did not bring about the cessation of discrimination, then the President could exclude any or all products of the offending country. Because of its flexibility, this was regarded as an improvement over the 1909 provision, and it was thought that it would be more effective in obtaining nondiscriminatory treatment of United States exports.

Section 317 was retained without significant change as Section 338 in the Tariff Act of 1930. Neither has ever been applied. One reason is that the United States adopted a fourth method to obtain nondiscriminatory treatment—inclusion of the unconditional MFN clause in commercial treaties.

SECTION 317 AND THE 1923 POLICY CHANGE

Section 317 played an important part in the historic change of MFN policy in 1923. It was interpreted by the Administration as applying to all types of discrimination against United States products, including differential treatment resulting from reciprocity agreements. In other words the Administration viewed Section 317 as opposing the practice of conditional MFN treatment and as expressing the will of Congress in this respect. Section 317 was regarded as a Congressional mandate for a change from conditional to unconditional MFN policy.

In a letter occasioned by enactment of Section 317, the vice-chairman of the Tariff Commission, William S. Culbertson, wrote Secretary of State Hughes in September, 1922, that this provision expressed "the desire of Congress to extend the principle of equality of treatment in commercial relations."[108] Culbertson looked upon Section 317 as Congressional support for the change to the unconditional MFN policy that he had already advocated several months earlier.[109] Another letter to Hughes from Culbertson, dated December 14, 1922, urged that the unconditional MFN clause be included in future commercial treaties. It stated that in enacting Section 317 Congress had taken "a definite stand for the policy of equality of treatment" and that "it would seem to follow

108. William S. Culbertson, *Reciprocity* (New York: McGraw-Hill Book Company, Inc., 1937), p. 245.

109. See letter of Culbertson to Secretary Hughes, dated May 21, 1922. *Ibid.,* pp. 238-43.

logically that in the revision of our commercial treaties we should adopt the unconditional form of the most-favored-nation clause."[110]

On January 15, 1923, Secretary Hughes wrote President Harding suggesting that the unconditional form of the MFN clause be included in future commercial treaties and enclosed Culbertson's letter of December 14.[111] In a reply, dated February 27, 1923, the President approved adoption of this new policy.[112] Thus, the unconditional MFN clause, one of the most important bases of present-day United States commercial policy, was adopted.

A circular letter of August 18, 1923, to United States diplomatic officers announced that future commercial treaties of the United States would contain the unconditional MFN clause. Reference to Section 317 in this circular implied that Congress intended such a change in policy.[113]

The thesis that Section 317 was a mandate from Congress for a change in United States MFN policy has been widely accepted by writers on this subject.[114] As recent and authoritative a publication on United States trade policy as the Randall Commission *Staff Papers* states that "the unconditional most-favored-nation policy was adopted, in fact, when Congress enacted Section 317 (a) of the Fordney-McCumber Tariff Act of 1922."[115] However, an examination of the evidence available indicates that the intention of Congress was just the opposite. Because the unconditional MFN clause is such an important part of present United States commercial policy, the record should be set straight.

There is little difference between Section 317 and the maximum-minimum provision of the Tariff Act of 1909. Both had the same purpose of obtaining nondiscriminatory treatment for United States exports by threat of penalty duties. The penalty provision of the 1909 Act was not looked upon as a Congressional mandate for a change in United States MFN policy because differential treatment resulting from nongeneralized tariff reductions made in reciprocity agreements was not considered discriminatory from the conditional MFN viewpoint. Senator

110. Culbertson, *Reciprocity*, pp. 248-49.

111. *Ibid.*, pp. 256-58.   112. *Ibid.*, pp. 258-59.

113. *Ibid.*, p. 277. This circular letter; Culbertson's letter of December 14, 1922; Secretary Hughes's letter of January 8, 1923; and the President's reply of February 27, 1923, are also published in *Foreign Relations*, 1923, Vol. I, pp. 121-29 and pp. 131-33.

114. See, for example, McClure, *New Commercial Policy*, p. 117. See, also, Culbertson, *Reciprocity*, pp. 167-68, and *International Economic Policies: A Survey of the Economics of Diplomacy* (New York: D. Appleton and Company, 1925), pp. 98-99; and Henry J. Tasca, *The Reciprocal Trade Policy of the United States: A Study in Trade Philosophy* (Philadelphia: University of Pennsylvania Press, 1938), pp. 116-17.

115. Commission on Foreign Economic Policy, *Staff Papers* (Washington, D.C.: February, 1954), p. 260.

Smoot (R., Ut.), who introduced Section 317 and the other flexible provisions as an amendment to the Fordney Bill, favorably compared Section 317 with its 1909 predecessor. He said that it allowed the President greater flexibility in the imposition of penalty duties and that it was based on Secretary Knox's suggested revision.[116] If the 1909 penalty provision was not considered a Congressional mandate for a MFN policy change, then Section 317 should not be regarded as such a mandate, unless Congressional thinking on what constituted discrimination had changed and Congress intended Section 317 to apply to differential treatment resulting from reciprocity agreements.

Determination of Congressional intent is usually difficult. It is even more difficult with respect to Section 317, which received little Congressional or public attention. There is no mention of Section 317 in either the House or Senate hearings on the tariff bill, nor was there any discussion of this provision in the House. Except for the explanatory statement by Senator Smoot, referred to above, there was no discussion of Section 317 in the Senate until it was called up for adoption or rejection.

When Section 317 was voted upon in the Senate, the major question with which this body was concerned was the compatibility of Section 317 with United States MFN treaty policy. Upon examination, the Senate found that Section 317, as recommended by the Finance Committee, appeared to be inconsistent with the United States version of the MFN clause, because it would have penalized as discriminatory nongeneralized tariff reductions made by other countries in reciprocity agreements. Accordingly, the text of Section 317 was revised with the intention of eliminating any conflict with United States conditional MFN policy.

Senator Lenroot (R., Wis.) opened the debate on this question. He said:

. . . I think this section [Section 317] . . . presents a most dangerous situation for the United States, because if the United States is to enter upon this policy no man can tell where the end will be. For instance . . . [it] provides that the President shall increase duties—he must increase duties—if any other country enters into a reciprocity arrangement with a third country whereby the goods of such country shall be admitted at a lower rate than the general customs tariff rate in return for the other country admitting the goods of the second country at a lower rate. That is a right upon which the United States has insisted in times past. Such provisions have been found in former Republican tariff bills. But this provision says if any country in the world shall enter into such an arrangement in the future the President of the

116. U.S. *Congressional Record,* 67th Cong., 2nd Sess., Vol. LXII, Pt. 6 (April 24, 1922), p. 5879.

United States must increase the duties fixed in this bill upon imports from such country.[117]

Senator Walsh (D., Mont.) also criticized the Finance Committee version of Section 317, because it appeared to apply to differential treatment resulting from reciprocity agreements.[118]

Senator McCumber (R., N. Dak.), chairman of the Finance Committee, replied in effect that penalty duties under Section 317 would not be applicable to differential treatment resulting from reciprocity agreements because "it has always been held that a reciprocal arrangement made between two countries, whereby one for due consideration receives special favors from another and pays for them in granting special favors, is not in conflict with the favored-nation clauses of the treaty." He continued: "And therefore, where reciprocity treaties have been made between nations it would not be a discrimination against the United States for the reason that just and proper consideration is supposed to pass between the countries in making those reciprocal arrangements."[119]

Senator Lodge (R., Mass.), chairman of the Foreign Relations Committee, agreed that "the favored-nation clause is not violated by a reciprocity treaty, of course."[120] He admitted that the Finance Committee text of Section 317 could be interpreted as applicable to a reciprocity treaty, but he insisted that that could not be the intention. He said that "the reciprocal arrangement never has been held, and never can be held, to be a violation of the favored-nation clause."[121] He continued: "Discrimination exists only when a nation has been treated differently from all other nations which have no reciprocity treaties."[122] His final point was that Section 317 needed some rewording in order to make it clear that penalty duties would not be applicable to differential treatment resulting from reciprocity agreements because "we cannot undertake to interfere with reciprocity treaties, of course. We have them ourselves."[123]

The senators were agreed that nongeneralized tariff reductions in reciprocity agreements did not constitute discrimination and, therefore, that they were not applicable to the penalty provisions of Section 317. The only controversy involved in this discussion was whether the Finance Committee wording of Section 317 made this clear. Accordingly, Section 317 was amended to eliminate all language that the Senate regarded as

117. U.S. *Congressional Record*, 67th Cong., 2nd Sess., Vol. LXII, Pt. 11 (August 11, 1922), p. 11245.

118. *Ibid.*, pp. 11245 and 11246.   119. *Ibid.*, p. 11246.
120. *Ibid.*, p. 11247.   121. *Ibid.*
122. *Ibid.*   123. *Ibid.*

being inconsistent with United States conditional MFN policy. Because Section 317, as amended, continued to apply to the products of any foreign country that "discriminates against the commerce of the United States,"[124] a literal reading, without taking account of the senators' views of what constituted discrimination, conveys the impression that Section 317 is applicable to all discrimination, including that resulting from reciprocity agreements. Clearly, however, this was not the intention of the senators when voting affirmatively on this provision.

Because most other countries regarded nongeneralized tariff reductions made in reciprocity agreements as discriminatory, the Senate's definition of discrimination was somewhat unique. It was no departure, however, from traditional United States usage. But, whether or not the "position taken by the Senators appears a bit strained and unnatural,"[125] as one writer has suggested, this does not alter the fact that in debating Section 317 the Senate did not regard differential treatment resulting from reciprocity agreements as discriminatory and therefore subject to Section 317.

The Conference Committee accepted the Senate version of Section 317 with little substantive alteration. The only significant change bearing on this discussion was the addition of the words "in fact" after the word "discriminates" in the statement of the circumstances that would make the penalty duties applicable. One can only speculate what the intent of this addition might have been. It has been suggested that it was intended "to deprive the word 'discriminates' of any legal connotation that might cling to it because of the American interpretation of most-favored-nation treatment."[126] It might be held equally that this addition was intended to exclude from the application of Section 317 differential treatment resulting from reciprocity treaties, which the Senate had not regarded as constituting discrimination.

The United States had adhered to a conditional MFN policy for 144 years. If it were the intent of Congress, directly or indirectly, to inaugurate a new and different MFN policy, it is reasonable to expect that there would have been some discussion of this intent. In the light of Senate debate, Section 317 should be regarded as a Congressional mandate for continued adherence to the conditional policy, rather than as one for adoption of an unconditional policy.

124. The text of Section 317, as originally presented in the Smoot amendment, as reported by the Finance Committee, as passed by the Senate, and as finally enacted after amendment by the Conference Committee, can be found in McClure, *New Commercial Policy*, pp. 337-40, 76-79, 341-43, and 23-26.

125. McClure, *New Commercial Policy*, p. 89.

126. *Ibid.*, p. 84.

The United States Tariff Commission, however, whose members drafted Section 317 of the 1922 Act, may very well have contemplated the adoption of a new MFN policy. In 1918, the commission, under the chairmanship of Taussig, issued a report that recommended equality of treatment as the guiding principle of postwar United States commercial policy and the use of penalty duties to enforce such treatment for United States exports.[127]

In referring to Section 317 in its *Annual Report* of 1922, the Tariff Commission said:

Section 317, as finally enacted with certain House amendments, provides, in effect, that the President shall endeavor to secure the removal of all discriminations which foreign countries may inflict upon the commerce of the United States. The law recognizes that there may be cases (sanitary regulations may afford instances) in which a discrimination between American and certain other products is reasonable, but aside from such reasonable exceptions, every country which 'discriminates in fact . . . in such manner as to place the commerce of the United States at a disadvantage compared with the commerce of any foreign country' is liable to discrimination against its commerce by the United States. The law itself thus defines discrimination and makes it clear that the point to be regarded is the effect upon American commerce and not the motive or intent of the foreign country in adopting its legislation or in adjusting its rates.[128]

It appears that the commission's view of what constituted discrimination differed from that of the Senate as reflected in Senate debate. Apparently, the commission regarded Section 317 as applicable to all kinds of discrimination, including differential treatment resulting from reciprocity agreements. Such an interpretation was inconsistent with United States conditional MFN policy and consequently implied the need for a change in this policy. Commissioner Culbertson, it will be recalled, used this interpretation as an argument for supporting the MFN policy change.[129]

127. U.S. Tariff Commission, *Reciprocity and Commercial Treaties*, 1919, pp. 10 and 14. The commission reiterated these views in its *Second Annual Report*, 1918, pp. 27-28.

128. U.S. Tariff Commission, *Sixth Annual Report*, 1922, pp. 5-6.

129. See above, pp. 38-39. In his correspondence with Hughes advocating a change in United States MFN policy and citing Section 317 as evidence of Congressional intent for a change in policy, Culbertson enclosed a memorandum in support of this view. This memorandum related to additional remarks made by Senator Smoot in the statement referred to in the text and to a statement by the House managers of the 1922 tariff bill appended to the Conference Committee *Report*. He might also have included similar excerpts from the *Report* of the Finance Committee on the tariff bill relating to Section 317. But like the text of Section 317 itself, the bearing of this material on the question of Congressional intent in regard to United States MFN policy depends upon its interpretation, particularly on what was meant by discrimination. Research on this point has failed to produce evidence that the Congress regarded differential treatment resulting from

Section 317, then, played a part in the 1923 change to an unconditional MFN policy, but not the role that has been assigned to it. Section 317 was used by the Harding Administration to justify, in part, this policy change, but it did not express the intention of Congress for such a change. Congress, however, voiced no objection to the new unconditional policy when it was announced by the Administration, and within a few years the Senate consented to treaties containing the unconditional MFN clause.[130]

REASONS FOR ADOPTION OF UNCONDITIONAL MFN POLICY

The Administration needed no justification for the 1923 policy change. There were sound reasons for this change with or without the existence of Section 317. After the middle of the nineteenth century, United States conditional MFN policy lost any practical value that it may have had in earlier years. The navigation laws and colonial trade policies that had prompted its adoption had largely disappeared, and most European countries had adopted an unconditional MFN policy in regard to tariffs. In these changed circumstances the conditional policy, because of its inherently discriminatory nature, was unsuited to obtain nondiscriminatory treatment for United States exports. Even when coupled with the threat of penalty duties, authorized in the Tariff Acts of 1890, 1897, and 1909, or when sweetened with the tariff reductions of the "argol" agreements, conditional MFN was not an effective instrument for obtaining nondiscrimination. The relative immunity from discrimination that United States products enjoyed in the latter years of the nineteenth and early years of the twentieth centuries was due to reasons other than United States conditional policy.

In the first place, by maintaining a single-column tariff, the United States, despite its conditional policy, did not discriminate against the products of other countries except in those few cases where reciprocity agreements were concluded. There was little occasion, therefore, for retaliation by other countries.

Secondly, United States exports were protected against discrimination in many cases where the United States had MFN treaty rights, even though these rights were of the conditional variety. Since the Cobden Treaty of 1860, it had become common European practice to make com-

---

reciprocity agreements as constituting discrimination and, therefore, subject to the penalty duties of Section 317.

130. Senator Lodge even supported adoption of the new policy. Secretary Hughes in his letter of January 15, 1923, to President Harding, suggesting a change in United States MFN policy, enclosed a letter from Senator Lodge, dated January 8, 1923, which was favorable to Culbertson's views. See Culbertson, *Reciprocity*, p. 258.

mercial treaties containing the unconditional MFN clause. Many of the countries with which the United States had conditional MFN agreements had unconditional MFN commitments to third countries. In such cases it could be argued that any tariff benefits freely extended to such third countries having unconditional rights also had to be extended freely to the United States under the terms of the conditional clause. Under these circumstances United States conditional rights were, in effect, unconditional.

Thirdly, United States exports consisted largely of agricultural goods and raw materials, which were much desired by the industrialized European countries that purchased them and which were largely noncompetitive with their own more finished production. Except for a few foodstuffs there was little desire either to protect or discriminate against such United States exports. This was particularly true from a payments viewpoint because until 1874 the United States had a consistent over-all merchandise trade deficit, and even after this date no difficulty was experienced in countries' payments positions vis-à-vis the United States.

About the turn of the century, however, these conditions that had shielded the United States from the consequences of its conditional policy began to change.

Firstly, in the 1890's and afterwards United States practice of nondiscrimination within the framework of conditional MFN underwent several aberrations that caused much hostility. In many cases the agreements negotiated under threat of penalties (authorized in the Tariff Act of 1890) obtained preferential treatment for United States exports, and in three instances, where agreements were not concluded, the United States discriminated against products of the countries concerned. The exclusive preferential treaty with Cuba, the arrangement with Brazil granting preferential treatment of certain United States products, and the imposition of contingent duties were further deviations from nondiscriminatory practice. The enactment of a double-column tariff in 1909, although it was never applied, was a major departure from the historic single-column policy, and it resulted in a number of negotiations with other countries that caused considerable friction.[131]

Secondly, the United States experienced difficulty in renewing or revising old commercial treaties and agreements or negotiating new ones on the conditional basis, so that in many cases United States exports were not afforded even conditional MFN protection against discrimina-

131. The "argol" agreements also caused friction with some countries. Even though these agreements were made effective within the framework of United States conditional MFN policy, third countries objected to the discrimination against their exports caused by tariff reductions in these agreements.

tion. As of 1922 the United States had "no commercial treaty with France, Russia nor the greater number of the secondary states of Europe; no commercial treaty with Mexico, Chile, nor many other states of Latin America; and no commercial treaty with India nor the five self-governing British dominions."[132] Most of the treaties in effect were more than fifty years old.[133] Furthermore, countries, including some with which the United States had commercial treaties, were threatening to adopt the conditional MFN practice, so that the advantages that the United States had enjoyed in the past from the unconditional practice of other countries might soon disappear. Such a widespread conditional system would also create difficulties for the United States because of the non-negotiable nature of the United States tariff. Apart from practical objections to the "equivalent-concession" bargaining inherent in such a system,[134] Congressional control of a tariff based on the cost-equalization principle would make it most difficult, if not impossible, for the United States to engage in the negotiations necessary under such a system to obtain nondiscriminatory treatment for its exports.

Thirdly, around the turn of the century the United States became more and more an exporter of manufactured goods. Agricultural products and raw materials, which made up 80 per cent or more of United States exports before the Civil War, still accounted for around 75 per cent in 1890, but by the outbreak of World War I they constituted less than 60 per cent. By 1920 exports of manufactures were half of total exports.[135] Because these manufactured goods were highly competitive with those of European countries, United States exports had lost one of the characteristics that had tended to immunize them from protective measures and from discrimination.

The changed international financial position of the United States from a debtor to a creditor also tended to make United States exports more liable to restrictive and discriminatory measures. The very discrimination to which United States products had become more liable had also become more objectionable, because of the increasing dependence on foreign markets by some segments of United States industry. This changed international financial position and increasing dependence of industry on foreign markets, which argued for a change in United States tariff policy at the end of World War I, also argued for a change in MFN policy.

The United States adopted an unconditional MFN policy because officials like Secretary Hughes and Commissioner Culbertson recognized

132. Culbertson, *Reciprocity*, p. 253.   133. *Ibid.*
134. See above, pp. 30-31.   135. *Statistical Abstract*, 1922, p. 354.

that in the changed postwar situation the conditional policy was unlikely to secure the relative immunity from discrimination that, for reasons other than adherence to this policy, United States exports had enjoyed in the past.[136] Since most European and other countries regarded the conditional MFN clause as discriminatory in nature, inclusion of the unconditional clause in future commercial treaties appeared to be a better way of securing nondiscriminatory treatment for United States exports. In explaining this change of policy in 1924, Secretary Hughes said:

. . . It was the interest and fundamental aim of this country to secure equality of treatment but the conditional most-favored-nation clause was not in fact productive of equality of treatment and could not guarantee it. It merely promised an opportunity to bargain for such treatment. Moreover, the ascertaining of what might constitute equivalent compensation in the application of the conditional most-favored-nation principle was found to be difficult or impracticable. Reciprocal commercial arrangements were but temporary makeshifts; they caused constant negotiation and created uncertainty. Under present conditions, the expanding foreign commerce of the United States needs a guarantee of equality of treatment which cannot be furnished by the conditional form of the most-favored-nations clause.

. . . To be consistent with our professions, and to conserve our interests it has become important that we make our commercial practice square in fact with the theory upon which our policy has been based. This explains the reason why, having examined with most minute care the history of the application of our conditional most-favored-nation principle, the Administration decided to abandon this practice and in its place to adopt the practice of unconditional most-favored-nation treatment. . . .

. . . As we seek pledges from other foreign countries that they will refrain from practicing discrimination, we must be ready to give such pledges, and history has shown that these pledges can be made adequate only in terms of unconditional most-favored-nation treatment. . . .[137]

The decision for this change in policy was made easier because it involved nothing more than guaranteeing by treaty commitment the treatment that the United States was already extending to other countries. The preferential Cuban treaty and duty-free importation of goods from United States dependencies were to be specifically excepted from the application of the clause. President Harding was prepared to cancel the

136. In addition to Section 317, most of the reasons discussed above were cited or referred to by Culbertson and Hughes in their various published statements urging or explaining the adoption of the unconditional policy.

137. Letter from Secretary Hughes to Senator Lodge, urging Senate consent to ratification of the Treaty of Friendship, Commerce, and Consular Rights with Germany signed on December 8, 1923. This letter is published in *Foreign Relations,* 1924, Vol. II, pp. 183-92. Sections quoted above can be found on pp. 190 and 191.

Cuban treaty if it were going to affect our entire foreign trade. The Department of State, however, concluded that since Congress in special provisions in the Tariff Acts of 1909, 1913, and 1922 had expressed its concern about preserving the Cuban arrangement, it would be better to request other countries to make an exception to it. In return the United States would permit similar exceptions.[138]

The new policy, however, was broader than adoption of the unconditional MFN clause in future commercial treaties. It embraced the entire principle of nondiscrimination; therefore, it marked a return to traditional United States practice in this respect. In line with this broader concept, in January, 1923, the United States requested that Brazil extend unconditional MFN treatment to United States products instead of the preferential treatment that had been requested annually and that Brazil had granted since 1904.[139] With the termination of the Brazilian arrangement, the last remnant of the penalty-preferential bargaining policy of the 1890's came to an end. Except for the Cuban treaty and the treatment of goods from United States dependencies, the only deviation of any significance from the unconditional MFN principle that remained was provision for contingent duties on a few products contained in the 1922 Tariff Act.[140]

IMPLEMENTATION OF THE 1923 POLICY

United States tariff policy for the next decade became firmly established in 1923. That policy was a high, non-negotiable, but nondiscriminatory tariff. The high tariff based on the cost-equalization principle was regarded as a matter of strictly domestic concern. Only if it were discriminatory was a tariff regarded as concerning other countries.

From this policy base, Secretary Hughes set out to negotiate commercial treaties incorporating the unconditional MFN clause with the purpose of obtaining nondiscriminatory treatment for United States exports. By mid-1923 negotiations had been initiated with Spain, Austria, Germany, Hungary, and Czechoslovakia.

The German treaty was the first to be signed, and it became the prototype for others. Article VII of this treaty provided for unconditional MFN treatment. It said in part:

138. Culbertson, *Reciprocity,* pp. 259 and 260.

139. *Foreign Relations,* 1923, Vol. I, p. 454.

140. The general provisions for contingent duties that would have been applicable to all products was deleted from the Fordney Bill along with the reciprocity provisions by the Senate Finance Committee, but a few provisions for contingent duties on specific products were included in the tariff bill as it was finally enacted. Provisions for contingent duties on a few products were included also in the Tariff Act of 1930, but these were repealed in the Trade Agreements Act of 1934.

Each of the High Contracting Parties binds itself unconditionally to impose no higher or other duties or conditions and no prohibition on the importation of any article, the growth, produce or manufacture, of the territories of the other than are or shall be imposed on the importation of any like article, the growth, produce or manufacture of any other foreign country.

Each of the High Contracting Parties also binds itself unconditionally to impose no higher or other charges or other restrictions or prohibitions on goods exported to the territories of the other High Contracting Party than are imposed on goods exported to any other foreign country.

Any advantage of whatsoever kind which either High Contracting Party may extend to any article, the growth, produce, or manufacture of any other foreign country shall simultaneously and unconditionally, without request and without compensation, be extended to the like article the growth, produce or manufacture of the other High Contracting Party.[141]

The Senate did not give its advice and consent to ratification until 1925, when the treaty entered into force, but this delay was not due to the treaty's unconditional MFN clause. In considering this treaty, the Foreign Relations Committee and the Senate voiced no objection to the new unconditional MFN clause.[142] As indicated earlier, even though passage of Section 317 did not reflect any desire of the Senate for a change in MFN policy, the Senate had no objection to this policy change once it was effected.

From the very beginning Secretary Hughes experienced difficulty in implementing the new MFN policy in treaties. In 1923, for example, Spain refused to grant United States products unconditional MFN treatment unless the United States would reduce its tariff on certain products of interest to Spain. United States tariff policy did not allow for such reductions, and no treaty was concluded. The Spanish had suggested that reductions might be made under Section 315 of the 1922 Tariff Act, but they were told that Section 315 was intended as a means of equalizing foreign and domestic production costs, that the Tariff Act did not associate tariff reductions under Section 315 with treaty negotiations, and that the United States government would not want to include in a treaty any provision dealing with such an essentially domestic matter. A modus vivendi, prolonging a 1906 commercial agreement, was effected, extended from time to time, and finally made of indefinite duration,

141. U.S. Dept. of State, *Treaty Series,* No. 725, Treaty between the United States and Germany, Friendship, Commerce and Consular Rights, 1925.

142. U.S. Congress, Senate Committee on Foreign Relations, *Hearings* on the Treaty of Commerce and Consular Rights with Germany, 68th Cong., 1st Sess., January 25–March 11, 1924. U.S. *Congressional Record,* 68th Cong., 2nd Sess., Vol. LXVI, Pt. 4 (February 10, 1925), pp. 3385-90.

but despite the threat of penalties under Section 317, Spain continued to refuse to grant unconditional MFN treatment to United States exports.[143]

The most dramatic instance in which the new policy encountered difficulty concerned France. French postwar commercial policy had been conducted on the basis of MFN bargaining in which French minimum tariff rates were granted in exchange for tariff concessions by other countries. However, United States goods, for the most part, had been extended the lowest French rates under arrangements agreed upon in 1910 and 1921. After enactment of a new tariff law in 1927 and the simultaneous entry into force of a reciprocity agreement with Germany, this favorable treatment ceased. Not only were United States goods subjected to the very high rates of the French tariff revision but also in many cases these rates were discriminatory because of lower rates accorded to Germany. It was estimated that from $40 million to $60 million of United States trade might be diverted to Germany.[144]

After the French government announced the new rates on August 31, 1927, the United States protested on the grounds that they were discriminatory because they were not applicable to Germany. The United States admitted that in the absence of a commercial treaty it had no right to demand unconditional MFN treatment, but it requested such treatment on the grounds that the United States accorded nondiscriminatory treatment to French products. At the same time the United States expressed its desire to proceed with negotiations for a commercial treaty and submitted a draft, similar to the German-United States prototype, for French consideration.

France objected to the unconditional MFN clause, contending that unconditional MFN treatment by the United States was not comparable to similar treatment by France, because high United States tariff rates were not equivalent to the moderate rates of the French minimum tariff. France would not consider the United States draft treaty as a basis for negotiation unless tariff reductions on French export products were made. France suggested that such reductions might be made under Section 315 of the 1922 Tariff Act.

The United States was unable to assure France of tariff reductions under Section 315. There was even the embarrassing possibility that cost investigations made under Section 315 would require that higher rather than lower duties be imposed. Penalty duties under Section 317 were

143. For an account of commercial treaty negotiations with Spain, see *Foreign Relations*, 1923, Vol. II, pp. 831-74; 1924, Vol. II, pp. 684-92; 1925, Vol. II, pp. 707-13; 1927, Vol. III, pp. 729-33; and 1929, Vol. III, pp. 788-96.

144. *The New York Times*, September 13, 1927.

threatened if France continued to discriminate against United States products.[145]

The positions of the two governments were irreconcilable. The United States under its unconditional MFN policy regarded nondiscriminatory treatment as a principle of international conduct and not a matter for bargaining. To obtain unconditional MFN treatment for its exports, the United States was willing to grant unconditional MFN treatment to the exports of other countries, but nothing else. Tariffs, as long as they were not discriminatory, were regarded as a domestic matter. France regarded nondiscriminatory treatment as something to be bargained against high tariff rates. Equality of bad treatment was not considered good enough to obtain the French minimum rates.

No commercial treaty was concluded. A compromise agreement to continue during the period of further negotiations provided that tariff treatment of United States goods by France would be restored substantially to that which existed before the new tariff came into effect. On its part the United States agreed to transmit to the Tariff Commission French requests for cost-of-production investigations under Section 315.[146] No cost investigations were ever made, however, and some United States goods continued to be subject to discrimination under the compromise agreement.[147]

The controversy with France illustrates the practical difficulty that the United States experienced in implementing Secretary Hughes's program of negotiating unconditional MFN treaties while at the same time maintaining a high, non-negotiable tariff. Negotiations for unconditional MFN treatment were actively carried on with countries in all parts of the world until late 1929. In 1933 the United States had unconditional MFN

145. For a general account of this tariff dispute with France, see "The Franco-American Tariff Dispute," *Foreign Policy Association Information Service*, III (October 26, 1927), 241-60. For a detailed account of the diplomatic correspondence involved in this dispute, see *Foreign Relations,* 1927, Vol. II, pp. 631-702.

146. The United States also agreed to examine in the most friendly spirit any French complaints concerning United States sanitary regulations, to discontinue cost investigations by United States officials in French territory, and to lower the contingent duties that had been placed on some French products as the result of the tariff increases made by France.

147. No cost investigations were made under Section 315 by the Tariff Commission, because the principle of foreign and domestic cost equalization, upon which any duty reductions had to be based, made such reductions improbable. In addition, the rigid statutory language of this "flexible" provision made the satisfaction of French requests virtually impossible. Section 315 required that costs in the principal competing country should be compared with United States costs. The French request for reduction in the duty on peanut oil, therefore, would have had to depend upon the investigation of costs in China rather than in France. In the case of silk velvet and plush ribbons, there was no domestic production of comparable articles, and therefore, neither a cost study nor tariff relief was possible. Percy W. Bidwell, *Tariff Policy of the United States* (New York: The Council on Foreign Relations, 1933), p. 66.

pledges from twenty-nine countries, twelve of which were included in treaties and seventeen in executive agreements.[148] These countries, however, accounted for only about 20 per cent of United States exports. Conditional MFN pledges or pledges that were not expressly unconditional were still in effect with fifteen countries,[149] accounting for less than 40 per cent of United States exports. More than 40 per cent of United States exports went to countries with which the United States had no MFN commitments of any kind.[150] Among the countries in this latter group were Canada, France,[151] the Soviet Union, Mexico, Sweden, Venezuela, Switzerland, and the other British Dominions and Crown Colonies. Germany was the only country of major importance to United States export trade with which a commercial treaty or agreement providing for unconditional MFN treatment had been concluded. More than 80 per cent of United States exports remained unprotected by expressly unconditional MFN assurances after the program of active negotiation of commercial treaties ceased.

The relative lack of success of this program was due in large part to United States maintenance of a high, non-negotiable tariff. Taussig refers to this difficulty in implementing Secretary Hughes's treaty program:

. . . while we offer everybody the same treatment, we merely offer the same bad treatment all around. Our rates are so high, our policy of protection is so intolerant, so all-embracing, so inclined to extension to every blessed article on the demands of each interested group of producers, that our most-favored-nation policy amounts to universal severity and universal ill treatment. Under such circumstances can we expect any warmth of feeling, any cordial response to our newly taken basis of negotiation?[152]

148. The countries with which treaties had been concluded were Austria, China, Estonia, El Salvador, Germany, Honduras, Hungary, Latvia, Norway, Siam, Turkey, and Yugoslavia.

The countries with which executive agreements had been concluded were Albania, Brazil, Bulgaria, Chile, Czechoslovakia, Dominican Republic, Egypt, Finland, Greece, Guatemala, Haiti, Lithuania, Nicaragua, Persia, Poland, Rumania, and Spain. U.S. Tariff Commission, *Tariff Bargaining Under Most-Favored-Nations Treaties*, Rep. No. 65, 2nd Ser., 1933, p. 3.

149. These countries were Argentina, Belgium, Bolivia, Borneo, Colombia, Costa Rica, Denmark, Ethiopia, Luxemburg, the United Kingdom, Italy, Japan, Liberia, Paraguay, and Portugal. *Ibid.,* p. 4.

150. Calculated from Tables No. 459 and 484, *Statistical Abstract*, 1934, pp. 402 and 424-29.

151. The *modus vivendi* concluded with France in 1927 provided that certain United States products would receive the French minimum tariff rates, but it did not assure MFN treatment to all United States exports.

152. F. W. Taussig, "The Tariff Controversy with France," *Foreign Affairs*, VI (January, 1928), 185.

It was even suggested that United States unconditional MFN policy was a shield for its high-tariff policy. In commenting on the policies of France and the United States during the tariff dispute between these countries, Cordell Hull, then a member of Congress, said that "the primary purpose of the French bargaining tariff policy was to promote foreign trade, while that of the United States in changing its policy [MFN] was to fortify the Fordney Tariffs against the slightest assault, with minor concern for foreign trade."[153]

In the diplomatic correspondence of the tariff dispute with France, the United States had referred to the unanimous endorsement of the unconditional MFN principle by the members of the 1927 World Economic Conference, including the French participants.[154] France was quick to point out that the World Economic Conference also associated the reduction of excessive tariffs with equality of treatment.[155] French bargaining policy, which frequently resulted in discrimination and which infrequently resulted in more than the removal of the padding in French tariff rates, was not in the interest of expanding world trade. But neither was United States tariff policy, even though nondiscriminatory. Nor was United States unconditional MFN policy able to obtain widespread assurances of nondiscriminatory treatment for United States exports.

This inconsistency in United States trade policy was remedied in 1934, when in the Trade Agreements Act the United States tariff became negotiable while at the same time the unconditional MFN policy was retained.

3. OPPOSITION TO QUANTITATIVE RESTRICTIONS

In 1927 the United States signed and in 1929 ratified the International Convention on the Abolition of Import and Export Prohibitions and Restrictions.[156] This multilateral agreement outlawed the use of quantitative restrictions to protect domestic industries. Adherence to the Convention crystallized United States policy toward quantitative restrictions, a policy that, despite some subsequent deviations, remains United States policy today.[157]

153. *The New York Times,* October 4, 1927.
154. *Foreign Relations,* 1927, Vol. II, p. 679.
155. *Ibid.,* pp. 683-84.
156. Hereafter, referred to as the Prohibitions Convention.
157. The following discussion is based upon William B. Kelly, Jr., *The 1927 Convention on the Abolition of Import and Export Prohibitions and Restrictions and Its Significance in United States Commercial Policy* (Ann Arbor, Mich.: University Microfilms, Inc., 1963).

BACKGROUND OF THE PROHIBITIONS CONVENTION

Before World War I, tariffs were the principal barrier to international trade. Not since mercantilist times had quantitative restrictions on trade been used extensively for protective purposes. During World War I quantitative restrictions were used widely to control exports and imports.[158] However, they were regarded as emergency wartime measures to be discontinued after the end of hostilities.

After the Armistice the removal of quantitative restrictions, particularly import restrictions, was not as easy a task as had been anticipated. One effect of import controls had been to protect domestic industries, even though they had not been imposed for this purpose. Producers who had benefited from this protection resisted the relaxation of restrictions and exerted political pressure to prevent it.[159] Within a few years of the Armistice, however, quantitative restrictions were no longer of major importance outside of Central and Eastern Europe.

Extremely adverse conditions in Central and Eastern Europe retarded the relaxation of quantitative restrictions that occurred elsewhere. Acute shortages of food, raw materials, and manufactured articles led governments to retain quantitative controls on exports. Quantitative controls on imports were retained because of extreme currency disorders. Countries whose currencies were depreciating in the foreign-exchange market attempted to prevent or slow down this depreciation by limiting imports to necessities. (The balance-of-payments arguments used by many countries after World War II to justify the retention or imposition of quantitative restrictions on imports were similar to those used in the early 1920's by countries with depreciating currencies.) Behind such controls vested interests became firmly entrenched, making the ultimate problem of decontrol more difficult.

A partial relaxation of quantitative restrictions in Central and Eastern Europe was effected through contingent agreements in which contracting states mutually allowed the importation or exportation of fixed quantities of specified commodities. These agreements amounted to a form of barter, and they closely resembled similar agreements negotiated for the same purpose after World War II. Provisions for contingents even became involved in negotiations of permanent treaties with such distant

158. For an account of wartime trade controls of European belligerents, see O. Delle-Donne, *European Tariff Policies: Since the World War* (New York: Adelphi Company, 1928), Pt. I, Chaps. II and III.

159. Quantitative restrictions were advocated also to protect industries from the goods of countries with depreciating currencies. It may be recalled in this connection that one of the reasons for the very high rates in the United States Tariff Act of 1922 was the fear of exchange dumping by countries with depreciated currencies. See above, p. 8.

countries as the United States.[160] Contingent agreements were a far cry from the prewar system of multilateral trade to which European countries aspired and which they considered normal and proper.

Gradually, many quantitative restrictions were withdrawn as the conditions that prompted their retention passed away. After 1925, they were no longer a dominant feature of commercial policies even in Central and Eastern Europe. But the process of elimination was never completed, and important prohibitions and restrictions were retained throughout the 1920's. These restrictions, like those retained after World War II, had the effect, if not the purpose, of protecting domestic industries.

In this post World War I period, governments generally were opposed in principle to the use of quantitative restrictions, and they desired to abolish them and to return to prewar trading practices. Use was made of them largely because they provided a more precise and certain control of imports and exports than customs duties.[161] Prompt and frequent adjustment of numerous duties to meet postwar conditions was regarded as an impossible administrative task. It was widely recognized, however, that even though quantitative restrictions might have been better suited than customs duties to meet the extreme economic difficulties of this period, they did not shed themselves of their objectionable features.[162]

The desire to abolish quantitative restrictions as soon as possible was reflected repeatedly in the declarations of postwar international economic conferences. The Brussels Financial Conference of 1920, the Portorose Conference of 1921, and the Genoa Conference of 1922 urged the abolition of import and export prohibitions and restrictions. An agreement concluded at the 1923 Geneva Conference on the Simplification of Customs Formalities committed its signatories to reduce quantitative restrictions "as soon as circumstances permit . . . to the smallest number."[163] But it did not pass on the principle of quantitative restrictions as a form of trade control nor did it set a definite date for their removal. Finally, on the initiative of the Assembly of the League of Nations, the Economic

160. For example, in United States negotiations with Czechoslovakia in 1923 for a general treaty of amity, commerce, and consular rights, contingents for imports of automobiles were discussed. See *Foreign Relations,* 1923, Vol. I, pp. 866-75.

161. Furthermore, European trade at the end of World War I was almost completely under government control. Retention of wartime restrictions was the least line of resistance. This situation was very different from that which arose in the 1930's, when a system of trade regulated primarily by tariffs was then supplemented and in large measure superseded by a system of quantitative restrictions.

162. For a brief discussion of objections to quantitative restrictions as compared with tariffs, and for references to other sources, see below, pp. 58-59.

163. League of Nations, *International Convention Relating to the Simplification of Customs Formalities* (Geneva: November 3, 1923), C.678. M.241. 1924.II., p. 4.

Committee of the League drafted an international convention for the suppression of quantitative restrictions, and the Council of the League convened an international conference to consider adoption of this convention. The conference met from October 17 to November 8, 1927, with thirty-four countries, including the United States, represented; it marked the culmination of the many international efforts after 1920 to abolish quantitative restrictions.

THE UNITED STATES AND THE PROHIBITIONS CONVENTION

The United States imposed no restrictions of the type with which the 1927 Conference on the Abolition of Import and Export Prohibitions and Restrictions was concerned, nor had it ever done so, except in rare instances. Through the War Trade Board, various prohibitions and restrictions had been imposed during World War I, but these were abolished soon after the Armistice. In the postwar period the United States rejected quantitative restrictions as a means of protecting domestic industries in favor of high tariffs, which were legislated in the Tariff Act of 1922. Great pressure was exerted by the United States chemical industry to protect warborn production of dyestuffs by an import prohibition, but such drastic legislation was never made permanent.[164]

The United States had declined to be represented or had been represented only by an observer at the postwar international conferences at which quantitative restrictions had been considered. Quantitative restrictions were primarily a European problem, and since the end of World War I the United States had largely detached itself from European affairs and had had even less to do with activities of the League of Nations.

However, even though the United States had not actively participated in the earlier international efforts to abolish quantitative restrictions, it was most interested in their suppression. United States exports, particularly of automobiles, had been hurt by import prohibitions and restrictions imposed by other countries. These restrictions not only had curtailed exports but had discriminated against them as well, because of

164. The Dye and Chemical Control Act, approved May 27, 1921, imposed a qualified prohibition on imports of dyestuffs and other coal-tar products for a period of three months. This prohibition was later extended for another three months, and then indefinitely, but it was repealed by the Tariff Act of 1922 in favor of high ad valorem duties assessed upon a very high valuation basis, the American selling price (see above, pp. 16-17). What amounted to a policy of nearly prohibitive duties was thereby substituted for quantitative restrictions.

The Tariff Act of 1930 continued protecting coal-tar products with high duties based upon the American selling price. If such protection could be justified after World War I, it is more difficult to justify today when the coal-tar sector of the United States chemical industry exports twice as much of such products as the United States imports.

the manner in which they had been applied. They had also hampered the negotiation of commercial treaties in which the United States sought to obtain nondiscriminatory treatment of its exports. The very fact that the United States was willing to participate fully in a League-sponsored conference indicates the importance it attached to the abolition of quantitative restrictions.[165]

The draft convention of the Economic Committee of the League of Nations, which was the basis of the deliberations of the 1927 conference, provided for the abolition of all import and export prohibitions and restrictions within a period of six months subject to two types of exceptions. The first was prohibitions or restrictions based on non-economic considerations and generally recognized as indispensable and compatible with freedom of trade. These related to national defense, public health, public morality, and the like. The second, provided for under Article 5, was prohibitions or restrictions necessary to meet "extraordinary and abnormal circumstances and to protect the vital economic and financial interests of the State."[166]

At the 1927 conference much controversy concerned the general exception of Article 5. Some countries that wanted as tight a convention as possible would have eliminated Article 5 or amended it, so as to limit its use. Others favored a much less rigid convention with a loose interpretation of Article 5. As in most international controversies, a compromise was made. Article 5 was included, but it was tightened. To placate those countries that favored a broader general exception, a new Article 6 exempted prohibitions or restrictions on products to be listed in an annex to the convention. This compromise necessitated a second conference, held from July 3 to July 11, 1928, which considered and attempted to limit the specific exceptions allowed under Article 6.

At both the 1927 and 1928 conferences, the United States sided with those countries that wanted a tightly drawn convention. In addition to limiting the scope of the general exception of Article 5, the United States also wanted to limit the number of specific exceptions allowed under Article 6. The United States was concerned especially about proposed reservations on imports of automobiles (Czechoslovakia and Portugal) and on exports of raw cork (Portugal)—products in which it had a

---

165. At the 1927 World Economic Conference, which was sponsored by the League of Nations, the United States was represented by a delegation, but delegates attended this conference in their individual capacities and not as representatives of their governments.

166. For the text of the Economic Committee's draft convention, see League of Nations, International Conference for the Abolition of Import and Export Prohibitions and Restrictions, Geneva, October 17 to November 8, 1927, *Proceedings of the Conference* (Geneva: February 1, 1928), C.21. M.12. 1928.II., pp. 224-26.

trading interest. The United States was also concerned about a proposed export reservation by Czechoslovakia on rounded timber, not because Czechoslovakia was an important supply source, but because, if once recognized, similar restrictions might also be invoked by other countries, such as by Canada in the case of pulpwood. All of these proposed reservations, except that on raw cork, were withdrawn. The withdrawal of reservations on automobiles was particularly gratifying.

The United States was also most interested in the abolition of restrictions, imposed by France and other countries, that limited the showing of foreign films. However, these restrictions were never put forward as exceptions to the Prohibitions Convention. They were regarded by the countries resorting to them as legitimate restrictions to preserve their culture and traditions and not within the scope of the convention's provisions.

United States opposition to a loosely drawn convention was motivated only partly by its economic interest in limiting quantitative restrictions imposed by other countries on its exports and imports. The position of the United States at the 1927 and 1928 Prohibitions Conferences cannot be explained solely in these terms. An adequate explanation must include opposition to quantitative restrictions as a matter of principle.

During the 1920's the United States, probably even more than other countries, regarded quantitative restrictions as an improper form of trade control. Indeed, if at any time in its history the United States had been required to formulate a position on this type of trade restriction, it would have been opposed to its use. The United States view was that if domestic industries were to be protected from foreign competition, then this protection should take the form of tariffs.

The reasons for this United States preference for tariffs as a means of protection were not so fully formulated at the time of the Prohibitions Convention as they later came to be. It can be accounted for in part, however, as a reflection of United States devotion to the free-enterprise economic system. Unlike tariffs, quantitative restrictions are completely alien to the price mechanism upon which this system is based. Quantitative restrictions tend to destroy the price relationship between foreign and domestic markets. Because of their absolute nature, which prohibits all trade in a commodity after the allowed amount has entered the country, quantitative restrictions do not permit price adjustments via changes in trade volume to take place. Tariffs, on the other hand, are more flexible instruments of trade restriction. A product subject to a tariff may be imported as long as the prescribed duty is paid. Price adjustments can take place between the world market and the country imposing a tariff because trade in the commodity concerned may continue. Price changes in the world market or in the tariff-imposing country may be transmitted to each other via changes in import volume. A price differential between the tariff-imposing country and the world market is created, but the price mechanism is not destroyed.[167]

The United States also opposed quantitative restrictions as a matter of principle because of their inherently discriminatory nature. No matter how administered, quantitative restrictions almost always discriminate among supplying countries and among domestic importers. Trade restrictions are nondiscriminatory only if the patterns of trade among supplying countries and among domestic importers are the same as they would be in the absence of the restrictions. Seldom, if ever, will such nondiscriminatory trade patterns follow the imposition of quantitative restrictions. Tariffs, on the other hand, are not by their nature discriminatory. They afford equal treatment to supplying countries and to traders if the same rates are applicable to all countries.[168]

Apart from principle, United States concern over the discriminatory aspects of quantitative restrictions stemmed from their discriminatory effects on United States exports and from their conflict with United States unconditional MFN policy.

During the 1920's quantitative restrictions usually took the form of prohibitions to which governments made exceptions by granting licenses. In a few cases, however, they were of the quota type, and permitted imports were allocated among supplying countries. United States exports were discriminated against under both these practices, which frequently resulted in arbitrary actions. Even when quotas were allocated in equal amounts among supplying countries, as sometimes was the case, they were a greater restriction on United States exports than on the exports of other countries in instances where United States products occupied a

167. For a discussion of the price and other effects of quantitative restrictions as opposed to tariffs, see Kurt Häfner, "Zur Theorie der mengenmässigen Einfuhrregulierung," *Weltwirtschaftliches Archiv*, 41. Band (1935I), pp. 190-223, upon which much of the writing on the theoretical aspects of quantitative restrictions is based. See also Heinrich Heuser, *Control of International Trade* (Philadelphia: P. Blakiston's Son & Co., Inc., 1939), pp. 149-67; Margaret S. Gordon, *Barriers to World Trade* (New York: The Macmillan Company, 1941), pp. 232-43; and J. N. Reedman, "Some Notes on the Theoretical Aspects of Import Quotas," *The South African Journal of Economics*, IV (December, 1936), 425-35.

168. For a discussion of the discriminatory nature and other characteristics of quantitative restrictions, see League of Nations, *Quantitative Trade Controls: Their Causes and Nature*, prepared by Gottfried Haberler in collaboration with Martin Hill (Princeton, N.J.: Princeton University Press, 1943), 1943. II. A. 5, pp. 20-27, and League of Nations, *Trade Relations Between Free-Market and Controlled Economies*, prepared by Jacob Viner (Princeton, N.J.: Princeton University Press, 1943), 1943. II. A. 4, pp. 54-70.

more prominent position in the trade. Austria, Czechoslovakia, and Poland, for example, imposed quotas on automobile imports and allocated them in equal amounts among supplying countries even though the United States was by far the principal supplier.

In the negotiation of the Prohibitions Convention and commercial treaties, the United States experienced difficulties in applying the MFN principle to quantitative restrictions. In bilateral negotiations with Austria, France, and Sweden prior to and simultaneous with the 1927 Prohibitions Conference, the United States proposed provisions that attempted to prevent the arbitrary issuance of licenses and that required quota allocations to be based on equitable shares in view of the normal volume of trade of supplying countries.[169] At the 1927 conference the United States attempted to apply this same equitable-share doctrine to the allocation of quantitative restrictions allowed by the convention. The draft convention already contained provisions regarding licensing formalities very similar to those proposed in bilateral negotiations.

At the 1927 Prohibitions Conference the United States proposal on quota allocations was strongly opposed because it would have required an end to arbitrary allocation practices favored by some countries. Furthermore, it was looked upon as an attempt to apply the MFN clause to quota allocations. The MFN clause was not regarded generally as applying to quantitative restrictions, particularly to their allocation.

The United States effort to apply the MFN principle to quota allocations was only partly successful. The Protocol to the Prohibitions Convention implied that quota allocations were to be equitable, but "equitable" was not defined further and no mention was made of "normal volume of trade." United States bilateral efforts at this time also were only partly successful. The only treaty proclaimed that included an equitable-

169. United States views on nondiscriminatory treatment in regard to quantitative restrictions were more clearly defined in a 1935 policy statement, which recognized the undesirability of quotas and their basic inconsistency with an MFN policy and defined nondiscriminatory treatment as proportional allocation of quotas based on the trade in a commodity during a previous "representative" period. By "representative" period was meant "a series of years during which trade in the particular article under consideration was free from restrictive measures of a discriminatory character, and was not affected by unusual circumstances such as, for example, a crop failure in the case of an agricultural product." See Foreign Relations, 1935, Vol. I, p. 538. The term "representative," therefore, was flexible enough to take into account all circumstances affecting the trade in any commodity. The chief difficulty with this term is its ambiguity; it is impossible to determine a "representative" period in any completely precise or objective way. Such a period, therefore, is always subject to negotiation. Nevertheless, this representative-period formula "comes closer to a generally applicable formula which would prevent deliberate discriminatory treatment in the allotment of quotas by countries than any other formula which has so far been used or suggested." League of Nations, Trade Relations, p. 66.

share formula was with Austria, and it contained a provision comparable to the convention's Protocol.[170]

Just as United States MFN policy became involved in the United States position at the 1927 Prohibitions Conference, so did United States tariff policy. Tariffs, as already noted, were regarded as a matter of strictly domestic concern and not a subject for international discussion or negotiation.

The invitation of the League of Nations and the Economic Committee's draft convention had clearly implied that the 1927 Prohibitions Conference was to be concerned only with quantitative restrictions. However, once the conference convened, the question of tariffs played a prominent part in some of the proceedings. Many countries emphasized that what was really to be desired was greater freedom of trade and that this could not be accomplished by the elimination of quantitative restrictions alone. The Netherlands, in particular, wanted an expression from the conference that high import duties were as injurious to trade as import prohibitions and restrictions, and it submitted a proposal along these lines. The Final Act of the conference declared that excessive export or import duties or hindrances of any other kind should not replace the quantitative restrictions to be abolished by the Prohibitions Convention. It declared further that an elimination of quantitative restrictions entails correlative obligations in regard to export and import duties, especially in regard to import duties on articles manufactured from raw materials freed from quantitative export restrictions by the convention.

The inclusion of this declaration relating to tariffs in the Final Act prompted a speech by the United States delegate, Hugh Wilson, who said that this reference to customs duties was "like the ghost in Hamlet," which "continues to appear when least expected."[171] He stated further that United States policy "does not foresee the granting of reductions in duties as compensation for favours given" and that "we extend equality of treatment to all nations and endeavor to persuade them to do likewise."[172] But, as in the tariff controversy with France, United States policy of equality of treatment when it amounted to equality of bad treatment was not good enough to obtain the support of other governments. Only Rumania voted with the United States to suppress this

170. In bilateral trade agreements, concluded during the 1930's, and in the multilateral GATT, concluded in 1947, the United States was successful in including provisions for equitable quota allocations based on previous trade volume.

171. League of Nations, *Proceedings of the* [1927] *Conference*, p. 141.

172. *Ibid.*, pp. 141-42. He explained further that there was no method under the United States tariff by which the United States could respond to the implied moral obligation contained in the Final Act to reduce import duties.

declaration. Thereupon, members of the United States delegation refused to sign the Final Act even though it had no binding force.[173] To make the United States position completely clear, Wilson, when signing the Prohibitions Convention itself, attached a reservation to the effect that the convention in no way affected the tariff systems of contracting parties. Only Chile attached a similar reservation.

UNITED STATES RATIFICATION

Even though the United States did not succeed in keeping the subject of tariffs from consideration at the 1927 conference nor from inclusion in the Final Act, this never threatened United States ratification of the Prohibitions Convention. On January 2, 1929, Secretary of State Kellogg recommended to President Coolidge that the convention and its supplementary documents be ratified. The President concurred, and on January 3 he submitted these instruments to the Senate for its advice and consent to ratification. The Foreign Relations Committee, to which they had been referred, gave its unanimous approval on September 18, 1929; the Senate gave its advice and consent on the following day. President Hoover formally ratified these instruments on September 20, 1929, and he proclaimed the convention in effect on March 6, 1930.[174]

The Prohibitions Convention never came into force except in a few countries. Of the twenty countries that eventually ratified the convention, only eight did so without making their ratifications conditional on the ratification of others. Ten states made their ratifications contingent upon that of Poland, which refused to ratify. Besides the United States, only Denmark, Great Britain, Japan, the Netherlands, Norway, and Portugal were bound by the convention after July 1, 1930, when, according to an agreement reached at a third conference, held in December, 1929, quantitative restrictions were to be abolished. By June 30, 1934, all seven of the countries that had given effect to the convention, including the United States, had withdrawn.

Although the Prohibitions Convention was a failure, it is a landmark in United States commercial policy. The United States had no laws nor regulations that had to be changed in order to give effect to the convention, but nonresort to quantitative restrictions was less a matter of considered policy than of habit. Adherence to the convention formalized

173. The Final Act was not signed by delegates as plenipotentiaries of their governments, but it was open for signature to any person who attended the conference. Thus, members of the International Chamber of Commerce delegation, who attended the conference only in a consultative capacity, signed the Final Act.

174. The convention actually came into force on the part of the United States on January 1, 1930.

United States policy in regard to quantitative restrictions[175] just as adoption of the unconditional form of the MFN clause in 1923 formalized United States policy of nondiscrimination. It made deliberate a policy that heretofore had been followed as a matter of course. It made this policy definite at a time when quantitative restrictions had again become a means of restricting trade and in the 1930's were to become a most formidable trade barrier. The United States practiced a policy of high protection, but it drew the line at resort to this most drastic form of trade restriction. Tariffs alone were regarded as the proper means of furnishing protection to domestic industries. In later years, the elimination of quantitative restrictions imposed by foreign countries became a prime objective of United States trade policy.

4. POLICY REVERSAL

After the Democrats came to power in the White House in 1933, United States high, "flexible," non-negotiable tariff policy was changed. There was not a complete reversal of commercial policy, however, because the Democrats adopted the Republican policies of unconditional MFN treatment and opposition to quantitative restrictions.

THE 1933 WORLD MONETARY AND ECONOMIC CONFERENCE

The policies of the new Administration came to the fore in connection with the 1933 World Monetary and Economic Conference, held in London. Instructions by President Roosevelt to the United States delegation to this conference outlined future United States commercial policy. One of the resolutions to be proposed by the delegation read:

(a) That it is against the common interest for any nation to adopt or continue a policy of extreme economic nationalism and to raise additional trade barriers and discriminations;

(b) That embargoes, import quotas and various other arbitrary restrictions should be removed completely as quickly as possible; and

(c) That tariff barriers should be reduced as quickly as possible by

175. No official statement of United States policy in regard to quantitative restrictions was published in connection with the Prohibitions Convention, but the following quotation from an unpublished memorandum clearly indicates what this policy was: "Señor Muñoz [of the Argentine Embassy] called at the Treaty Division on July 24, 1931, for the purpose of inquiring whether there existed an official statement of the policy of the United States with reference to prohibitions and restrictions. Señor Muñoz was informed that the United States was a party to the convention for the abolition of import and export prohibitions and restrictions and that the maintenance of this treaty on the part of the United States would seem to constitute the best expression of its policy with reference to it." U.S. National Archives, Dept. of State, Treaty Division, "Import and Export Prohibitions and Restrictions, Conversation: Señor Muñoz of the Argentine Embassy," July 25, 1931, Policy Memorandum No. 544.

reciprocal bilateral agreements or by multilateral agreements to a point where trade can once more move in a free and normal manner; and

(d) That care should be taken in making bilateral or multilateral agreements not to introduce discriminatory features which, while providing an advantage to the contracting parties, would react disadvantageously upon world trade as a whole.[176]

Under United States leadership, an international tariff truce (more accurately a trade-barriers truce, because it included all trade restrictions) was instituted prior to and during the London Conference. At the conference, the United States introduced the commercial-policy resolution quoted above and also a comprehensive proposal, which outlined a possible international agreement on restrictive trade measures. This proposal prohibited the introduction of any new trade barriers and called for "bilateral (or plurilateral) negotiations for the removal of prohibitions and restrictions and for the reduction of tariff rates."[177] All agreements resulting from such negotiations were to "have incorporated in them the most-favoured-nation principle in its unconditional and unrestricted form—to be applied to all forms and methods of control of imports, and not only to import duties."[178]

Nothing of substance was accomplished at the London Conference in regard to tariffs or quantitative restrictions. Failure of the conference to reach any agreement on the stabilization of currencies precluded any meaningful agreement on trade matters. The United States position at the conference, however, reflected changed tariff policy and continued adherence to the principles of nondiscrimination and opposition to quantitative restrictions.

While the London Conference was in session, the United States withdrew from the Prohibitions Convention. However, this withdrawal did not signify any change in policy. The United States withdrew only after it became obvious that the Convention would obtain no new adherents and that other measures were needed if effective action on quantitative restrictions were to be taken.[179]

Later in 1933 the new turn that United States trade policy had taken at the London Conference was affirmed. At the Seventh International Conference of American States at Montevideo, Uruguay, the United

176. *Foreign Relations, 1933*, Vol. I, p. 627.

177. League of Nations, Monetary and Economic Conference, *Reports Approved by the Conference on July 27, 1933, and Resolutions Adopted by the Bureau and the Executive Committee* (London: July 27, 1933), C.435. M.220. 1933.II., p. 42.

178. *Ibid.*, p. 43.

179. See U.S. Dept. of State, *Treaty Information*, Bulletin No. 45 (June 30, 1933), p. 32, and *Foreign Relations, 1933*, Vol. I, pp. 784-85.

States introduced a comprehensive resolution on commercial policy based upon the earlier London proposal. This resolution, unanimously adopted by the conference, called for the reduction of tariffs and the removal of quantitative restrictions through bilateral or multilateral agreements, all such agreements to include the unconditional MFN clause.[180] Specific reference was made to the revival and revision of the 1927 Prohibitions Convention or to agreement upon a new convention that would abolish quantitative restrictions.[181]

The United States proposals at the London and Montevideo Conferences were designed to lay the groundwork for a future program of trade expansion through the reduction of tariffs and the abolition of quantitative restrictions. They were not drafts of agreements presented for adoption but statements of United States policy to which other governments were urged to adhere. This policy was to be implemented through subsequent bilateral or multilateral agreements.

In 1933 Secretary Hull had desired that legislation be passed similar to that subsequently enacted in 1934, authorizing the President to enter into trade agreements based on the unconditional MFN principle for the mutual lowering of trade barriers. These agreements were to become operative if not disapproved by Congress within sixty days. A bill to this effect was drafted, but it was never introduced, because of the Administration's preoccupation with domestic matters.[182]

The efforts of the Roosevelt Administration in 1933 to extricate the United States from the world depression compromised the trade policy put forward by Secretary Hull at London and Montevideo. In potential

180. However, unless they assumed corresponding obligations, countries were not to invoke the MFN clause in bilateral treaties with countries that were parties to a multilateral agreement that had as its purpose the liberalization of trade and that was open to all parties. The United States commercial policy proposal introduced at the London Conference contained a similar stipulation in regard to the MFN clause. Its purpose was to encourage the use of multilateral agreements for the reduction of trade barriers by reserving their advantages for countries assuming their obligations.

Under United States initiative a draft international agreement requiring contracting parties to refrain from invoking the MFN clause in respect of certain multilateral conventions was approved by the Montevideo Conference. After clarifying amendments by the Governing Board of the Pan-American Union, this agreement was opened to signature by all countries on July 15, 1934. Although signed subsequently by nine countries, it is in force today only on the part of Cuba, Greece, and the United States.

181. For the text of the United States commercial policy resolution adopted at the Montevideo Conference, see Seventh International Conference of American States, *Plenary Sessions*, Minutes and Antecedents, Montevideo, 1933, pp. 40-41.

182. However, during 1933, preliminary discussions or negotiations on treaties for the reduction of trade barriers were conducted by the United States with Argentina, Brazil, Canada, Colombia, Cuba, New Zealand, Norway, Portugal, and Sweden. A treaty with Colombia was signed, but it never received the requisite legislative approval of either government.

conflict with this policy were the National Industrial Recovery Act (NIRA) and the Agricultural Adjustment Act (AAA), which authorized the imposition of higher tariffs and quantitative restrictions on imports if they interfered with domestic programs designed to raise prices of industrial and agricultural products. Consequently, the United States commercial policy proposals introduced at the London and Montevideo Conferences included exceptions for this legislation.

In 1934, largely due to the persistence of Secretary Hull, a dual approach to depression problems was adopted. Domestic measures such as the NIRA and AAA were still to be given priority, but an attempt to stimulate United States exports was also to be made through the negotiation of agreements for the mutual lowering of trade barriers. Tariff reductions made under these agreements were to be generalized to third countries, and Section 336, the "flexible" cost-equalization provision of the 1930 Tariff Act was not to apply to items subject to tariff concessions. Congressional approval of these agreements was given in advance in the Trade Agreements Act of 1934.[183] This Act gave legislative sanction to and provided the means for carrying out the trade policy proposed by the United States at the London and Montevideo Conferences.

SUMMARY

The years between 1922 and 1934 are important in a study of United States commercial policy because they saw the development of two features of present-day policy, the unconditional MFN principle and opposition to quantitative restrictions for protective purposes.

Adoption of the unconditional MFN policy under Secretary Hughes in 1923 was a historic change. This policy of the Republicans under the Harding, Coolidge, and Hoover Administrations was accepted by the Democrats when they came to power in 1933 and was put into legislative form in the 1934 Trade Agreements Act. The 1954 report of the Republican-sponsored Commission on Foreign Economic Policy (Randall Commission) recommended specifically that this unconditional MFN policy be continued, thereby reaffirming earlier Republican policy of the 1920's. In 1955 the Eisenhower Administration and the Congress tacitly accepted this recommendation by extending the Trade Agreements Act. The 1962 trade legislation of the Kennedy Administration continues this policy.

Republican policy in regard to quantitative restrictions was also accepted by the Democrats in 1933, when at the London and Montevideo Conferences the United States sought more effective multilateral action

183. For a discussion of the 1934 Trade Agreements Act, see Chap. II.

in regard to quantitative restrictions than had been achieved by the 1927 Prohibitions Convention. During the 1930's bilateral trade agreements negotiated under the trade-agreements program included provisions prohibiting quantitative restrictions on scheduled items, i.e., on products upon which tariff concessions had been made. In 1947 under the Democrats, the United States furnished the impetus for the outlawing of these restrictions in the GATT. The Republican Administration of President Eisenhower was reluctant to impose quantitative restrictions and, in general, adhered to earlier Republican policy. President Eisenhower, for example, when questioned at a press conference on February 8, 1956, about his views on quotas, said, "I have always been against quotas. I think quotas are a very bad way to handle our foreign trade, if we can get out of it. Now, I realize that in a few products we haven't. But I don't believe in them."[184] He gave evidence of this belief in 1957 when he rejected the Tariff Commission's recommendation in an escape-clause action for a quota on clothespins and raised the tariff instead.[185] Despite deviations, mostly due to domestic agricultural programs,[186] United States policy since the Prohibitions Convention has generally opposed the use of quantitative restrictions for protective purposes.[187]

The third feature of United States commercial policy during the 1920's and early 1930's, the high, "flexible," non-negotiable tariff, established in the Republican Tariff Act of 1922 and retained in the Tariff Act of 1930, was changed under the Democrats. Indications of this change were evident at the 1933 London and Montevideo Conferences. In the Trade Agreements Act of 1934 the United States high tariff was made negotiable, and products, the subject of trade-agreement con-

184. *The New York Times,* February 9, 1956.

185. See White House Press Release, November 22, 1954, for a statement by President Eisenhower when he rejected a recommendation for quotas in an earlier escape-clause action on spring clothespins.

186. See Chap. IV.

187. In recent years, however, there has been a noticeable shift in United States policy in regard to quantitative restrictions. For example, in September, 1958, President Eisenhower upon recommendation of the Tariff Commission in an escape-clause action imposed quotas on imports of lead and zinc. All five previous recommendations of the commission for quotas in escape-clause actions had been rejected by Presidents Truman and Eisenhower. In March, 1959, President Eisenhower imposed quotas on imports of petroleum and petroleum products under the 1958 national-defense amendment to the Trade Agreements Act. These are important and significant deviations from previous United States policy, which had limited the imposition of quantitative restrictions to imports of agricultural products interfering with a domestic agricultural program.

Quantitative limitations by other countries on exports to the United States of textiles and other manufactured products have been negotiated under both the Eisenhower and Kennedy Administrations. Similar limitations had been negotiated during the 1930's but on a smaller scale. In 1962 Congress enacted legislation authorizing the President to impose quantitative restrictions on imports to assure the effectiveness of such agreements.

cessions, were exempted from the "flexible" cost-equalization provisions of the 1930 Tariff Act. In bilateral and multilateral negotiations conducted under both Democratic and Republican auspices since 1934, United States tariffs have been reduced substantially. The Trade Expansion Act of 1962 anticipates further reductions.

By 1934, therefore, the principal features of present-day United States commercial policy had been adopted. Since 1934 the United States has been concerned with the implementation of this policy in negotiations conducted under the authority of the trade-agreements legislation.

CHAPTER II

The Legislative Basis of United States Commercial Policy

The legislative basis of United States commercial policy has been the Trade Agreements Act of June 12, 1934. This Act authorized the President to lower duties in trade agreements with foreign countries. It thereby gave a new direction to United States commercial policy, which had considered the tariff as virtually "untouchable" and not subject to negotiation with foreign countries. This direction has been maintained, but with some uncertainty and considerable wavering. This chapter is concerned with (1) considerations underlying the original Act; (2) administrative decisions following its enactment; (3) significant changes in the law; and (4) the 1962 trade legislation.

1. CONSIDERATIONS UNDERLYING THE TRADE AGREEMENTS ACT OF 1934

The Administration of Franklin D. Roosevelt, which succeeded that of Herbert Hoover on March 4, 1933, was pledged to the reduction of the United States tariff. In the 1932 Presidential campaign, the Democratic platform had condemned the Hawley-Smoot Tariff Act and had advocated a policy of freer international trade. However, as is frequently the case with party platforms, it had dealt in generalities, and there was no clear outline as to how the policy was to be implemented. Several alternatives presented themselves as to how much and by what means the tariff should be reduced.[1]

NEGOTIATED VS. UNILATERAL TARIFF REDUCTION

There were two means of lowering the United States tariff—by negotiations with other countries for reciprocal reductions or by unilateral action. Generally, sentiment favored reciprocal tariff reductions, though there were important objections to this policy. There was the possibility

1. Leading Democrats were not clear or certain as to what their trade policy should be. Some favored tariff reduction by reciprocal trade treaties. Others were strongly for high tariffs and protection for any and all United States industries. Roosevelt was not well versed in tariff matters, and he straddled the issue, at times calling for protectionism and the cost-equalization formula and at other times advocating the lowering of tariff barriers in order to increase trade. See, Franklin D. Roosevelt, *Looking Forward* (New York: The John Day Company, Inc., 1933), pp. 177-90.

that foreign tariffs and restrictions would be "padded" for bargaining purposes—that other countries, knowing that they would be required to make tariff concessions in order to obtain concessions from the United States, might raise their tariffs, so that the result of negotiations would be merely the removal of the padding and would leave barriers against United States exports the same as before. While subsequent experience under the Trade Agreements Act did not bear out these fears, the problem of padding has always been present. Several times during the development of the trade-agreements program, the United States warned other countries against padding rates or erecting other restrictions for the purpose of improving their bargaining position.[2] In general, padding has been dealt with by making it clear that the United States would not continue to negotiate with countries that increased rates after negotiations have begun. When rates or restrictions have been increased before the beginning of negotiations, such changes have been disregarded by the United States in formulating requests for tariff concessions. In this concern for foreign padding of rates there was apparently little recognition by the United States that its own rates were already padded by the Hawley-Smoot Tariff Act.

A further objection to a policy of reciprocal tariff reductions was that if it were strictly applied with a view to producing a dollar's worth of increased exports for every dollar's worth of increased imports, it promised to do nothing to correct the imbalance in United States international accounts.[3] During the 1930's the United States export surplus of goods and services continued, but it was paid for largely by exports of gold to the United States rather than as in the 1920's by the receipts from United States private investment abroad. Foreign countries whose requirements for dollars to pay for United States goods and services were already in excess of their dollar earnings could not afford to increase their imports from the United States to the same extent that they increased their exports to the United States. They first had to apply their larger dollar earnings to existing dollar obligations before importing more United States goods. Although in the short run this could be avoided or mitigated by private United States investment abroad or by government loans or grants, these were not forthcoming. Therefore, given the imbalance in United States international accounts, reciprocal tariff reduction

2. See, for example, *Papers Relating to the Foreign Relations of the United States,* 1934, Vol. II, pp. 176 and 737; 1935, Vol. II, p. 231; 1936, Vol. V, p. 975; and 1937, Vol. II, p. 90.

3. For an excellent account of the United States balance-of-payments position in the interwar period, see U.S. Dept. of Commerce, Bureau of Foreign and Domestic Commerce, *The United States in the World Economy,* prepared by Hal B. Lary and associates, 1943.

by foreign countries would encourage the continuation of exchange controls or quantitative trade restrictions. Strict tariff reciprocity would not mitigate the financial stringencies abroad on which foreign exchange and quota controls were based, whereas a policy of unilateral tariff reduction by the United States would help this situation. Later experience under the Trade Agreements Act after World War II bore this out. The United States obtained extensive tariff concessions from foreign countries during this period, but for many years the effect of such concessions on the flow of trade was largely offset by quantitative import restrictions and exchange controls imposed on balance-of-payments grounds.

These were arguments against the strict application of the reciprocity idea but not necessarily against a moderate and judicious application of it. If, where circumstances warranted, the United States were to grant tariff concessions that were somewhat greater than those given in return, foreign protectionist tendencies might in some degree be held in check and at the same time the application of the harsher trade controls to which countries in balance-of-payments difficulties usually resort might be averted. But, in practice, once the reciprocity idea has been adopted, it is seldom applied in this judicious manner. Negotiators tend to seek bargains that will reflect public credit on them as negotiators, even though they gain no credit as economists in the eyes of the discerning minority. There is a tendency in such negotiations to "get" as much and to "give" as little as possible. In commenting on this method of tariff bargaining, Taussig suggests that it leads often to "bargaining and bickering" and that it lends itself to "pressure by interested persons." "The negotiators are tempted to try to get the better of each other, to make a show of doing a smart thing."[4]

There was much to be said in favor of unilateral tariff reduction as a United States policy. It would increase not only imports but exports as well because of its effect on foreign incomes.[5] The availability of dollars

4. F. W. Taussig, "Necessary Changes in our Commercial Policy," *Foreign Affairs,* XI (April, 1933), 402-03.

5. As one British writer observed: "There is, however, a way in which Britain's buying power can be increased very greatly, and that is by a substantial reduction of the tariffs imposed by America and other high protectionist countries on her exports. Ever since the war Great Britain has never had less than one to one-and-a-half million unemployed, the larger proportion of whom are normally employed in our export trades. If these potential consumers of American goods could be set to work on goods for export, there would be a considerable rise in American exports both of finished goods and of materials for production. More than one pound out of every eight spent by Great Britain on imports goes to the United States. A comparatively slight increase in British prosperity would, therefore, bring more benefits to America than the complete disappearance of British import duties" (Walter Layton, "The Tasks of the World Economic Conference," *Foreign Affairs,* XI [April, 1933], 417).

was also a limiting factor on foreign purchases of United States goods. In addition to exporters, United States consumers would benefit because of the lower prices that ought to result.

In general, however, the main argument for unilateral tariff reductions by the United States was that reciprocal reductions might become an illusory and self-defeating process. There was some favorable feeling in Congress for a unilateral lowering of the tariff, but generally, sentiment there and elsewhere, insofar as it supported tariff reduction under any conditions, was heavily in favor of negotiated reductions.

There were a number of arguments for reciprocal tariff reductions. Perhaps the domestic economic situation in 1934 was the most persuasive. The United States was in the grip of the most severe depression in its history, with widespread unemployment and commodity surpluses. Most foreign countries had erected, and were busily adding to, barbed-wire entanglements around their domestic markets. Moreover, all of these barricades could not be justified by balance-of-payments difficulties and other external factors; they were in substantial part the product of pro-tectionist pressures and nationalistic philosophies. United States exports were severely curtailed at a time when they were most urgently needed. It was necessary to find a way to cut through these entanglements and provide quick relief rather than to wait for the slow disintegration of the barriers over a period of years. Action by foreign governments to reduce trade barriers promptly could only be obtained by a policy of reciprocal tariff reductions. Also, unilateral reductions in the United States tariff, resulting in increased imports, would aggravate the domestic price, surplus, and unemployment situation unless they were immediately com-pensated for by increased exports. This argument for reciprocal as against unilateral tariff reductions under conditions prevailing in 1934 was well stated in 1936 by Henry F. Grady:

. . . Unilateral action by the American Congress would undoubtedly be a quick and effective method if the system under which the world operated before the war, and to some extent after the war, were still in use. If the world's commerce were free from the many restrictive devices which have been instituted in recent years, and if some sort of an international gold standard were in operation, the lowering of our own tariffs would result in an increase in export commerce more or less corresponding to the increase in imports facilitated by our own tariff reductions. But with conditions as they are today, I am convinced that a unilateral tariff reduction program, even if politically feasible, would not have this effect. In view of the possibility that exports would not increase quickly enough to compensate for disturbances to certain branches of American industry, there would be a strong probability that the tariff reductions would be quickly withdrawn and replaced by still higher tariffs. At a time when we are just emerging from the depression it would be particularly difficult to make tariff adjustments downward without some assurance of immediate compensations in the form of increased exports. Under present conditions, unilateral tariff action is not economically and politically a practicable alternative to the program now in operation.[6]

Political considerations also argued compellingly for reciprocal rather than unilateral action. The principle of tariff protection was deeply embedded in United States thinking through a long period of rigorous practice. The tariff, in law and practice, had been virtually "untouchable," i.e., not subject to negotiation with foreign countries; and it had come to be regarded as "untouchable" (unless to raise it) by anyone who valued his political life.[7] A break from the protectionist policy, particularly in time of depression, would have to be based on an appeal to basic preoccupations and prejudices, such as the prevailing preoccupation with producing and selling rather than with increasing consumption. Protectionism draws much of its strength from this attitude of mind, and reciprocal tariff reduction also capitalizes on it. For a producer-minded public, export opportunities are the sugar coating that enables them to swallow the pill of increased imports. This practical consideration of political acceptability argued strongly for reciprocal rather than unilateral action.

The Democratic party platform had advocated "a competitive tariff for revenue" and "reciprocal tariff agreements with other nations." This could have been construed as meaning primarily unilateral tariff reduction with occasional tariff treaties or agreements. However, when translated into specific legislative terms in the Trade Agreements Act of 1934, the policy adopted was one of reciprocal agreements only.

THE SELECTIVE VS. HORIZONTAL APPROACH

The selective approach to the tariff laid down in the Trade Agreements Act of 1934 was one of the most important features of the Act. It meant that separate consideration had to be given to each of the thousands of rates in the tariff law, with varying reductions or with no reduction at all, as indicated by all relevant considerations, such as the height of the rate, the competitive strength of the protected industry concerned, and the probable effect a duty reduction would have on it. The alternative approach, to which some consideration was given, was the horizontal reduction of all duties by some uniform percentage or

6. "The New Trade Policy of the United States," *Foreign Affairs*, XIV (January, 1936), 284.

7. See Chap. I, pp. 25-29.

down to some uniform ad valorem equivalent. The decision in favor of the selective approach had important consequences both in the amount of duty reduction later effected and in the kinds of agreements negotiated.

The selective approach causes concentration of attention on the problems and needs of each protected industry, with a strong tendency to see the tariff problem narrowly through the eyes of the particular producers concerned rather than broadly from the standpoint of the national interest as a whole. The horizontal approach tends to view the national interest as a whole from a broader perspective.

Either approach depends, of course, on how it is applied. A shallow horizontal cut affects special interests but little, if at all, and it does correspondingly little good from the standpoint of promoting international trade. On the other hand, despite the natural inhibitions mentioned above, a selective approach can be so applied as to result in a substantial general tariff reduction. But the distinction, nevertheless, remains between them. There is a strong tendency for the selective approach to be more moderate and to be more considerate of domestic protected interests with correspondingly less effectiveness in promoting foreign trade; the horizontal approach, because it gives less attention to special interests, tends to be more effective in reducing barriers to trade generally and in promoting the national interest as a whole.

The nature of the negotiations and the kinds of agreements concluded also differ materially under these two approaches. If a horizontal cut of substantial size had been decided upon and made effective in 1934, it would have led not only to a quick reduction in all United States tariff rates but also might have been the basis for a broad multilateral agreement reducing quickly and simultaneously all the tariffs and other restrictions of a large number of countries—at one stroke going far toward unshackling world trade. The idea had a strong appeal because of the seriousness of the international trade-barrier problem and the importance of releasing pent-up surpluses and surplus productive capacity. Moreover, it was believed in 1934 that only by the horizontal approach could these sweeping results be achieved on a wide scale. The selective approach was considered impracticable as a basis for negotiating a broad multilateral agreement, owing to the complexity of product-by-product negotiations conducted simultaneously among a large number of countries. This view was expressed by the United States Tariff Commission in a report to the United States Senate: "The Congress may desire the United States to participate in a multilateral agreement with some or all foreign countries for a general and simultaneous reduction of tariffs. If so, it must be remembered that tariffs are so complicated that multilateral bargaining on individual articles must be regarded as impossible; no multilateral bargaining can be envisaged unless the nations can agree on some simple formula applicable to all tariffs."[8]

For all these reasons the horizontal approach had a strong appeal for those concerned about the barriers to international trade. In fact, this approach did receive some consideration within the Executive branch. A bill drafted by the Administration included a provision for a 10 per cent horizontal reduction combined with authority for further selective reductions. But the horizontal-cut proposal was never submitted to Congress, and the idea was entirely abandoned. Under the disturbed economic conditions of the time, the horizontal approach involving a duty reduction of any significance was considered too drastic. Secretary Hull commented to this effect in his *Memoirs*:

> In earlier years I had been in favor of any action or agreement that would lower tariff barriers, whether the agreement was multilateral, signed by many or all nations, whether it was regional, embracing only a few, or whether it was bilateral, embracing only two. . . . As the London Economic Conference approached I was still prepared to use this [multilateral] method if other nations were willing. The world-wide tariff truce I proposed and saw adopted was a step in this direction. But during and after the London Conference it was manifest that public opinion in no country, especially our own, would at that time support a worth-while multilateral undertaking. My associates and I therefore agreed that we should try to secure the enactment of the next best method of reducing trade barriers, that is, by bilateral trade agreements which embraced the most-favored-nation policy in its unconditional form—meaning a policy of nondiscrimination and equality of treatment.[9]

The Trade Agreements Act of 1934, as introduced and as enacted, adopted the principle that tariff adjustments be made selectively. This principle was embodied in the law, along with the requirement of reciprocity:

> Section 350. (a) For the purpose of expanding foreign markets for the products of the United States (as a means of assisting in the present emergency in restoring the American standard of living, in overcoming domestic unemployment and the present depression, in increasing the purchasing power of the American public, and in establishing and maintaining a better relationship among the various branches of American agriculture, industry, mining, and commerce) by regulating the admission of foreign goods into the United States in accordance with the characteristics and needs of the

8. U.S. Tariff Commission, *Tariff Bargaining Under Most-Favored-Nation Treaties*, Rep. No. 65, 2nd Ser., 1933, p. 3.

9. Cordell Hull, *Memoirs* (New York: The Macmillan Company, 1948), 2 vols., I, 356.

various branches of American production so that foreign markets will be made available to those branches of American production which require and are capable of developing such outlets by affording corresponding market opportunities for foreign products in the United States, the President, whenever he finds as a fact that any existing duties or other import restrictions of the United States or any foreign country are unduly burdening and restricting the foreign trade of the United States and that the purpose above declared will be promoted by the means hereinafter specified, is authorized from time to time—(1) To enter into foreign trade agreements with foreign governments or instrumentalities thereof, and (2) To proclaim such modifications of existing duties . . . as are required or appropriate to carry out any foreign trade agreement that the President has entered into hereunder. . . .[10]

The language most directly relevant to the selective approach was that duty reductions must be made "in accordance with the characteristics and needs of the various branches of American production." The language of the law was somewhat general and involved, but if there were any doubt about the meaning of the law itself, this would be dispelled by an examination of its legislative history. The President in his message on the bill stated that "in a time of difficulty and unemployment such as this, the highest consideration of the position of the different branches of American production is required."[11] Secretary Hull, as chief Administration spokesman during hearings on the bill, spoke of "singling out items that could be made the subject of profitable arrangements," and of "picking out one item very carefully here, another commodity over there very carefully."[12] These and numerous other similar statements by Administration spokesmen leave no room whatever for doubt as to the intent of the law that the approach was to be a careful selective one and that any indiscriminate horizontal reduction was precluded.

Some misunderstanding that selective action precluded multilateral action may arise from the fact that in 1934 it was assumed universally that selective tariff reduction must necessarily be expected through bilateral agreements. This assumption was made because the complexities of product-by-product negotiations simultaneously among a large number of countries would make a multilateral agreement by this method wholly impracticable. Actually, some years later a means was found to negotiate

10. Public Law 316, 73rd Cong. (48 Stat. 943; 19 U.S.C. 1351-1354). The Trade Agreements Act of 1934 amended the Tariff Act of 1930 by adding to Title III a new section, Part III, Promotion of Foreign Trade.

11. U.S. Tariff Commission, *Operation of the Trade Agreements Program*, June, 1934, to April, 1948, Pt. II, p. 65.

12. U.S. Congress, House Committee on Ways and Means, *Hearings* on H.R. 8430, 73rd Cong., 2nd Sess., 1934, p. 24.

selective tariff concessions through a multilateral agreement, and the General Agreement on Tariffs and Trade (GATT) was the result. The claim has been made that in negotiating GATT the President exceeded his authority because the Trade Agreements Act authorized only bilateral agreements.[13] Any such claim rests on a technical misreading of the Act and its history. The intention of Congress that has significance was that duty reductions should be selective. Congress was not concerned about the number of parties to an agreement in which selective reductions were made.

DELEGATION OF AUTHORITY TO THE PRESIDENT

Another important feature of the Trade Agreements Act of 1934 was the delegation of tariff-adjusting authority to the President, so that agreements negotiated under the law, together with the reductions in duties, could be made effective without specific approval by the Senate or the Congress. This feature naturally followed from the decision in favor of reciprocal tariff reduction since negotiations with foreign governments were involved. Such negotiations fall within the President's constitutional function of conducting foreign relations and require the use of facilities that only the Executive has for this purpose.

However, a range of choice as to the extent to which the President would exercise decision-making authority had to be delimited. The role of the Executive might have been confined to that of a negotiating agent. Congress might have laid down detailed specifications, product by product, as to the duty concessions to be offered, leaving to the President only the task of getting the most he could from foreign countries in return.

The decision of Congress regarding the role of the Executive was circumscribed by its desire for a selective approach. It could not legislate selectively without going through another general tariff revision, and the experience with the general revision that resulted in the Hawley-Smoot tariff law was unpleasantly fresh in mind. In commenting on this legislation, President Hoover had said that "Congressional revisions are not only disturbing to business but with all their necessary collateral surroundings in lobbies, logrolling, and the activities of group interests, are disturbing to public confidence."[14] In his veto message on the Collier Bill, Hoover had also referred to the "politics and logrolling" involved

13. Richard B. Anthony, "Foreign Trade Troubles Ahead," *Commercial and Financial Chronicle*, September 5, 1954. Mr. Anthony is Executive Vice-President of the Trade Relations Council, formerly the American Tariff League, a leading protectionist organization.

14. U.S. Dept. of State, *Press Releases*, Weekly Issue No. 38 (June 21, 1930), p. 311.

in a general revision.[15] Senator Vandenberg in later years referred to tariff rate-making in Congress as an "atrocity," saying that "it lacks any element of economic science or validity. I suspect that 10 members of the Senate, including myself, who struggled through the 11 months it took to write the last congressional tariff act, would join me in resigning before they would be willing to tackle another general congressional tariff revision."[16] There was little enthusiasm in 1934 for basing tariff reductions on a detailed consideration of tariff schedules by Congress. Therefore, the desire for selective adjustments and the aversion to such adjustments being made by Congress itself left the delegation of tariff-adjusting authority to the President as the only alternative.

With the decision to delegate such authority, consideration had to be given to the range of duty changes within which the authority could be exercised. This range could be anything from 1 per cent of the existing rate to the complete elimination of the duty. The point midway between these extremes was decided upon. The relevant provision of the law as enacted reads: "No proclamation shall be made increasing or decreasing by more than 50 per centum any existing rate of duty or transferring any article between the dutiable and free lists."[17]

Constitutional Questions.—The decision to delegate authority to the Executive to change the tariff within the 50 per cent limitation and to make such changes effective by international agreement without further action or decision by Congress involved two constitutional questions: the treaty issue and the delegation issue.

The treaty issue arose from the contention that trade agreements concluded under the Act would be treaties and hence subject to the constitutional requirement of advice and consent of the Senate with two-thirds of the senators present concurring. The answer to this contention was that there are international agreements that are not treaties in the constitutional sense and that there is ample legal authority for the view that the agreements contemplated by the Trade Agreements Act

15. *Ibid.*, Weekly Issue No. 137 (May 14, 1932), p. 478.

16. Quoted in The Public Advisory Board for Mutual Security, *A Trade and Tariff Policy in the National Interest* (Washington: February, 1953), p. 43.

17. It will be noted that the 50 per cent limitation applied to increases as well as to decreases in duties. Since the purpose of the Act was to promote the foreign trade of the United States, and since only such changes could be made in the tariff as were required or appropriate to carry out any foreign trade-agreement entered into thereunder, and since foreign countries would not be likely to enter into agreements providing for duty increases on their products, the provision for duty increases may appear entirely meaningless. Actually, however, a foreign government might agree to an increased rate, in the case of a tariff quota under which a duty might be reduced on a specified quantity of imports with a higher rate than the pre-existing one applicable to imports in excess of that quantity.

would not be treaties in this sense. As it is pointed out by Francis B. Sayre, Assistant Secretary of State at the time the Act was under consideration:

> The United States Supreme Court has expressly recognized the validity and constitutionality of executive agreements entered into without Senate approval.

Executive agreements within the field of tariff duties have twice come before the Supreme Court. The case of *Field* v. *Clark*, 143 U.S. 649 (1892), involved Section 3 of the Tariff Act of 1890. . . . Under the authority of this legislation twelve executive agreements became effective, without Senate ratification, binding the United States to admit certain articles free of duty when coming from the other country. Three of these had been concluded at the time of the argument of *Field* v. *Clark*. The Act was challenged, in the language of the Supreme Court, "as delegating to him [the President] both legislative and treaty-making powers" (143 U.S. 681). After holding that the Act did not constitute an improper delegation of legislative power, the Court went on to say (p. 694):

> "What has been said is equally applicable to the objection that the third section of the act invests the President with treaty-making power."[18]

Senator George pointed out during the debate on the original trade-agreements legislation that the "Constitution places a check upon the President's power to enter into treaties by imposing the requirement" of senatorial advice and consent, "but no such extraordinary requirement exists with respect to commitments with foreign governments when such commitments give effect to the will of the people as expressed by previous acts of Congress."[19]

The second Constitutional question raised by the Act was the delegation issue—whether Congress could delegate to the President authority to change tariff rates. This issue is discussed in Chapter I in connection with Section 315 of the Tariff Act of 1922.[20] In commenting on this question Sayre writes, "The Constitution vests in the President the execution and administration of the laws passed by Congress; this by necessity means the placing in the President's hands of large discretionary powers which he must exercise in order effectively to enforce and execute Congressional laws and policies. In other words, once Congress enacts a law and lays down a policy, large discretionary power may constitu-

18. Francis Bowes Sayre, *The Way Forward,* The American Trade Agreements Program (New York: The Macmillan Company, 1939), p. 66. See pp. 65-68 for a discussion of the treaty issue.

19. U.S. *Congressional Record,* 73rd Cong., 2nd Sess., Vol. LXXVIII, Pt. 9, p. 10072.

20. See Chap. I, pp. 24-25.

tionally be vested in the President for carrying out the law and the declared policy."[21]

Since the trade-agreements bill was introduced in Congress in 1934, protectionists, who oppose any tariff reduction, have attacked the legislation on constitutional grounds. In the earlier years of the program the attacks centered on the constitutional question, and even today, after a quarter of a century, this argument is still used.[22]

Checks on President's Authority.—The latitude allowed the Executive by the law was subject to important checks. One of the most important of these provided for termination of the authority after three years, thus necessitating Congressional review of the way in which the authority was being exercised. This provision was not in the bill proposed by the Administration, but it was added in Congress. It read: "The authority of the President to enter into foreign trade agreements under Section 1 of this Act shall terminate on the expiration of three years from the date of the enactment of this Act."

This provision insured a periodic check-up by Congress, Congressional satisfaction with past performance being the price of exercising the authority in the future. It made the nonrenewal threat more effective by facilitating withdrawal of the authority in the event of dissatisfaction with the way it was being used. Without such a provision, the authority could be terminated only by legislation repealing it. Such legislation would require the President's signature, and if he clung to his authority and resisted repealing legislation to the point of vetoing it, Congress might find that the authority conferred by a majority vote could be withdrawn only by a two-thirds vote overriding a Presidential veto. Provision whereby the authority would lapse automatically at the end of three years overcame this difficulty, since positive legislative action would be necessary to extend the authority; if either House failed to approve the extension, the authority would terminate.

This automatic-termination provision has markedly affected the development of the policy laid down in the Act. While there are certain advantages from a freer trade point of view, these have probably been more than offset by the disadvantages.

Periodic Congressional review has served to provide opportunities for all friends of liberal trade in and out of Congress, for the Administration, and for public-service organizations to undertake a campaign to

21. Sayre, *The Way Forward*, p. 69. See pp. 68-83 for a discussion of the delegation issue.

22. For a recent discussion of the constitutional question, see "United States Participation in the General Agreement on Tariffs and Trade," *Columbia Law Review*, LXI (March, 1961), 510-30.

educate the general public on the importance to the United States of an enlightened trade policy. Also, it had afforded the Executive the opportunity to obtain increased authority. The automatic-termination provision, however, has had some serious disadvantages. The re-opening of the question of United States commercial policy at relatively short intervals has resulted in the interruption of negotiations, and it has laid the law open periodically to restrictive amendment. It has given the trade program an aspect of instability because of the periodic uncertainty as to whether efforts to free international trade would continue or would come to an abrupt halt.

The least objectionable of the disadvantages is the interruption of negotiations. However, the interruption has been of some consequence because of the magnitude of the problem presented by international barriers to trade and the need for persistent effort in dealing with that problem. The trade-agreements authority has expired at the end of each one-to-four-year extension period. Each time it has come up for review, much of the interval between the convening of Congress in January and the expiration of the authority in June has been occupied with Congressional hearings, debates, consideration of amendments, and all the legislative process entailed in reaching a determination as to whether the authority should be renewed. In addition, a slow-down has taken place in advance and in anticipation of Congressional review in order to provide fewer targets for opposition attack. The strongest weapon of attack against the trade agreements has always been fear rather then reality. The actual effects of the agreements that have been in force for some time are known, and they can be defended on the record. But fear of the consequences of an agreement just concluded or about to be concluded can be exploited with telling effect. Hence, there has been a strong tendency to suspend negotiating activities well in advance of the lapse of authority so as to avoid prejudicing its renewal. Of the thirty-one bilateral trade agreements signed between 1934 and 1945, only two unimportant agreements were signed in the period between January and June of any year in which the authority had to be renewed. Only seven of the thirty-one agreements were concluded within a year preceding the expiration of the authority.

With the trade-agreements legislation coming up for Congressional renewal at frequent intervals, a ready means has been provided for opponents to cripple it if they cannot defeat it. Protected interests have availed themselves fully of this opportunity. The national need for a freer trade policy has been widely recognized, and the trade-agreements program has acquired strong public support. Unable to defeat the program, its opponents have turned their efforts toward impeding its application. And in this they have achieved a large measure of success, principally through the peril-point and escape-clause amendments, which are discussed in Chapter III.

The purpose of the law has been to promote the foreign trade of the United States, thus benefiting the nation as a whole. The purpose of the protected interests has been to safeguard their own position more fully than was done in the 1934 enactment, and their efforts have brought them a share of government solicitude out of proportion to the size and importance of the interests thus favored. Obviously, a law should be amended in response to a demonstrated need. But a law dealing with the tariff is notoriously subject to pressures, and the automatic-termination provision has invited such pressures and provided periodic opportunities for applying them.

The international-trade policy of the most important trading country in the world has been made a highly unpredictable one in consequence of the automatic-termination provision. The policies of other countries have been affected accordingly, since they must be adjusted to those of the principal trading nation, at least to a considerable degree. If the United States pursues a policy of freer trade, other countries are better able to orient their policies in that direction. If the United States pursues a highly protectionist policy, other countries must rely more on their domestic and less on their international trade, or on bilateral or regional arrangements rather than on broader expectations. Because of the periodic consideration of the trade legislation, other countries in considering their trade-policy orientation have been uncertain as to whether the freer trade policy of the United States would be continued or abandoned, or be so seriously emasculated under protectionist attack as to be of little effect.[23] The extent to which this consideration has had a material effect on international commercial policies throughout the world can only be a matter of conjecture. But it is a fact that doubt about the permanence of United States freer trade policy has been frequently expressed abroad.

The provision for the automatic termination of the President's authority applied only to the authority to negotiate agreements and to make them effective, not to the entire Trade Agreements Act nor to agreements already concluded under it. This distinction was made deliberately. The bill as it came from the House provided that all the provisions of the Act should terminate three years after the date of

---

23. Another factor contributing to the uncertainty of United States trade policy was the avowed "emergency" character of the legislation. See below, pp. 84-85.

enactment. The report of the Senate Finance Committee pointed out that under the House version agreements might remain in force thereafter and that provisions such as those for generalizing tariff concessions or for the non-applicability of the "flexible" cost-equalization provision in the Tariff Act of 1930 (Section 336) would lapse, whereas they ought to be kept in effect as long as agreements were in effect. Accordingly, the Finance Committee recommended and the Congress adopted an amendment whereby only the President's authority to enter into agreements would lapse on the expiration of three years.

While agreements negotiated and in effect would not automatically terminate if the authority should lapse, the law did prevent the Executive from committing the United States internationally in such a way that it could not free itself within a reasonable period of time from international obligations assumed pursuant to the Act. The agreements had to be terminable, not terminated, within three years from the date they came into force. The Act provided that "every foreign trade agreement concluded pursuant to this Act shall be subject to termination, upon due notice to the foreign government concerned, at the end of not more than three years from the date on which the agreement comes into force, and, if not then terminated, shall be subject to termination thereafter upon not more than six months' notice." The language took account of the usual provisions for the duration of international treaties or agreements, which, in the interest of stability, commonly provide for an initial term during which they must run (in this case not more than three years), after which they may be terminated on shorter notice (in this case not more than six months).

THE ROLE OF CONGRESS

The Trade Agreements Act of 1934 placed in the hands of the Executive the adjustment of tariff rates by reciprocal agreement, subject to general Congressional directions and to periodic review by Congress of past executive activities. Congressional control over what would be done would be mainly derived from this periodic review, the cost of Congressional dissatisfaction being the non-renewal of the Executive's authority. In the event of non-renewal, however, the tariff adjustments already made would remain in effect until the President would give notice of termination of the agreements embodying them. Under the Trade Agreements Act, therefore, the power of Congress was a power to prevent all new tariff adjustments by executive action, not a power to terminate those already made.[24]

24. Congress has means outside the provisions of the Trade Agreements Act to put an

The Trade Agreements Act was introduced and supported in 1934 mainly as an emergency measure. President Roosevelt in his message on March 2, 1934, said: "Legislation such as this is an essential step in the program of national economic recovery which the Congress has elaborated during the past year. It is part of an emergency program necessitated by the economic crisis through which we are passing. . . ."[25] The same point was emphasized by Secretary Hull at the Senate hearings on the 1934 Act, when he said: "There should, I repeat, be no misunderstanding as to the nature or the purpose of this measure. It is not an extraordinary plan to deal with ordinary or normal conditions, nor an ordinary plan to deal with extraordinary conditions. Its support is only urged as an emergency measure to deal with a dangerous and threatening emergency situation. . . ."[26]

The reasons for treating the legislation as an emergency measure were doubtless in part to reduce resistance to it. Any long-established policy, such as the protectionist policy that had long been pursued, tends to become accepted as normal, and a new policy must overcome the inertia of established patterns of thought and resistance to change. Stiff resistance to the kind of change proposed could be counted on from well-organized tariff beneficiaries and their spokesmen in Congress.

An economic emergency, which could be regarded as demanding a close look at established policies and which created mental receptivity to tariff reform, certainly existed. But reciprocal tariff reduction cannot be regarded as an emergency type of policy. It is not a quick-acting remedy such as emergencies require. Even Secretary Hull's long-held and well-known views on the tariff would not lead him to advocate such a policy as a measure to be employed briefly to meet the economic emergency and to be abandoned when the emergency was over. Reciprocal tariff reduction is a long-range, evolutionary type of policy, the utility of which is not confined to special conditions such as existed in 1934. It has in fact been adhered to by both Democratic and Re-

---

end to agreements that it does not like. Congress could get rid of an agreement without violating it by enacting legislation whereby, after an interval sufficient to allow for the giving of the required notice of termination, the agreement would no longer have effect in the United States. Such legislation, however, would require the President's signature, and if this were withheld, a two-thirds vote in Congress would be needed to enact the law. Congress could also get rid of an agreement by enacting legislation that violated it. Congress might get around the obstacle of a Presidential veto to such legislation by including it as a rider to legislation of a broader character that the President would find difficult to veto, such as an appropriation bill.

25. U.S. Tariff Commission, *Operation of the Trade Agreements Program,* June, 1934, to April, 1948, Pt. II, p. 66.

26. U.S. Congress, Senate Committee on Finance, *Hearings* on H.R. 8687, 73rd Cong., 2nd Sess., 1934, p. 5.

publican Administrations for almost three decades of depression, boom, recession, and war.

While the policy of reciprocal tariff reduction could hardly have been regarded as a short-run emergency measure, the method by which it was effected might conceivably have been so regarded. As already indicated, the constitutional authority over the tariff lies with Congress. The proposed Trade Agreements Act gave the Executive more tariff-cutting authority than Presidents have usually had. The question as to whether the proposed delegation of authority was desirable in more normal times was one that Secretary Hull apparently felt could be left for final determination when the emergency had passed. At the House hearing on the 1934 Act, Hull said: "There will be ample time and opportunity after the crisis shall have been met and passed and the unprecedented emergency coped with, for a thorough review, re-examination, and discussion of any and all methods, policies, plans, and programs that may have been placed in operation during the panic period in desperate endeavors to curb, control, and cure conditions."[27] Secretary Hull may have felt, however, that the United States system of government ought to be adaptable to the national needs; that, given the nature of the tariff issue, nothing short of delegated authority to the Executive would work; and that to treat the Act as an emergency measure until thinking had become accustomed to the new policy and the method of carrying it out would help in the transition from the old backward-looking policy to his new and forward-looking one.

It was not until fifteen years later that the "emergency" tariff-making process established in the Trade Agreements Act was formally accepted as a normal process. This was done during a Democratic administration when, in renewing the authority in 1949, the language in the preamble referring to "the present emergency" was removed from the Act. The "emergency" label was also omitted in later renewals, including those under Republican administrations.

Concern was expressed in 1934 and later regarding the extent to which Congress had given up control over tariff adjustments under the process established by the Trade Agreements Act. Some critics, as indicated above, have been concerned about the constitutionality of the delegation of authority. Others have been less concerned with its legality than with its desirability. In the decision on the *Hampton* case, which also has a bearing on the legality of the Trade Agreements Act,[28] the Supreme Court said that "in determining what Congress may do in seeking as-

27. U.S. Congress, House Committee on Ways and Means, *Hearings* on H.R. 8430, 73rd Cong., 2nd Sess., 1934, p. 6.
28. See Chap. I, pp. 24-25.

sistance from another branch, the extent and character of that assistance must be fixed according to common sense and the inherent necessities of governmental coordination."[29]

But some have questioned whether "governmental coordination" might not have been more satisfactorily accomplished by some other means than that laid down in the Trade Agreements Act. Senator McClellan gave expression to this misgiving in 1945 on the occasion of the renewal of the authority. He said that he was "going along on the passage of the bill" but that he "could not vote for it without first having at least made the last plea to retain some authority in the United States Senate or the Congress."[30] Many who object to the Trade Agreements Act on constitutional grounds may in reality be concerned primarily with the loss of tariff benefits that may result from the Act. Senator McClellan, however, was ready to vote for the Act, which seems to indicate not only that he favored the policy but felt that the Act could be defended on strict constitutional grounds. His doubts apparently related not so much to the legality as to the desirability, under our system of government, of such a delegation of authority to the Executive.

Experience with the operation of the Trade Agreements Act does in fact raise some question as to the desirability of the executive-legislative relationships established by the law. General review by Congress of agreements already made effective, rather than a direct sharing of responsibility for each agreement before it becomes effective, may have had some tendency to divide the legislative and executive branches rather than to co-ordinate and unify their efforts. The system whereby Congress merely has conducted periodic reviews of past executive action has tended to place Congress in the role of a critical bystander, free to criticize agreements that it has had no direct share in making, to disassociate itself from responsibility for them, and to treat the international commitments as obligations of the Executive rather than as obligations of the United States. Congress has even enacted legislation in violation of trade agreements.[31] A striking illustration of the tendency of Congress to divest itself of responsibility has been its formal disavowal in connection with later renewals of the authority of either approval or disapproval of the GATT, which embodies most of the results of almost three decades of negotiations pursuant to the law.[32]

29. *J. W. Hampton, Jr. & Co.* v. *United States* (T.D. 41478), 49 Treas., Dec. 626, and 276 U.S. 394.

30. U.S. *Congressional Record,* 79th Cong., 1st Sess, Vol. XCI, Pt. 5 (June 20, 1945), p. 6364.

31. See Chap. IV, pp. 208-9.

32. For a further discussion of this Congressional "caveat," see below, pp. 106-9.

An alternative to periodic Congressional review of past action would be some form of Congressional acceptance of each agreement prior to its becoming effective. Various proposals of this kind were advanced in 1934 and later, sometimes by people favorable to the ends in view but who were also genuinely concerned about the means.

One method that had some support was simply to treat trade agreements as treaties, to be negotiated by the Executive and approved by a two-thirds vote of the Senate. Another was to treat them as executive agreements that would be made effective in each case by joint resolution of Congress, involving a majority vote of both Houses. Advocacy of these methods comes to much the same thing as advocating no special trade-agreements legislation at all, since either could be employed by using the constitutional authority that both the executive and legislative branches already have. Moreover, it can be stated with considerable confidence that in the case of tariff action, which is so notoriously subject to politics, pressures, and logrolling, neither of these normal processes would work. One of the grounds on which President Hoover vetoed the Collier Bill in 1932 was that the treaty method of tariff reduction was unworkable.[33] He pointed out that this had been tried in the Kasson treaties concluded pursuant to Congressional request in the Tariff Act of 1897. In the House hearings on the Trade Agreements Act of 1934, Secretary Hull took the same position, saying: "Our Government, for example, negotiated the 10 commercial agreements known as the John A. Kasson commercial treaties, under the Dingley Act of 1897, which according to current public opinion at the time would have doubled our foreign trade if allowed to operate. They were, however, filibustered to death in another body, as we are accustomed here in the House to say...."[34] A requirement of subsequent Congressional approval of individual agreements by joint resolution is open to objection on similar grounds. It is doubtful whether anyone really believed in 1934 that a requirement of subsequent Senate or Congressional approval of trade agreements, irrespective of their nature or the general benefits to be derived from them, would have any other result than their being pigeonholed or defeated for the most part.

Another idea, presented at a later time, was the approval of such agreements by majority vote of the Senate only.[35] Such a provision

33. See Chap. I, pp. 27-29.

34. U.S. Congress, House Committee on Ways and Means, *Hearings* on H.R. 8430, 73rd Cong., 2nd Sess., 1934, p. 5.

35. See U.S. *Congressional Record*, 79th Cong., 1st Sess., Vol. XCI, Pt. 5 (June 20, 1945), pp. 6363-64.

would be of dubious validity in view of the exclusive right of the House to originate revenue legislation, unless this requirement were superimposed on the Trade Agreements Act as drawn, with all the checks and limitations that have been accepted by the House. But the requirement of positive approval by the Senate, even by only a majority vote, would probably result in most cases in the agreements being pigeonholed, as happened in the case of the Kasson treaties.

Another device that was considered in the Executive branch prior to the 1934 enactment and on later occasions, was the legislative veto. Although it was not actually submitted to Congress, a bill authorizing reduction in duties by trade agreements, prepared in the Executive branch in 1933, provided in part: "Any agreement . . . shall enter into force on the date provided therein, unless disapproval of the terms of such agreement shall, before such date, have been signified by Act of Congress, in which case such agreement shall not enter into force. The day fixed in such an agreement for its entry into force shall not be earlier than the thirtieth occurring while Congress is in Session, following the day of signature thereof." A legislative veto provision of this kind might have brought about more effective co-ordination of legislative and executive functions and greater unity of purpose by associating Congress more closely with the Executive in the actual agreement-making process. Of more tangible importance, the legislative veto would have made it logical to dispense with the arbitrary uniform limitation on duty changes applicable to rates varying greatly in height, restrictiveness, and importance. At least the check on each agreement would have made logical the creation of much wider latitude for tariff reductions than was given by the law as drawn. It would also have made it logical to dispense with the periodic termination of the authority, and it would have avoided in some degree the attending slow-down and instability and the ready-made opportunity to bring protectionist pressures to bear on this basic legislation. It is true that protectionist pressures would have concentrated on each agreement. But this would have brought more sharply into focus the conflict between protected interests and the export and other interests. Those standing to gain from a trade agreement would have been confronted with the jeopardy of very visible prospective benefits if protectionist pressures should succeed in defeating an agreement already negotiated and signed. The resistance to protectionist pressures, therefore, might have been somewhat stronger than when, under the law as enacted, the issue periodically arising was the legislative basis for freer trade in general; and the jeopardy took the form of crippling amendments, the effects of which are less imminent, less tangible, and less clearly understood.

Probably the draft of the legislative veto provision, quoted above, would have been changed if presented in 1934, at least to the extent of insuring that Congress would not be prevented by filibuster tactics from acting within the prescribed period. Also it might have been changed so that an agreement could have been defeated by a vote of either House.[36] However, since the tariff is so notoriously subject to pressures, politics, and logrolling, there is serious doubt as to whether the legislative-veto idea in any form likely to be given legislative expression would not have resulted in the defeat of so many agreements as to defeat the policy.

A further revival of the legislative-veto idea took place in connection with the renewal of the trade-agreements authority in 1955, when Senator Morse proposed it as a further limitation on top of the peril-point and escape-clause amendments and all the other checks and limitations with which the Act had by that time become encumbered.[37] In such circumstances the legislative-veto idea has neither logic nor utility if freer international trade is the end in view.[38]

36. In the Reorganization Acts, which later employed the legislative-veto device, a motion to discharge a committee from consideration of a resolution to disapprove a reorganization plan is in order ten days after such a resolution has been referred to the committee in order to prevent a resolution to disapprove from being bottled up in a committee. Under the Reorganization Act of 1949 and subsequent extensions, a plan could be defeated by either House but with the important qualification that there had to be a majority of its total membership, not simply a majority of those present and voting.

In the Reorganization Acts the legislative-veto device seems to have worked fairly well. Under the Reorganization Act of 1949, with a majority of the total membership of either House able to defeat a plan, nine out of forty-one plans were disapproved. Under the earlier Acts of 1939 and 1945, with a majority (present and voting) of both Houses required to defeat a plan, three out of twelve plans submitted were disapproved.

37. See U.S. Congressional Record, 84th Cong., 1st Sess., Vol. CI, Pt. 4 (May 4, 1955), p. 5604.

38. A legislative-veto provision in a limited form came up in Congress in 1948 in a bill introduced by Representative Gearhart. It provided in substance that if the President did not follow the Tariff Commission's peril-point recommendations, an agreement would not become effective until sixty days after the President had transmitted it to both houses of Congress and it would "thereafter take effect only if . . . [during the sixty-day period] there has not been passed by the two Houses a concurrent resolution stating in substance that the Congress does not favor the foreign trade agreement." See U.S. Congress, Senate Committee on Finance, Hearings on H.R. 6566, 80th Cong., 2nd Sess., 1948, p. 2. This veto provision was in the bill as passed by the House but was stricken by the Senate Finance Committee. It was in connection with this limited Congressional veto provision that Senator Vandenberg described Congressional tariff-making as an "atrocity." The action of the Senate Finance Committee, with a Republican majority, in eliminating even this limited Congressional veto is further evidence of the strong feeling, held even by protectionist-minded senators, against bringing the details of tariff rate-making back into Congress.

THE MOST-FAVORED-NATION (MFN) POLICY

The policy of nondiscrimination or unconditional MFN treatment was formally adopted by the United States during the Republican Administration of President Harding in 1923, and it had been given effect in treaties and agreements since that time.[39] With the adoption of the policy of reciprocal tariff-reduction, the question presented was whether to continue the MFN policy.

The alternatives to the policy would be: (a) abandonment of the unconditional MFN policy and the negotiation of exclusive preferential agreements, such as the treaty of 1902 with Cuba, which remained in force as an exception to the general policy; or (b) the use of discrimination as a bargaining weapon for reducing foreign tariffs and restrictions, which would result in temporary suspension by the United States of nondiscriminatory treatment with respect to each country pending the conclusion of a satisfactory reciprocity agreement; or (c) the maintenance of the principle of unconditional MFN treatment without substantial permanent or temporary deviation from it.

Permanently preferential agreements would involve a radical change in traditional United States policy. In theory the benefits that such agreements would give United States exporters would be increased in that they would obtain from the parties to the agreements lower duties than those paid by foreign competitors supplying these markets. In other words, the competitive position of United States exporters would be improved not only in relation to domestic producers in the foreign countries but also in relation to other foreign competitors. To obtain such advantages, the United States would have to offer similar preferential treatment. However, countries thereby discriminated against inevitably would take counter measures against United States exports by granting exclusive benefits to competitors' products so that the special advantages gained for United States exporters in one country would be lost through discrimination against them in other countries. Since the United States could not embark on such a policy without terminating the treaties and agreements providing for MFN treatment, the way to foreign discriminations against the United States would be wide open. Such a policy would be a prolific breeder of trade war and hostile trading blocs—in brief a recipe for commercial chaos. This alternative could not be reconciled with the broad objective of reducing barriers to world trade.

The second alternative would be to avoid the granting of unconditional MFN treatment to a particular country until discrimination had been used as a lever to obtain a satisfactory reciprocity agreement. Under

39. See Chap. I, pp. 29-53.

such a scheme, similar to that pursued up to that time by France, MFN treatment would be one of the desiderata held out to foreign countries as an inducement to signing a reciprocity agreement on United States terms. Duty reductions under an agreement with one country would be withheld from others with the idea of making them more amenable to requests for concessions from them. The United States would be able to offer not only duty reductions, which would improve the competitive position of such third countries in relation to United States domestic producers, but also to offer the removal of a handicap placed on them by discrimination in favor of their foreign competitors.[40] Such a policy would also be a breeder of trade wars and a stumbling block to any real relaxation of trade barriers. Countries discriminated against would seek to match the United States bargaining position by withholding MFN benefits, thereby placing themselves in a position to trade MFN rights for MFN rights. Such a policy would do little or nothing to lower international barriers to trade. Indeed, it probably would make the trade-barrier situation worse. Since it would require the termination of all United States unconditional MFN treaties and agreements, foreign countries would be free to apply discriminatory counter measures. This alternative did not receive serious consideration, although some sentiment for it was implicit in the view that in combining the MFN policy with tariff reduction we were "giving something for nothing."

The third alternative would be to continue to adhere to the principle of unconditional MFN treatment. Secretary Hull, as leading Administration spokesman during the House hearings on the Trade Agreements Act, stated the views of the Administration in favor of this alternative: "The favored-nation doctrine in its unconditional form, or the principle of equality of treatment would be continued as a policy of our Government. There would be no occasion therefore for the denouncement of existing treaties before our Government could proceed with negotiations. . . ."[41]

The law as enacted reaffirmed the policy of unconditional MFN treatment. It said: "The proclaimed duties and other import restrictions shall apply to articles the growth, produce, or manufacture of all foreign countries, whether imported directly, or indirectly: Provided, That the President may suspend the application to articles the growth, produce, or manufacture of any country because of its discriminatory treatment of American commerce or because of other acts or policies which in his

40. An example of this kind of maneuvering is the tariff dispute between the United States and France in 1927. See Chap. I, pp. 50-53.

41. U.S. Congress, House Committee on Ways and Means, *Hearings* on H.R. 8430, 73rd Cong., 2nd Sess., 1934, p. 4.

opinion tend to defeat the purpose set forth in this section. . . ." Under these provisions, the policy reaffirmed was not merely *de jure* unconditional MFN treatment, whereby rates reduced under a trade agreement with one country are applied only to products of countries entitled to such treatment by virtue of a treaty or agreement with the United States. The law reaffirmed a policy of *de facto* unconditional MFN treatment, whereby the reduced rates apply to imports from all countries regardless of whether they are entitled by international agreement to receive MFN treatment (subject to the provisos quoted above).

As noted above, some consideration was given in the process of formulating the policy laid down in the Trade Agreements Act to the possibility of negotiating a broad multilateral agreement involving a horizontal reduction of tariffs. The MFN commitments in bilateral treaties and agreements were regarded as an obstacle to such a multilateral agreement. If, by invoking the MFN clause in its bilateral treaties with countries participating in a multilateral agreement, a country could obtain the benefits of that agreement without adhering to it, this would tend to put a premium on abstention. The possibility of obtaining the benefits without making the commitments might cause some countries to hold back and consequently increase the difficulty of concluding broad multilateral agreements.[42] With these considerations in mind, and taking account of the possibility that a broad horizontal-cut agreement might become a possibility, the United States at the Seventh International Conference of American States held in Montevideo in 1933 took the initiative in negotiating a convention in which the signatories would agree not to "invoke the obligations of the most-favored-nation clause for the purpose of obtaining from Parties to multilateral conventions . . . the advantages or benefits enjoyed by the Parties thereto."[43]

The trade-agreements program developed, however, in such a way as to make such a waiver unnecessary. The problem presented by the MFN clause in bilateral treaties and agreements arises acutely only in connection with multilateral agreements involving horizontal reduction of all

42. The effect on multilateral agreements of MFN commitments of member parties had recently been demonstrated in the case of the 1932 Ouchy Convention, signed by Belgium, Luxembourg, and the Netherlands, which was intended as a nucleus for much wider undertakings. The convention provided that the parties would lower their tariffs on each others' products by 10 per cent a year for five years, subject to certain provisos. The convention did not become effective because of failure of certain countries having MFN rights with the parties to the convention to waive those rights. See Jacob Viner, *The Customs Union Issue* (New York: Carnegie Endowment for International Peace, 1950), pp. 30-31.

43. U.S. Dept. of State, *Treaty Series*, No. 898, p. 2. For the fate of this convention, see Chap. I, footnote 180.

rates. The selective principal-supplier approach of the trade-agreements program, under which each party to a bilateral agreement granted concessions only on products of primary importance to the other party, permitted the generalization of concessions under the MFN clause without serious loss of bargaining position. Under this same approach used in negotiating the multilateral GATT, the products selected were in general those of primary interest to the participating countries; and while the MFN clause would give non-participating countries some benefit, they could only be sure of duty concessions on products of primary interest to them by joining the agreement and negotiating concessions on such products.

2. ADMINISTRATIVE DECISIONS

Executive decisions following the enactment of the Trade Agreements Act played an important part in shaping United States commercial policy. Innumerable questions of policy, method, and procedure obviously had to be dealt with in administering a law of this kind, but executive decisions of two kinds were of particular significance. These were decisions relating to the application of the MFN principle and those relating to the organizational arrangements for administering the law.

APPLICATION OF THE MFN PRINCIPLE

The Trade Agreements Act, as already indicated, laid down the principle that tariff concessions made on products of a country party to a trade agreement (Cuba excepted) should be extended to the like products of all other foreign countries. In applying this principle, however, the Administration found that it had to resolve an internal conflict over its application and to adopt policies in regard to discretionary exceptions provided for in the Act and in regard to the maintenance of a negotiating position with other countries.

The Hull-Peek Controversy.—Shortly after the Act became law, a conflict arose within the Administration on the general application of the MFN principle. The chief parties to this conflict were Secretary Hull, representing the broad view, and George N. Peek, special adviser to the President on foreign trade, representing the narrow view.

Peek was a prominent and capable businessman who had been brought into the government to assist in solving the critical economic problems of a nation in the throes of a depression and who conscientiously sought to serve his country in the emergency. Soon after Roosevelt became President, Peek was appointed administrator of the Agricultural Adjustment Act; he was deeply committed to domestic programs envisaged by that Act and the National Industrial Recovery Act. He believed in the abandonment of the unconditional MFN principle and in bargaining with foreign countries on a strictly bilateral basis. In March, 1934, before the enactment of the Trade Agreements Act, he was designated by Executive Order as head of the Office of the Special Adviser to the President on Foreign Trade.[44] His reports in that capacity frequently attacked the State Department for a trade liberalization policy that he regarded as mistaken.[45] After the enactment of the Trade Agreements Act (which he had an important part in formulating), Peek negotiated several agreements with foreign countries that conflicted with the principle of equality of treatment. Consequently, he found himself increasingly in conflict with Secretary Hull.

Peek saw commercial policy narrowly, at close range. The prosperity of the country was being stifled by surpluses, especially agricultural surpluses. If these surpluses could be moved by bartering them with foreign countries, this was to him the sensible, businesslike thing to do. The effect of such barter deals, however, was to pre-empt portions of the markets of the two parties and thereby to discriminate against third countries by precluding free international competition for the segments monopolized by the parties to such deals. Peek apparently considered that United States trade relations with third countries or United States export interests that might suffer from similar deals between other countries were relatively unimportant. To him, it was a matter of seizing immediate advantages as opportunities offered, without too much concern for the remote and problematical consequences, especially in view of the current domestic unemployment situation and the pressing need for outlets for agricultural surpluses.

Secretary Hull took a longer view. He saw commercial policy in broader perspective—not as a series of unrelated intergovernmental transactions but as a pattern into which day-to-day decisions should fit. Opportunism might be suitable for an individual businessman if his responsibilities to his stockholders and employees can best be met in this way. But the affairs of a nation are vastly more complex and involve a

44. Executive Order 6651, March 23, 1934. The special adviser was authorized by the order not only to collect and co-ordinate information and statistics on foreign trade but also to carry on negotiations with respect to specific trade transactions with any individual, corporation, association, group or business agency interested in obtaining assistance from the federal government through financing transactions, or other forms of governmental participation authorized by law.

45. See George N. Peek with Samuel Crowther, *Why Quit Our Own* (New York: D. Van Nostrand Company, Inc., 1936). For a critical review of this book by Henry F. Grady, first chief of the Trade Agreements Division, Dept. of State, see *The Washington Post*, October 7, 1936.

great variety of interest and enterprises, each of which may be affected by intergovernmental dealings on behalf of other interests and enterprises. For these reasons, Hull felt that consistent policy based on sound principle from the standpoint of the general interest is essential and that opportunism in international affairs is bound to be costly sooner or later to the nation as a whole. As he frequently said, "You depart from principle at your peril."

The conflict between the Hull and Peek philosophies came to a head when late in 1934 Peek negotiated a barter agreement with Germany that would have created a special preferential arrangement for the disposal of United States cotton. Secretary Hull insisted that the President should not approve the agreement, and the President accepted his view. Peek resigned in November, 1935.

Discretionary Exceptions.—Policy decisions involving the MFN principle were also necessitated by specific provisions in the Trade Agreements Act. The Act provided that duty changes made in an agreement with any foreign country (Cuba excepted) should "apply to articles the growth, produce, or manufacture of all foreign countries." There were, however, two important discretionary exceptions. The President might suspend the application of reduced rates to "articles the growth, produce, or manufacture of any country because of its discriminatory treatment of American commerce." He might also, even in the absence of foreign discrimination against United States trade, suspend the application of the reduced rates to products of any country, "because of other acts or policies which in his opinion tend to defeat the purpose set forth" in the Act.

With the first agreement to which the generalization provision became applicable (Belgium), an official statement of policy regarding these exceptions was announced.[46] The United States would withhold trade-agreements concessions only on the ground of foreign discrimination against United States trade, not because of "other acts or policies," such as the height of nondiscriminatory tariffs or other trade barriers. With respect to foreign discrimination, the policy was one of using the power to suspend trade-agreements rates as a means of inducing foreign countries to cease such discrimination and to place their commercial relations with the United States on the basis of reciprocal acceptance and observance of the unconditional MFN principle.

Making this policy effective was another matter, largely because of the breakdown of the multilateral-payments system and the widely prevalent resort to bilateral-balancing arrangements from which the countries involved often could not extricate themselves at will. Under such condi-

46. See *Press Releases*, Vol. XII, No. 288 (April 6, 1935), pp. 212-20.

tions, to deny a country in balance-of-payments difficulties the benefit of United States trade-agreements concessions would, through diversion of its trade to competitors, reduce its earnings of one of the few convertible currencies—thereby worsening its balance-of-payments situation, binding it more tightly to its bilateral-balancing arrangements, and reducing its capacity to grant the nondiscriminatory treatment that the United States desired. Nevertheless, United States policy regarding the unconditional MFN principle was to press for the elimination of discriminations as circumstances might permit. The power to suspend generalization of trade-agreements rates probably served as some deterrent to the new discriminations.[47]

The law permitted denial of trade-agreements rates not only to combat foreign discriminations but also "other acts or policies," a phrase that would cover foreign tariff or other impediments to imports for protecting domestic producers or for easing balance-of-payments difficulties, even though such measures were applied impartially to imports of United States and of other foreign origin. Since a basic purpose of the Trade Agreements Act was to promote freer international trade, such non-discriminatory trade barriers could be regarded as tending to "defeat the purpose" of the Act.

One major objective of United States policy was to eliminate foreign discriminations. Another was to reduce the level of protection that countries afforded domestic producers. The question for decision was whether this latter purpose would be served by suspending trade-agreements rates and thereby discriminating against a country because its tariff or other barriers to trade, even though nondiscriminatory, were regarded as unduly high. It was decided that if trade-agreements concessions were withheld on this latter ground, both of these basic policy objectives would tend to be defeated. Suspension in such circumstances would be an attempt to use discrimination to put pressure on other countries to reduce high but nondiscriminatory trade barriers, which they had established in the belief that the welfare of their economies demanded such protection from outside competition. Such coercive action would be similar to that employed by France against the United States in 1927. United States reaction to the French action was illustrative of the kind of reaction that might be expected if similar pressure tactics were employed, namely, actual or threatened penalty duties or restrictions against the United States to offset the United States discrimination and to induce its abandonment. The trade warfare that might ensue would mean not only higher trade

---

47. The Executive found it feasible actually to suspend generalization of trade-agreements rates in the case of only two countries, Australia and Germany.

barriers abroad, rather than the lower ones sought by the Trade Agreements Act, but increased discrimination in international trade, which would likewise be contrary to the objectives of the Act.

In brief, the policy laid down by the Executive under the discretion allowed him by the Trade Agreements Act was that reductions in nondiscriminatory foreign trade barriers should be sought only by offers of concessions with respect to the height of the United States tariff and that nondiscrimination by foreign countries should be sought by offering nondiscriminatory treatment in return.

The Chief-Source Rule.—A further problem of administration growing out of adherence to the MFN principle was that of maintaining a negotiating position, a matter of some significance since the practical feasibility of adhering simultaneously to two highly desirable policies depended on its solution.

Negotiated tariff reductions and nondiscrimination had been combined previously in European practice, but in the United States there was a widely prevalent misconception until the enactment of the Trade Agreements Act that reciprocal tariff reductions of necessity involved the abandonment of the unconditional MFN policy.[48] This was one of the grounds on which President Hoover had vetoed the Collier Bill in 1932.[49] This misconception was probably due to a failure to examine closely enough the precise nature and purpose of the MFN principle.

The purpose of the MFN principle is to assure equality of treatment of each particular imported product irrespective of its national origin, rather than to assure equality of treatment of the commerce of each foreign country as a whole. It imposes no obligation, for example, to give to third countries general commercial benefits equal to those accruing to the other party to a trade agreement, which would indeed be impracticable. Its purpose is a much narrower one. It provides assurance that any particular product originating in one foreign country will not be subject to a higher tariff or otherwise be less favorably treated than the like product originating in another foreign country. The aim is to avoid placing producers of any product in one country at a disadvantage as compared with their competitors in another country.

This purpose of MFN treatment and the degree of specialization in production among the countries of the world make it possible to pursue a policy of reciprocal tariff reduction while adhering to the MFN principle. It is only necessary in making tariff concessions to a particular country to select products of primary interest to that country. The con-

48. See, for example, Taussig, "Necessary Changes," *Foreign Affairs,* p. 402.
49. See Chap. I, pp. 27-29.

cessions can then be extended to other countries that also supply the products but whose interest in them is less important than that of the country to which the concessions have been made. The less important suppliers obtain, as they should, benefits under the MFN principle, but they still have a motive for negotiating a trade agreement in order to obtain concessions on products of primary interest to them. Thus, to use a hypothetical example, a concession could be made to the United Kingdom on certain types of textiles of which that country had been the principal supplier of the United States market and the concession could be extended to France, with some benefit to that country; but the rates on wines would remain untouched and provide a basis for later negotiations with France. The *quid pro quo* for extending the textile and other concessions to France would be the general extension to the United States of concessions made by France in negotiations with other countries.

Adherence to the MFN principle is not only technically feasible but is highly desirable. It has the negative virtue of avoiding artificial trade diversion with resulting loss to and friction with countries with which negotiations are deferred or never undertaken, and it has the positive virtue of making a tariff-reduction policy of maximum value to world trade through a wide sharing of its benefits. To have abandoned the MFN principle upon the adoption of the tariff-reduction policy would have been to abandon it in the very circumstances in which it had its greatest practical applicability and value.

The method of selecting products on which to offer concessions in negotiations with each country came to be known as the chief-source rule. As the name implies, it consists simply of granting concessions to each country on products of which that country has been the chief or an important source of importations.[50]

The chief-source rule, however, has been a general guide for negotiations rather than a rigid rule, since in practice special circumstances have required exceptions to it. There are indeed instances in which strict adherence to the rule would be impossible, as, for example, when a product is of major importance to a number of countries that have few other products of outstanding export interest. Coffee, the main export of several Latin American countries, is an illustration in point. In this case an attempt was made to meet the situation by simultaneously negotiating and making effective agreements with the several countries in order to avoid making the concession available to any of them under the

---

50. Although the Trade Agreements Act does not specifically refer to the chief-source rule, its intended use was explained to Congress by Administration spokesmen, and Congress presumably anticipated that it would be used in exercising the authority conferred by the Act.

MFN principle until it had been used as a basis for negotiations with all of them. The plan did not work out, since simultaneous action proved impracticable. Nevertheless, agreements were successfully concluded with the principal coffee-producing countries. Each country wanted to obtain the concession on this product, of such importance to economy, in its own right rather than to rely on the MFN principle whereby the continued enjoyment of the concession depended on the continuance in effect of an agreement with the United States. Considerations of government prestige were also doubtless present. This experience illustrates a point of some consequence—that a direct right in a trade agreement is more valuable than an indirect right under the MFN principle and that the making of a concession to one country does not entirely destroy the value of the same concession on the same product as a basis for negotiations with another country.

Another means of using a concession on the same product for negotiations with different countries is to split the concession, giving part of the duty reduction that the United States is ultimately in a position to offer to one country and the remainder to another. For example, in a trade agreement with Sweden the duty on paving blocks was cut from 60 per cent to 40 per cent, and in a later agreement with Finland the rate was cut from 40 per cent to 30 per cent.

Another technique in applying the chief-source rule is the reclassification of products or greater tariff specialization, which, in effect, makes more products with which to operate the rule. This involves creating narrower classifications than appear in the tariff legislation, differentiating products within a given classification on the basis of the value, type, or quality of particular interest to the other party to the negotiations and leaving other values, types, or qualities as a basis for negotiating with other countries. In United States practice, however, reclassification has frequently had for its primary purpose not the preservation of negotiating position so much as the reduction of the impact of tariff concessions on domestic producers by confining the concessions to types of a product that are less competitive with domestic production.[51]

ORGANIZATIONAL ARRANGEMENTS

The Trade Agreements Act laid the basis for a trade policy, but the nature of the policy that was to emerge depended in very substantial

---

51. The reclassification technique has been used often. It has been estimated that by 1940 one-third of the paragraphs of the Tariff Act of 1930 had been modified in this way. There were 91 reclassifications in the trade agreement with the United Kingdom alone. In 1962 there were around 3,800 import classifications for dutiable purposes as compared with approximately 2,000 such classifications in the Tariff Act of 1930.

degree on the nature of the organization created for administering the law. The law itself touched on organizational matters only to the extent of providing that before concluding a trade agreement "the President shall seek information and advice with respect thereto from the United States Tariff Commission, the Departments of State, Agriculture, and Commerce and from such other sources as he may deem appropriate."[52]

There were sound reasons behind this requirement. Each of the various government agencies has its own sphere of responsibility which involves some particular aspect of the national life, and account had to be taken of these interests and responsibilities if a balanced approach to tariff adjustments was to result. The Department of State, for example, is naturally concerned with and tends to attach greatest importance to foreign policy considerations and objectives. The Department of Agriculture has general responsibilities relating to the welfare of farmers; it is concerned with improved export opportunities for farm products, with protection for those branches of agriculture that are vulnerable to foreign competition, and with the effect of industrial tariff rates on the farmers as consumers. The Department of Commerce with its interest in promoting exports not only has an interest in foreign trade barriers but in the reduction in the United States tariff as a means of dealing with them. The Tariff Commission, whose viewpoint reflects the interests of tariff-protected industries, has a proper concern lest reductions in the tariff should go too far. Other agencies, such as the Departments of Treasury and Defense, have responsibilities that make trade agreements a matter of proper interest and concern to them. Domination by one agency in the administration of the Act would tend to emphasize one aspect of the national interest at the expense of others.

The importance of this consideration is well recognized by the various interests concerned, as demonstrated by the determined and largely successful efforts that have been made by protected industries and their spokesmen in Congress to give the Tariff Commission a dominant voice in the administration of the Act. The law merely touched on this problem by requiring the President to consult with the several agencies before concluding a trade agreement. How effective such consultation would be in creating a balanced approach would depend largely on how the Executive would administer this provision.

The President could have met the letter of the consultation requirement in various ways. For example, he could have set up a separate

52. The law was later amended to include the Department of Defense, and the Tariff Commission was given a special role in connection with the peril-point and escape-clause amendments. See Chap. III.

agency staffed with its own commodity and other experts and could have directed the new agency to seek information and advice from other agencies at any time prior to the actual conclusion of a trade agreement. Apart from the cost of such duplication of personnel and effort, such a step would not have conformed to what might well be regarded as the spirit of the law. There would be a strong tendency for such an agency to set itself up as judge of the merits of views submitted to it by other agencies and to minimize the importance of considerations growing out of their respective interests and responsibilities. The President decided not to create a special agency but to pool the resources and responsibilities of the government in an interagency organization, the heart of which was the interdepartmental Committee on Trade Agreements, which would have responsibility for formulating recommendations and negotiating trade agreements under the authority of the Act of 1934.[53]

The Trade Agreements Committee was established in response to a letter from Secretary Hull in June, 1934, to the heads of the Departments of Agriculture, Commerce, and Treasury, and to the Tariff Commission, the National Recovery Administration, and the Office of the Special Adviser to the President on Foreign Trade, each of whom appointed a representative to it, the State Department representative serving as chairman.[54]

The function of the Trade Agreements Committee was to administer the Trade Agreements Act, subject, of course, to higher authority. It would serve as the "central base of strategy," utilizing such subcommittees on particular countries, commodities, or subjects, as it found useful. An elaborate system of subcommittees in due course developed. It would refer important questions of policy to the Executive Committee on Commercial Policy established in November, 1933, to carry primary responsibility for supervising trade policy. The core of the function of the Trade Agreements Committee was to pool interagency information and competence and to co-ordinate interagency activity insofar as the Trade Agreements Act was concerned—to weld United States trade policy into a coherent and balanced whole.[55]

53. The Trade Agreements Committee was successor to the Interdepartmental Advisory Board on Reciprocity Treaties, which had been formed prior to the Trade Agreements Act for the negotiation of trade agreements that would be submitted to the Senate or Congress. Negotiations for such agreements were conducted, but no agreements were made effective until later under authority of the Trade Agreements Act.

54. The Trade Agreements Committee was not formally established until February, 1947, by Executive Order 9832.

55. The Trade Agreements Committee originally included eight agencies: the Departments of State, Agriculture, Commerce, and Treasury, the Tariff Commission, the Agricultural Adjustments Administration, the National Recovery Administration, and the Office

The chairmanship of the committee by the representative of the State Department was inevitable and logical. More than anyone else Secretary Hull was responsible for the adoption of the policy, and it was appropriate that initiative and responsibility should be exercised by one of his subordinates. Moreover, the scope of the responsibilities of the State Department is wider than that of any other agency since the conduct of foreign relations touches virtually every aspect of the national life. Actions of the Departments of Agriculture, Commerce, and Treasury and of the Tariff Commission frequently affect seriously our foreign relations; and in the day-to-day conduct of foreign affairs the State Department, in discharging its own responsibilities, must have constant and intimate contact with these other agencies. The responsibilities of no other agency are so vitally affected by the activities of other parts of the government as are those of the State Department. A co-ordinating function in any field involving foreign affairs, such as the trade-agreements program, therefore, naturally falls to the State Department rather than to agencies that deal with more specialized subject matter and whose concern is primarily with domestic matters and only in small part with foreign affairs. Also, in the case of trade agreements, negotiations with foreign countries are involved, and this is a field in which the State Department has primary responsibility as well as the requisite personnel at home and abroad and the channels of communication with foreign governments.

However, opponents of the trade-agreements program have from the outset attacked the Trade Agreements Committee on grounds of State Department domination, professing to fear the influence of international diplomacy on the committee's deliberations. Actually, there is no point at which the administration of the Trade Agreements Act is less vulnerable to criticism. The State Department fully realized that a balanced approach was required and, to this end, that there must be a leveling of agency influence on a full and equal partnership basis. This objective was achieved by practices and procedures that were largely initiated by the State Department itself.

---

of the Special Adviser to the President on Foreign Trade. By 1940 this number had been reduced to five, the latter three having dropped out. During World War II the Office of Price Administration was added. The membership was again enlarged after the war when the Departments of Interior, Labor, War, and Navy, and the Economic Co-operation Administration were added. The Trade Agreements Extension Act of 1948 prohibited any member of the Tariff Commission or its staff from participating in the decisions of the committees advising the President on trade-agreements matters or in the negotiation of any trade agreement, but this provision was repealed by the Trade Agreements Extension Act of 1949. In 1962 members of the committee were the Departments of State, Defense, Agriculture, Commerce, Treasury, Labor, and Interior; the Administration for International Development (nonvoting); and the Tariff Commission.

The actual administration of the Trade Agreements Act went far beyond the consultation required by the letter of the law and became full interagency collaboration. No action of any kind relating to trade agreements was taken without submitting the matter for decision by the Trade Agreements Committee. To insure full opportunity for consideration by all members and to remove any fear of State Department "steam-rollering," all meetings were announced and papers to be considered were distributed not less than forty-eight hours in advance, except in urgent cases. To assist committee members in preparations for meetings, matters for consideration included the recommended action. In order to promote unity and to insure full account being taken of the particular aspect of the national interest for which each agency was spokesman, an effort was made to secure unanimity, and it nearly always was successful. Where this failed and the State Department was in the minority, the majority views were the ones presented as committee recommendations to the Secretary of State and to the President. Where another agency was in a minority, its spokesman was given the opportunity to present his views along with those of the majority. In 1947, along with other changes in trade-agreements procedure provided by Executive Order, the President directed that all Trade Agreements Committee dissents were to be sent to the President.[56]

In consequence of these procedures, the Trade Agreements Committee was in due course welded into an interagency body with an entity virtually separate from that of the agencies comprising it. It was the committee, therefore, rather than the State Department, that came to be regarded as the authority to which United States negotiators at home or abroad looked as the initial source for their instructions on trade-agreements matters.[57]

3. SIGNIFICANT CHANGES IN THE LAW

From 1934 until 1945, the trade-agreements legislation was renewed without important changes.[58] In 1945, however, the President's authority

56. In recent years recommendations of the Trade Agreements Committee have been subject to review by the Cabinet-level Trade Policy Committee before being sent to the President. This committee, established by Executive Order in November, 1957, is chaired by the Secretary of Commerce or his alternate. Other members are the Secretaries of State, Treasury, Defense, Interior, Agriculture, and Labor, or their alternates.

57. For an early example of this development, see *Foreign Relations, 1936*, Vol. V, pp. 388 and 404. For further discussion of the Trade Agreements Committee, see Mary Trackett Reynolds, *Interdepartmental Committees in the National Administration* (New York: Columbia University Press, 1939), pp. 47-70, and Harry C. Hawkins, "Administration of the Trade Agreements Act," *Wisconsin Law Review* (January, 1944), pp. 3-14. See also U.S. Congress, House Committee on Ways and Means, *Hearings* on H.R. 2652 superseded by H.R. 3240, 2 vols., 1945. The index to these volumes contains numerous references to the Trade Agreements Committee.

58. The authority contained in the Act was renewed in 1937 for three years, in 1940 for

to reduce rates was increased significantly. In subsequent renewals the protectionists gained ground, as evidenced by a number of restrictive amendments and by no really important increases in negotiating authority.

NEW TARIFF-CUTTING AUTHORITY IN 1945

The important increase in negotiating authority in 1945 was effected by making the President's authority to reduce rates by 50 per cent applicable to rates in force on January 1, 1945, rather than, as theretofore, to rates in effect in 1934. This allowed further reductions in rates previously reduced. In the case of a rate already reduced by the full 50 per cent, authority was given to reduce it by another 50 per cent or 75 per cent below the 1934 level. This represented a very substantial increase in authority, since the maximum legal reduction of 50 per cent had been made on over 40 per cent of United States dutiable imports (based on 1939 trade data). Lesser reductions had been made on more than 20 per cent of such imports.[59] In all a reduction of 44 per cent had been made on 64 per cent of such imports.[60] The use made of the new authority is indicated by the fact that after the 1947 Geneva negotiations three-fourths of the total rate reductions made under the trade-agreements program were in excess of 45 per cent. Almost a third of these reductions were from 66 to 75 per cent.[61]

The 1945 renewal marks the high point in the legislative basis of the trade-agreements program. This enactment took place when the war was drawing to a close—at a time when there was a shortage of goods rather than serious market competition, when the creation of a permanent peace was still widely regarded as an attainable goal, and when peaceful trade among nations was widely recognized as an important foundation for international peace. Thereafter, market competition revived with the restoration of foreign production and the disappearance of shortages, and the development of the cold war dimmed the hope of permanent peace. The climate thus became favorable to a revival of protectionist strength, in consequence of which the effectiveness of the Trade Agreements Act was undermined by amendment, and even what had already

---

three years, and in 1943 for two years, the only change being that made in 1943 whereby the President's power to suspend the generalization of trade-agreements concessions was broadened to authorize such suspension, because of "the operations of international cartels." The apparent intent was to permit suspension of generalization to all imports from a country in which cartels were operating rather than to confine such suspension to products dealt with by the cartels. The provision has never been applied.

59. U.S. Tariff Commission, *Operation of the Trade Agreements Program*, June, 1934, to April, 1948 (1949), Pt. II, p. 14.

60. *Ibid.*, Pt. III, p. 13.   61. *Ibid.*, Pt. I, p. 21.

been accomplished under it came under severe and to some extent successful attack.

RESTRICTIVE AMENDMENTS OF 1951

The revision of the Trade Agreements Act began in 1948 when the Republicans were in control of Congress. Not only was the authority under the Act extended for only one year but the so-called peril-point amendment was adopted. The 1948 enactment was repealed in 1949 after the Democrats regained control of Congress, and the Trade Agreements Act as it previously existed was substantially restored with an extension of authority for three years, retroactively from June 12, 1948, or until June 12, 1951.[62] But this restoration was of brief duration. The revisionist trend that began in 1948 was resumed in 1951; and it is an indication of the growth of protectionist strength that the most serious emasculation of the Act took place with a Democratic President in the White House and with the Democrats in control of both Houses of Congress. Not only was the peril-point amendment restored but several other amendments hostile to freer trade were adopted. These were the escape-clause amendment, a significant amendment to the Agricultural Adjustment Act, and an amendment restoring the right of domestic producers to intervene in customs cases with a view to obtaining more tariff protection. Also there was included a disclaimer of Congressional responsibility with respect to the GATT.[63]

The peril-point and escape-clause amendments to the trade-agreements legislation are discussed at length in Chapter III. The amendment to the Agricultural Adjustment Act, which subordinated past and future trade agreements to import charges and restrictions in support of domestic agricultural programs is discussed in Chapter IV.

Restoration of Section 516(b).—The Trade Agreements Act as originally enacted in 1934 and as it stood down to 1951 had provided that the provisions of Section 516(b) of the Tariff Act of 1930 would not apply to articles upon which concessions had been granted in trade agreements.

Under Section 516(b) of the Tariff Act of 1930, a United States producer who was concerned about foreign competition could bring action

---

62. There were two nonrestrictive amendments to the Act in the 1949 legislation that were of some significance. One of these removed the emergency label from the law. The other modified the provisions regarding Cuban preferences to permit the elimination of those preferences by negotiation. The latter amendment reflected an undertaking in the pending International Trade Organization Charter for the ultimate elimination of preferences by all countries through the negotiating process.

63. Other 1951 amendments of some importance but of significance more for international-political than for commercial-policy reasons required the withdrawal of trade-agreements concessions from communist or communist-dominated countries and the embargo of imports of certain furs from the Soviet Union and Communist China.

in the Customs Court to contest the administrative tariff classification of an imported product with a view to obtaining a classification that would result in a higher rate. This is a right conferred by the law that a producer, not being a party to the transaction, would not otherwise have. The reason for the suspension of Section 516(b) was that the right of such legal intervention by producers could be used to harass importers, and hence it could impair the benefits of concessions granted in trade agreements.[64]

The suspension of Section 516(b) also had another effect: it created an obstacle to a court test of the constitutionality of the Trade Agreements Act. The courts would not consider customs cases instituted by domestic producers who no longer had legal rights in customs transactions. In an attempt to overcome this obstacle, certain producers of goods on which tariff concessions had been made temporarily became importers of such goods in order to avail themselves of importers' rights of appeal under Section 514 of the Tariff Act of 1930. They attacked the constitutional validity of the rate imposed. They were unsuccessful in these efforts because the court held, in effect, that a bona fide importer could not appeal against conditions favorable to him.[65]

Under the Trade Agreements Extension Act of 1951, producers' rights under Section 516(b) were restored. As a result, producers have availed themselves of the opportunity conferred by this amendment to test the constitutionality of the Trade Agreements Act in the courts.[66] The rights of producers under Section 516(b), however, have become less important since the availability of the escape-clause amendment as a means of restricting imports and, since 1955, of the national-security provision.

The GATT Disclaimer.—In addition to the other restrictive amendments enacted in 1951, Congress made the following declaration: "The enactment of this Act shall not be construed to determine or indicate

64. See U.S. Congress, Senate Committee on Finance, *Hearings* on H.S. Res. 96, 75th Cong., 1st Sess., 1937, pp. 79-82.

65. See *Fletcher* v. *United States,* 92 F. (2d) 713 and *Wislar* v. *United States,* 97 F. (2d) 152, Cert. den. 59 Sup. Ct. 93.

66. The first of these actions was brought in the District Court against the Secretary of the Treasury by the Morgantown Glassware Company of Morgantown, West Virginia (*Morgantown Glassware Guild, Inc.* v. *Humphrey, Secretary of the Treasury,* 236 F. 2d 670). This company questioned the assessment of duties on china and glassware on the grounds that the trade-agreements legislation is unconstitutional. The District Court found that the action should have been brought in the Customs Court, and accordingly, the Morgantown Glassware Company filed the complaint with the Customs Court. The Customs Court upheld the validity of the Trade Agreements Act, and the case was appealed to the Court of Customs and Patent Appeals. See also *Star-Kist Foods, Inc.* v. *United States,* 275 F. 2d 472 (1959), which is referred to in Chap. I, pp. 24-25.

the approval or disapproval by the Congress of the Executive Agreement known as the General Agreement on Tariffs and Trade." This declaration was another indication of the increasingly protectionist attitude of Congress. Though it had no concrete effect on the administration of the Act, it formally registered Congressional doubt about what had been done pursuant to it. The GATT had become the principal international instrument for promoting freer trade. It embodied most of the results of negotiations since 1934. The attitude toward GATT was a reflection of the Congressional attitude toward the policy of trade-barrier reduction and therefore significant to the trade-agreements program and its future.

This Congressional disclaimer of GATT was also included in the renewal legislation of 1953, 1954, 1955, and 1958. Such a provision is explicable only as a protectionist effort to undermine the trade program. Congress had passed and repeatedly renewed legislation laying down a policy and giving the President authority to carry it out. The purpose of requiring periodic renewal of the authority was to enable Congress to satisfy itself as to the manner in which the authority was being used. The results of this authority were largely embodied in GATT. Yet, five times, Congress renewed the authority while formally stating that it did not know whether it was satisfied or not.

That Congress was in reality satisfied with the administration of the Trade Agreements Act seems to be indicated by the fact that its disclaimer was accompanied by a renewal of the President's authority to carry on GATT negotiations. One explanation of the disclaimer is that Congress sought in this way to appease protectionist forces by saying, in effect, that it did not necessarily mean what its action so clearly implied. Or it may be that some Congressional opponents of the policy, being unable to defeat it outright, sought this means of undermining it and that others accepted this legislative equivocation in a spirit of compromise, a spirit that doubtless also owed something to protectionist pressures. If, however, confidence in GATT should be so undermined by such a Congressional attitude or by other acts as to bring about its collapse, the consequences would be the virtual end of the trade-agreements program.

The concentration of protectionist forces on the destruction of GATT is one of the most significant, and possibly portentous, features of United States commercial policy in the past decade. Protectionists have not in recent years generally advocated the repeal of the Trade Agreements Act and the return to the Hawley-Smoot Act of 1930. Instead, they have kept GATT under constant attack on various grounds, such as alleged subservience of United States tariff policy to foreign dictation; the basic issue of protectionism versus freer trade has been kept in the background. Yet, the attack on GATT has, in fact, been an attack on the trade-agreements program.

Most of the results of more than twenty-five years of negotiations under the trade-agreements program are embodied in GATT. At best, the consequences of the anti-GATT campaign might be to retard efforts to expand it and make it a more effective instrument for freeing international trade. At worst, confidence in GATT, both here and abroad, might be so shaken as to lead to its ultimate collapse. If this latter result were achieved, a reversion to tariff policy like that before 1934 might be accomplished without the onus of open advocacy of such a course.

In considering the effect of ultimate withdrawal of the United States from GATT, account must be taken of the fact that reductions in the rates of the Tariff Act of 1930 have been made pursuant to the Trade Agreements Act and can be maintained only through the instrumentality of agreements with foreign countries. If the principal agreement were to lapse, all rates established by it would revert to the pre-GATT rates. Some of them, which were reduced only in GATT, would revert all the way back to the Hawley-Smoot rates; others, which had been reduced in earlier bilateral agreements that were suspended (not terminated) by GATT and were reduced further in GATT, would revert to the rates established by the bilateral agreements. If GATT should lapse and not be replaced, there would be substantial tariff increases on over half of United States dutiable imports.

Reversion of United States rates upward to this extent assumes that there would be no successful efforts to maintain the GATT rates in bilateral negotiations. It is highly questionable, however, as to whether with the collapse of the multilateral agreement, any such bilateral efforts would be successful. Indeed, it is questionable as to whether even the rates in the old bilateral agreements that were suspended but not terminated by GATT could be maintained. These agreements might not survive the wave of economic nationalism that would follow the collapse of the major postwar instrument for freeing international trade and the loss of confidence in international as against domestic or other means of meeting national economic problems. Failure of the old bilateral agreements to stem the tide would mean a general reversion of the United States tariff to the pre-trade-agreement starting point and to the levels of the Hawley-Smoot Act of 1930.[67]

67. Any such result could, of course, be forestalled by act of Congress making the GATT rates the statutory rates. But if GATT should lapse, this would mean maintaining rates established by negotiations with the other parties for the benefit of their exports to the United States while releasing all the other parties from their negotiated commitments regarding the treatment of United States exports. Much can be said for unilateral tariff reduction, but those opposed to GATT do not favor such a policy.

The shape that the tariff controversy has taken since 1951, therefore, tends to obscure the real issue. The controversy goes far deeper than whether the United States should continue to participate in the "Executive Agreement known as the General Agreement on Tariffs and Trade." The war of attrition against GATT has been in reality a war against the trade-agreements program and the policy of freer international trade.

POLICY RE-EXAMINATION

After 1951, when protectionist forces and their spokesmen in Congress had achieved a large measure of success in their efforts to undermine the Trade Agreements Act and what had been accomplished under it, the Executive branch of the government sought to bring about a re-examination of the Act and policy from the standpoint of the national interest. Such re-examination was made on the initiative of both Democratic and Republican Administrations.

Trade policy was studied under the Democratic Administration shortly before it left office by the Public Advisory Board for Mutual Security (Bell Commission), which submitted its report to the President on February 24, 1953. The Commission on Foreign Economic Policy (Randall Commission) was established after the new Republican Administration took office, according to provisions in the Trade Agreements Extension Act of 1953. It reported to the President and to Congress on January 23, 1954. Another commission whose studies were relevant was the President's Materials Policy Commission (Paley Commission), which reported in 1952. Meanwhile, the authority in the Trade Agreements Act was extended for short periods—for two years in 1951 and for one year in 1953 and in 1954.

These reports brought out striking evidence as to the growing importance from the standpoint of the national interest of freer international trade and as to the relatively minor adverse effects of such trade on particular interests.[68] The conclusions to be drawn from these reports and

68. The Randall Commission *Staff Papers* indicated rather strikingly the limited number of United States workers who potentially would be adversely affected by a freer trade policy going far beyond anything contemplated in the Trade Agreements Act. It stated that "the number of workers involved in producing the equivalent of the maximum import increase anticipated by Piquet in the event of tariff suspension . . . comes to 405,000 nonfarm wage and salaried employees and farm workers . . . out of a total of 61,000,000 employed civilians in 1951." It pointed out that even this relatively small number of workers was overstated, because such dynamic factors as shifts in lines of production would reduce the impact of increased imports on employment. In contrast to the limited number of workers potentially affected adversely by freer trade, employment attributed to foreign trade was estimated at 4,376,000. The *Staff Papers* failed to point out, however, that the implication of such an estimate is also overstated, because it assumes that if there were no foreign trade, workers engaged in it would be unemployed rather

other sources are perhaps best, and most appropriately, summarized by President Eisenhower in his message to Congress of March 20, 1954: "If we fail in our trade policy, we may fail in all. Our domestic employment, our standard of living, our security, and the solidarity of the free world—all are involved. For our own economic growth we must have continuously expanding world markets; for our security we require that our allies become economically strong. Expanding trade is the only adequate solution for these two pressing problems confronting our country."[69]

THE TRADE AGREEMENTS EXTENSION ACT OF 1955

While the exhaustive studies had thrown a great deal of light on the national need for a freer trade policy, they threw no light on how the political obstacles presented by special and sectional interests could be surmounted. The Trade Agreements Extension Act of 1955, which was the end product of all these investigations, was equivocal toward the policy, full of compromises, and meager in its grant of authority. The tariff-reducing authority was not only meager, but it had to be gradual. The limit on reductions (except in the special case of Japan)[70] was only 15 per cent below the rates on January 1, 1955, to be made effective in three annual installments of 5 per cent each. A further provision, also to be applied on the same gradual basis, allowed the reduction to 50 per cent ad valorem or its equivalent of any rate in excess of that amount. This would provide in some cases considerably more than the 15 per cent authority. However, it was applicable to less than two hundred rates out of something over four thousand rates subject to the 15 per cent authority. These very high rates, however, doubtless had a disproportionate effect in restricting trade, and their reduction would be important from this standpoint. But the rates in question would still remain high after the authority had been used.

---

than producing formerly imported products. The purpose of trade is not to create employment but to make employment more productive. See *Staff Papers* Presented to the Commission on Foreign Economic Policy, February 1954, pp. 380-81 and 373-74, respectively.

For a recent scholarly study of the effects of imports on employment, see Walter S. Salant and Beatrice N. Vaccara, *Import Liberalization and Employment* (Washington, D.C.: The Brookings Institution, 1961).

69. "Recommendations Concerning Foreign Economic Policy," *The Department of State Bulletin*, XXX (April 19, 1954), 607.

70. The old tariff-reducing authority (50 per cent of the January 1, 1945, rates) was extended for the purpose of allowing the President to complete announced trade-agreement negotiations with Japan. However, rates of duty reduced by 15 per cent or more in the trade-agreement negotiations with Japan could not be further reduced under the new 15 per cent authority.

The Trade Agreements Extension Act of 1955 retained all of the restrictive amendments in the Act of 1951 and added a few of its own, such as those discussed in Chapter III, affecting the administration of the escape clause and tending to make it somewhat easier to invoke. It also contained a new amendment relating to national defense which was potentially a serious threat to freer trade:

In order to further the policy and purpose of this section, whenever the Director of the Office of Defense Mobilization has reason to believe that any article is being imported into the United States in such quantities as to threaten to impair the national security, he shall so advise the President, and if the President agrees that there is reason for such belief, the President shall cause an immediate investigation to be made to determine the facts. If, on the basis of such investigation, and the report to him of the findings and recommendations made in connection therewith, the President finds that the article is being imported into the United States in such quantities as to threaten to impair the national security, he shall take such action as he deems necessary to adjust the imports of such article to a level that will not threaten to impair the national security.

This provision conferred very wide authority on the President to regulate imports. The test laid down may be regarded as an intelligible one, since it required a finding of fact that imports were threatening to impair the national security. Yet it allowed for wide differences of opinion as to conclusions to be drawn from a given set of facts, and the President's judgment of necessity was to be a large ingredient in any decision reached. As Jere Cooper, chairman of the Ways and Means Committee, pointed out: "In arriving at his decision he [the President] must consider the impact of that decision on our total foreign policy, and on the economies of the nations of the free world that are allied with us. He must also consider the impact of any decision on our over-all strength and security, keeping in mind that any modification of a duty on imports or a quota would inevitably result in a curtailment of exports by the United States."[71] The provision in question is of particular interest in view of the earlier attacks on the constitutionality of the much more limited delegation of authority to the President under other provisions of the Trade Agreements Act.

Despite all the foregoing, however, there is one respect in which the Extension Act of 1955 and the discussion leading up to it were a landmark in the progress toward a freer trade policy in the national interest. This was the fact that a freer trade policy, and one more vigorous and less equivocal than that which found expression in the law, had been

71. U.S. *Congressional Record*, 84th Cong., 1st Sess., Vol. CI, Pt. 6 (June 14, 1955), p. 8161.

solidly endorsed by a Republican Administration and in that way had given a stronger bipartisan aspect to the policy of freer trade than it previously had had.[72]

THE TRADE AGREEMENTS EXTENSION ACT OF 1958

In the public discussion before and during the 1958 reconsideration of the trade-agreements legislation by Congress, it was widely expected that only a miracle could save the trade program from serious emasculation or outright defeat. If this widely prevailing impression was not actually propagated by astute opponents in order to soften resistance to restrictive amendments, it was most certainly a windfall for them. The Administration opened the campaign for renewal by advancing at the center and retreating on the flank. It asked for substantial tariff-reducing authority for a period of five years rather than the usual three because of the need for a longer period for negotiating with the newly-formed European Economic Community (EEC). At the same time it proposed measures that would facilitate tariff increases and would raise the limit on such increases. Whether due to the compromises offered or to unrealized strength of public support for the trade-agreements program, the final result was the renewal of the authority by heavy majorities in both Houses of Congress for four years from June 30, 1958, this being the longest extension in the history of the Act.

The duty reductions authorized were limited to: (1) 20 per cent of the July 1, 1958, rates, with no more than 10 per cent reduction in any one year; or (2) two percentage points with not more than one percentage point reduction in any one year, which would give greater than the 20 per cent authority in the case of low rates (e.g., a 5 per cent rate could be reduced to 3 per cent or by 40 per cent instead of 20 per cent under the general rule); or (3) reduction to 50 per cent ad valorem or its equivalent of any rate in excess of that level, with no more than one-third of the reduction being made in any one year.

Various other provisions had in view duty increases rather than duty reductions. The limit to which duties could be raised under the escape clause was increased to 50 per cent of the rates that existed on July 1, 1934, which in most cases were the rates of the Tariff Act of 1930. The previous limit had been 50 per cent of the rates in force on January 1, 1945. Authority was granted under the escape clause to transfer products from the free list to the dutiable list and to impose a duty up to 50 per cent ad valorem on products bound free of duty in a trade agreement.

72. For a further discussion and analysis of the Trade Agreements Extension Act of 1955, see U.S. Council of the International Chamber of Commerce, *Analysis of The Trade Agreements Extension Act of 1955*, staff paper by David W. MacEachron (August, 1955).

The justification advanced for this concession to protectionism was that the only action that could theretofore be taken in such cases was the undesirable alternative of imposing an import quota.[73] An amendment of the peril-point provision facilitated duty increases by requiring an immediate escape-clause investigation whenever a "peril-point" was found to be higher than the rate of duty on a product on which a tariff concession had been made.

Another provision created a means of overriding the President's authority in escape-clause cases. A crucial issue was whether the President would retain his discretion to act on Tariff Commission recommendations or whether (in effect) this aspect of foreign relations should be taken away from the President and turned over to the commission. The law as enacted left the President's discretionary authority unchanged, but it provided that within sixty days after the President's disapproval of a commission recommendation, Congress might by concurrent resolution, having privileged legislative status and supported by a two-thirds vote of both Houses, give effect to the commission's recommendation.

The provision relating to national security was amended to point more definitely in the direction of restrictions on imports. It provided for "adjustment of imports" to meet the needs of industries adversely affected by import competition when such industries were important to the national defense. Action on advice of the Director of the Office of Defense Mobilization (renamed the Office of Emergency Planning) was to be mandatory to the President unless he made a determination that the imports in question were not impairing or threatening the national security. The law laid down at some length the factors to be taken into account and referred to the "close relation of the economic welfare of the Nation to our national security"; but it did not mention the relation of foreign trade to economic welfare or of foreign relations to national security, although it did not specifically exclude these factors from consideration.[74]

73. This provision did not repeal the authority to impose quotas in escape-clause cases, but it added the alternative of a tariff in the case of free-list items. Several questions arise in connection with this grant and retention of quota authority, as follows: In a freer-trade act, should the President have authority to resort to such a drastic trade measure as import quotas? What limit, if any, is there in the law on the use of this authority? Could the President set the quota at any point he likes, down to a virtually complete embargo on imports of a product? Clearly, insofar as the limitation on duty increases is intended to limit the injury inflicted on importers, consumers, and others, such a limitation is wholly meaningless if the President is also given authority virtually to embargo imports entirely.

74. For a discussion of this national security amendment and its use, see Willard L. Thorp, "Trade Barriers and National Security," *The American Economic Review*, L, (May, 1960), 433-42.

Altogether, the Trade Agreements Extension Act of 1958 made a further and substantial contribution to the confusion of philosophy and purpose that had characterized the trade-agreements legislation from its inception and that since 1951 had become a bewildering maze of contradictions and cross purposes.[75]

4. THE TRADE EXPANSION ACT OF 1962[76]

In his message to Congress on the trade-agreements program, President Kennedy described the Administration's 1962 trade bill as "unprecedented in economic history."[77] In some respects, the 1962 trade legislation is "unprecedented." Authority to make duty reductions on categories of products and to eliminate some duties altogether is new. Adjustment assistance as an alternative to trade restrictions when injury results from tariff concessions is also new, and more importantly, it introduces a much needed philosophy into the trade program. However, the legislation is Janus-faced. Although the most restrictive features of the peril-point provision are missing, the substance of the escape clause is retained, and the national-security provision has not been altered. Also, other provisions restrict or qualify some of the Act's more liberal features. It is most significant, however, that the President is given much more authority and flexibility than formerly. Whether the Trade Expansion Act meets United States foreign-trade and foreign-policy needs of the next few years depends in large part upon the courage and vigor with which it is administered. It also depends upon the response of foreign countries to United States trade initiative.

NEGOTIATING AUTHORITIES

The Trade Expansion Act extends the President's authority to proclaim negotiated tariff concessions for five years or until June 30, 1967. Never before has Congress extended this authority for so long a period. Tariff reductions can be effected under any of four negotiating authorities:

50 Per cent Authority.—Rates of duty may be reduced by up to 50 per cent of their July 1, 1962, level. This is similar to previous grants of authority, except that negotiations need not be on an item-by-item basis.

EEC Authority.—In a trade agreement with the EEC, tariffs may be reduced by more than 50 per cent and even eliminated on industrial

75. For a further discussion and analysis of the Trade Agreements Extension Act of 1958, see U.S. Council of the International Chamber of Commerce, *United States Trade Policy in a Changing World Economy,* 1959.

76. This section was added by the editor after enactment in October of the Trade Expansion Act of 1962.

77. U.S. Congress, House Committee on Ways and Means, *Hearings* on H.R. 9900, 87th Cong., 2nd Sess., Pt. 1, 1962, p. 9.

products within categories in which the United States and the EEC together account for 80 per cent or more of the value of free-world exports during a representative period. Categories meeting this criteria would depend upon the membership of the EEC at the time of negotiations and upon the representative period selected. It is assumed that the United Nations three-digit Standard International Trade Classification (SITC) categories of products would be used, although this is not specified. Categories of products that might meet this criteria in future negotiations with an enlarged EEC are listed in Table 1, below.[78]

In a trade agreement with the EEC, tariffs may also be reduced to zero on agricultural products if such action will aid agricultural exports of like products.[79]

Tropical Products Authority.—Duties may be reduced by more than 50 per cent or eliminated on tropical agricultural or forestry commodities not produced in significant quantities in the United States provided that the EEC makes comparable commitments.[80]

Low Duty Authority.—Duties may be reduced by more than 50 per cent or eliminated on products dutiable at 5 per cent or less (or ad valorem equivalent).[81]

All articles are reserved from negotiations on which escape-clause action is in effect under this or previous legislation or on which an orderly marketing agreement has been negotiated under this new Act. Articles on which action is in effect under the national-security provision of this or previous legislation are also reserved.[82] Unless the Tariff Commission finds that economic conditions have substantially improved, all articles are reserved on which a majority of the commission has made a serious-injury finding under the old escape clause.[83] In addition, the President can reserve any other articles that he deems appropriate.

78. For a list of United States Schedule A commodity descriptions and numbers included within the SITC categories contained in Table 1, see *ibid.*, pp. 279-307.

79. For a list of agricultural products to which this provision could be applicable (depending upon export advantages), see *ibid.*, pp. 329-478.

80. For a list of dutiable tropical agricultural and forestry products not produced in significant quantities in the United States, see *ibid.*, pp. 308-11.

81. For a list of products dutiable at 5 per cent or less (or ad valorem equivalent), see *ibid.*, pp. 312-27.

82. When the Trade Expansion Act became law, the following articles met the criteria of this provision: dried figs, watches, toweling of flax, hemp, or ramie, safety pins, clinical thermometers, lead and zinc, stainless-steel table flatware, cotton typewriter-ribbon cloth, sheet glass, certain carpets and rugs, and crude petroleum and derivatives.

83. When the Trade Expansion Act became law, the following articles met the criteria of this provision: women's fur felt hats and hat bodies, hatters' fur, garlic, tobacco pipes and bowls, screen-printed silk scarves, scissors and shears, groundfish fillets, alsike clover seed, bicycles, ferrocerium (lighter flints), velveteen fabrics, violins and violas, straight pins, spring clothespins, umbrella frames, tartaric acid, cream of tartar, baseball and softball gloves, and ceramic mosaic tile.

TABLE I

COMMODITY GROUPS OF WHICH EXPORTS FROM THE UNITED STATES AND A POSSIBLE ENLARGED E.E.C.[a] TOTALED 80 PER CENT OR MORE OF FREE-WORLD EXPORTS IN 1960[b]

SITC, Revised, Group No.	Commodity Group	Free-World Exports (per cent)			U.S. Trade with Free World ($ million)		U.S. Trade with Enlarged E.E.C. ($ million)	
		U.S. and Enlarged E.E.C.	U.S.	Enlarged E.E.C.	U.S. Exports to Free World	U.S. Imports from Free World[c]	U.S. Imports from Enlarged E.E.C.[c]	Enlarged E.E.C. Imports from U.S.[c]
734	Aircraft	97	80	17	1,227	53	20	425
862	Photographic and cinematographic supplies, except cameras	93	37	56	62	29	28	13
321	Coal, coke, and briquettes	92	67	25	360	4	—	197
613	Fur skins	91	39	52	16	9	8	6
732	Road motor vehicles	91	29	62	1,237	643	596[d]	76
091	Margarine and shortenings	90	48	42	47	1		38
664	Glass, except glassware	89	17	72	34	54	44	5
533	Pigments and paints	88	35	53	77	4	3	20
552[e]	Perfumery, cosmetics, and cleansing preparations	88	30	58	74	8	7	7
731	Railway vehicles	87	39	48	126	1	7[d]	1
062	Sugar confectionery and other sugar preparations	86	19	67	10	15[d]	12[d]	1
111	Nonalcoholic beverages	86	5	81	1		27	—
715	Metalworking machinery	86	43	43	352	36	25	95
733	Road vehicles, except motor vehicles	86	14	72	24	33	38	1
712	Agricultural machinery, including tractors	85	47	38	520	136	34	30
891	Musical instruments, sound recorders, and parts	85	27	58	57	45	2	
612	Leather manufactures	83	19	64	6	5	26	19[d]
512	Organic chemicals	82	37	45	266	54		176

SITC, Revised, Group No.	Commodity Group	Free-World Exports (per cent)			U.S. Trade with Free World ($ million)		U.S. Trade with Enlarged E.E.C. ($ million)	
		U.S. and Enlarged E.E.C.	U.S.	Enlarged E.E.C.	U.S. Exports to Free World	U.S. Imports from Free World[e]	U.S. Imports from Enlarged E.E.C.[e]	Enlarged E.E.C. Imports from U.S.[e]
711	Power generating machinery, except electric machinery	82	25	57	280	24	17	130
599[e]	Miscellaneous chemicals, including plastics and insecticides	81	46	35	682	40[f]	20[f]	188
621	Materials of rubber	81	9	72	6			9
714	Office machinery	81	40	41	207	67	52	69
716[e]	Industrial machinery, except power, generating and metal-working machinery	81	39	42	1,817	170	92	340
122	Tobacco manufactures	80	51	29	97	1	1	11
629	Articles of rubber	80	32	48	152	47[f]	25[f]	13
721[e]	Electric machinery	80	33	47	1,066	284	122	216
	TOTAL (26 groups)				8,803	1,763	1,199	2,086

[a] Enlarged E.E.C. is present E.E.C. member countries (Belgium, France, Federal Republic of Germany, Italy, Luxembourg, and the Netherlands) plus Denmark, Greece, Ireland, Norway, and the United Kingdom.

[b] Free-world export value includes total exports of all countries of the free world except (1) exports from countries of a possible enlarged E.E.C. to each other; and (2) exports from free-world countries to countries dominated or controlled by international communism (Albania, Bulgaria, Czechoslovakia, Hungary, Poland, Rumania, U.S.S.R., China (mainland Communist), North Korea, North Viet-Nam, Outer Mongolia, Soviet Zone of Germany, and Cuba).

[d] United States imports are valued f.o.b.; enlarged E.E.C. imports are valued c.i.f.

[e] This is an original SITC group number, because separate data are not available according to the SITC, Revised, numbers.

[f] Less than $500,000.

[f] United States import statistics for articles of rubber include materials of rubber.

Source: International Trade Analysis Division, United States Department of Commerce.

In general, negotiated tariff reductions must be given effect in five equal annual stages. However, no such staging requirements are necessary for reductions made under the tropical-products authority.

As under previous legislation, reduced trade-agreements rates would usually be extended to third countries, except Communist countries. However, the Act denies the President the previous flexibility under which goods from Poland and Yugoslavia have been extended most-favored-nation treatment. The President may also withhold trade-agreements concessions from countries that discriminate against or that practice policies that inhibit United States exports. Greater emphasis is given to such possible retaliatory measures, including the authority to impose without limitation duties or other import restrictions on the products of any country that unjustifiably restricts exports of United States agricultural products.

Negotiations are to be conducted by a Special Representative to be appointed by the President. The Special Representative is to have ambassadorial rank and is to be chairman of the interagency Cabinet-level trade organization. This organization will administer the trade-agreements program, and it may be assisted in this task by the establishment of subordinate committees.

In some respects, the President's power under these negotiating authorities is far-reaching. The 50 per cent authority is the most notable, and if used on an across-the-board or linear basis, it could produce significant results.

The EEC authority appears to be more formidable than it is. Unless the United Kingdom joins the EEC, it will be virtually worthless, because as the EEC is presently constituted, the authority might apply to only two categories of products—aircraft and margarine and shortenings. This provision was intended to serve as an inducement for the United Kingdom to join the EEC. As illustrated in Table 1, if the EEC were enlarged to include the United Kingdom and other countries, some 26 categories of products might meet the 80 per cent criteria. An amendment introduced by Senator Douglas (D., Ill.) would have permitted the inclusion of the trade of the United Kingdom and other European Free Trade Association (EFTA) countries in the calculation of the 80 per cent criteria.[84] This amendment was adopted by the Senate, but it was not accepted by the House-Senate conference committee. As enacted, therefore, the legislation is not designed to deal significantly in any special way with the EEC unless its membership is expanded to include at least the United Kingdom.

84. Representative Reuss (D., Wis.) led the move for such an amendment in the House.

The purpose of the tropical-products authority is to induce the EEC to reduce or eliminate its duties on such tropical products as coffee. Duty-free entry of tropical products into the EEC from associated African countries discriminates against Latin American, Asian, and non-associated African countries. This discrimination would be reduced or eliminated to the extent that the EEC lowered its duties on tropical products. It is questionable, however, whether this authority gives the United States much bargaining power via the EEC. The United States imposes low duties or grants duty-free treatment on most of the products to which this authority applies. United States imports of such products in 1960 totaled $190 million. However, $120 million of these imports were dutiable at 5 per cent or less, and therefore they would be covered by the low-duty authority.

United States imports in 1960 of products subject to the low-duty authority totaled about $2.6 billion. Half of this total, however, would be exempt from negotiations because it consisted of crude petroleum and derivatives that are subject to quota restrictions on the grounds of national security. The principal benefit of the elimination of duties on the non-petroleum products would be to simplify customs administration because such low duties usually afford little, if any, protection. Nevertheless, such simplification can have a trade-stimulating effect.

SAFEGUARDS

The no-serious-injury philosophy, which has dominated the trade-agreements program since its beginning and which is reflected in the peril-point and escape-clause provisions of the trade legislation, has not been discarded, but it has been significantly modified. Concessions that might cause domestic adjustment problems or injury are no longer precluded by the legislation. Provision is made for adjustment assistance measures for industries, firms, and workers that may be injured by trade concessions.

Peril Points.—As under previous legislation, the Tariff Commission advises the President on the possible economic effects of proposed tariff concessions. In this connection public hearings must be held.[85] The all-important change in this procedure is that the commission's role is advisory. The commission no longer establishes peril points as such.

Escape Clause.—The new escape clause, referred to as "tariff ad-

85. Public hearings must also be held by an agency or an interagency committee designated by the President. These hearings are to be in connection with information and advice furnished the President by the Departments of Agriculture, Commerce, Defense, Interior, Labor, State, and Treasury.

justment," makes several changes in the criteria upon which the Tariff Commission makes injury findings. Probably the most important is that no definition of "industry" is given, thus eliminating the segmentation clause and permitting, though not ensuring, a broader definition than formerly.[86] The definition of competitive imports, however, is broadened so that they may include articles "at an earlier or later stage of processing" if such articles have an economic effect comparable to that of "articles in the same stage of processing as the domestic article." Thus, imports of lamb and mutton, as well as of the live animals, could be regarded as competitive with the sheep-raising industry. Under the new escape clause, imports injuring or threatening to injure an industry must be "in major part" the result of trade-agreements concessions instead of "in whole or in part" the result of concessions. There is a presumption that such imports must increase absolutely because the previous reference to "relative" increases is no longer included. Increased imports also must be "the major factor" in causing injury to an industry. The previous standard referred to imports having "contributed substantially" towards causing injury.

If the Tariff Commission finds serious injury or threat of serious injury to an industry, it recommends tariff or quantitative restrictions that it regards as necessary to prevent or remedy such injury. After receiving the commission's report, the President may take any of the following actions:

(1) He may impose increased duties up to 50 per cent of the rate existing on July 1, 1934, or, in the case of a duty-free article, impose a duty of up to 50 per cent ad valorem. He may also impose a quota. Such trade restrictions, unless extended by the President, are limited to a maximum of four years. Unless extended, escape-clause actions taken under previous legislation must be terminated no later than October 11, 1967.

(2) When deemed more appropriate, he may negotiate an interna-

86. However, the report of the House Ways and Means Committee defines industry as follows: "In general, the industry . . . will include those operations of those establishments in which the domestic article in question . . . is produced. If the domestic article in question is produced in an establishment along with several other articles, the overall operations of the establishment would be included in the domestic industry. Where a corporate entity has several establishments (e.g., divisions or plants) in only one of which the domestic article in question is produced, the establishments in which the domestic article is not produced would, as a general rule, not be included in the industry . . ." (U.S. Congress, House Committee on Ways and Means, *Report* to accompany H.R. 11970, 87th Cong., 2nd Sess., Rep. No. 1818, June 12, 1962, p. 23). This is a much broader definition of industry than that contained in the old law.

tional agreement with foreign countries limiting their exports of the article causing injury.

(3) He may allow firms and workers in the injured industry to request the Secretaries of Commerce and Labor, respectively, to certify their eligibility to apply for adjustment assistance.

(4) He may take any combination of these actions.

(5) He may not accept the Commission's injury finding.

If the President does not follow the recommendations of the Tariff Commission, he must explain his reasons for not doing so to the Congress. He may be overruled by a concurrent resolution by majority vote of both Houses of Congress. Under previous legislation, a two-thirds majority was required to overrule. However, such a resolution was to have privileged status, which it now would not enjoy.

Adjustment Assistance.—As indicated above, adjustment assistance may be made available to firms and workers when a finding of injury to an entire industry is made under the escape clause. However, such a finding is not required in order to make adjustment assistance available to individual firms and groups of workers. Such firms and workers may petition the Tariff Commission for an investigation to determine their eligibility to apply for adjustment assistance. If the commission, using essentially the same criteria as in escape-clause cases, finds that such firms or workers are being injured, it reports its finding to the President, who may certify that such firms or groups of workers are eligible to apply for adjustment assistance.

Before firms can obtain adjustment assistance after either an injury finding for an entire industry under the escape clause or an injury finding for individual firms, they must present an adjustment proposal that is designed to assist them. If such a proposal is approved by the Secretary of Commerce, firms may receive any or all of the following types of assistance: (1) technical assistance; (2) financial assistance in the form of loans, guarantees of loans, or agreements for deferred participation in loans; (3) tax assistance in the form of special carrybacks and carryovers of operating losses.

Groups of workers, determined by the Secretary of Labor to be entitled to adjustment assistance, may receive any or all of the following types of assistance: (1) allowances for partial or complete unemployment; (2) retraining for other types of employment; (3) allowances to assist families to relocate to an area where employment is available.

National Security Provision.—This provision is continued almost verbatim.

EVALUATION

The Trade Expansion Act extends to the President greater flexibility and tariff-reducing authority than any other legislation in the history of the trade-agreements program. Not only may tariffs be cut by up to 50 per cent but for the first time they may be eliminated on some products. Negotiations may be conducted on an across-the-board or linear basis, so that the rates on all products or on broad categories of products may be reduced and in some cases eliminated (except for those products that are specifically reserved from negotiation). Across-the-board negotiations should result in deeper cuts because they de-emphasize the attention given in item-by-item negotiations to the adjustment problems of individual industries and producers. Such problems may actually be less because across-the-board tariff cuts should have less of a distorting effect on the economy than selective cuts, i.e., the total level of protection would be lowered, but the relative protection of individual industries or producers would remain essentially the same.

The President is also given greater flexibility and authority in regard to safeguards to domestic producers. Import restrictions are no longer the sole relief for injured industries. Even more important, tariff reductions are not precluded when they might cause injury. If such tariff cuts are in the national interest, then adjustment assistance can be used to help the affected parties.

In sum, the opportunities for significant tariff reductions under the Trade Expansion Act are unparalleled. However, as already noted, there are a number of restrictions and qualifications on the use of the negotiating authorities. Most of these are not mandatory; they allow the President a great deal of discretion. The effectiveness of the Act in promoting freer trade appears to depend in very large part upon the willingness of the Administration to pursue vigorously a liberal trade policy. This will require great political courage.

Even if the United States is willing to use the trade act to the fullest, it is questionable how successful it will be in negotiations with other countries. In this regard, much depends on the outcome of the United Kingdom negotiations for accession to the EEC. As already indicated, the utility of the special EEC authority is dependent upon whether or not the United Kingdom joins. The European attitude toward negotiating with the United States will also be influenced by the success of these negotiations. Should the United Kingdom and others join, it may be difficult to negotiate with the countries of an enlarged EEC because they may want time to adjust to the greater intra-EEC competition before adjusting further to reduced duties on the goods of non-EEC countries.

Should the United Kingdom negotiations fail, it may be even more difficult to negotiate with the EEC. A little Europe under French hegemony may be less willing to reduce or eliminate its common external tariff, one of its most important cohesive elements. On the other hand, it may be less difficult to negotiate with the United Kingdom and other EFTA and Commonwealth countries, because they will be seeking alternative trade arrangements.

Whatever may be United States prospects for successful negotiations with other countries, the opportunity for such negotiations should not be missed. If the United States were to come to the tariff-negotiating table with a minimum proposal that other countries could use as an excuse for not negotiating significant concessions, all the effort put into enacting the Trade Expansion Act will have been in vain.

CHAPTER III

The Escape Clause and Peril Points Under the Trade-Agreements Program

The most important legislative limitations on the power of the President to negotiate tariff reductions under the Trade Agreements Act have been the escape-clause and peril-point provisions. These provisions, however, are statutory formulations of the principle of no serious injury to domestic industries which has underlaid the trade-agreements program since its beginning. This chapter deals with (1) the formalization of escape-clause and peril-point procedures; (2) the administration of the escape-clause and peril-point provisions; and (3) an assessment of these provisions. An account of the outcome or current status of all escape-clause investigations is contained in an appendix.

1. FORMALIZATION OF ESCAPE-CLAUSE AND PERIL-POINT PROCEDURES

The principle that trade-agreements concessions should not and would not be made for the purpose or with the anticipation of doing "serious injury" to a domestic industry has been present since the original enactment of the trade-agreements law in 1934. This concept was implicit in the manner in which the legislation contemplated that tariff negotiations would be conducted, i.e., on a selective, product-by-product basis. It was elaborated on in the Congressional hearings during which Administration spokesmen promised to avoid damage to domestic industries.

From 1934 to 1942 the methods of avoiding damage took the form of (a) interdepartmental administrative procedures designed to assure the careful weighing of facts and probabilities with respect to proposed tariff concessions; (b) the use of qualified concessions, i.e., tariff reductions on foreign merchandise limited to types, qualities, quantities, grades, or seasonal periods of importation, which offered less competition with domestic production than unqualified concessions would have; (c) the use of special escape clauses aimed at specific risks, such as foreign currency devaluations, which encouraged imports by lowering their prices in terms of dollars; and (d) willingness to renegotiate concessions that occasionally turned out to be more painful than had been expected.

In 1942, in the trade agreement with Mexico,[1] the various special escape clauses aimed at specific future risks were replaced by a general clause permitting the modification or withdrawal of trade-agreements concessions in order to remedy serious injury to a domestic industry from increased imports resulting from the concession.

During the postwar period, the escape-clause and peril-point procedures assumed an increasing degree of prominence in United States commercial policy. What had been a matter of administrative policy was made a Congressional requirement. The power of investigating to determine whether escape-clause action is warranted was vested in the Tariff Commission, some of the factors to be taken into account by the commission in making this determination were specified by statute, and the power of domestic industries to require investigations leading to possible escape action was enhanced.

THE EXECUTIVE ORDER OF 1947

From the Mexican trade agreement in 1942 until the issuance of an Executive Order in 1947, no special procedure existed within the Executive branch for determining whether to invoke escape clauses in trade agreements entered into by the United States. In 1945 when the Congress was considering legislation to renew and strengthen the Trade Agreements Act, the Administration agreed to include in all future agreements a general escape clause of the kind included in the agreement with Mexico but made no announcement of procedures for the implementation of this policy.[2] Complaints of injury brought by domestic industry were consequently handled along with all other trade-agreements matters by the interdepartmental Trade Agreements Committee. There is no information available as to the number of applications for escape-clause relief made to the Trade Agreements Committee during this period, but it is likely that they were very few. The fact that no public announcement of procedures was made may well have tended to limit the number of applications. Moreover, potential applicants for escape-clause action were undoubtedly influenced by the belief that the Trade Agreements Committee would not give them a sympathetic hearing.[3]

1. Article XI, Reciprocal Trade Agreement between the United States of America and Mexico, U.S. *Executive Agreement Series,* No. 311.

2. See U.S. Congress, Senate Committee On Finance, *Hearings* on H.R. 3240, 79th Cong., 1st Sess., 1945, pp. 179-80. The escape clause has been included in the bilateral trade agreement between the United States and Paraguay (1947); in the General Agreement on Tariffs and Trade (GATT) (1948); in the 1936 agreement between the United States and Switzerland (effective October, 1950); and in the 1939 agreement between the United States and Venezuela (effective October, 1952).

3. For example, in a brief presented to the Senate Finance Committee in connection

These factors, together with the circumstance that no tariff had been raised as a result of an escape-clause action, led protectionist groups, who had hoped that the escape clause might become a vehicle for increasing protection for United States industries, to urge modification of the procedures for determination of injury so as to make relief under the escape clause more readily available. One of the most significant of their proposals was that jurisdiction over the escape clause should be transferred from the Trade Agreements Committee, which represented the co-ordinated views of the Executive departments, to the Tariff Commission, an independent bipartisan agency closer to the Congress.

The publication by the Administration in the fall of 1946 of a long list of products upon which tariff changes would be considered at negotiations with eighteen foreign countries, contemplated for the spring of 1947 at Geneva, greatly alarmed protectionist elements. Encouraged by the Republican Congressional victory in 1946 they intensified their activities, demanding the curtailment of the President's trade-agreements authority and the revision of escape-clause procedures.

Early in the first session of the new Congress, a bill was introduced which would have stopped the Geneva negotiations until the Tariff Commission had completed a special report on the program. This bill, the Jenkins resolution,[4] received considerable support from Republican members of the House Ways and Means Committee who appeared to be in a strong enough position to report the bill to the House. At the same time, several influential Republicans in the Senate as well as in the House urged modification of the Trade Agreements Act before its expiration in June, 1948.[5]

Meanwhile, discussions were proceeding between Republican senators Vandenberg (R., Mich.) and Millikin (R., Colo.) and Undersecretaries of State William L. Clayton and Dean Acheson. The senators were anxious to avoid an open break on the tariff issue within their own party so early in its career as the majority party in the Congress. At the same time, they were impressed by the arguments of the Executive branch regarding the serious effects of a long tariff debate on the international

---

with the renewal of the Trade Agreement Act in 1951, the Independent Petroleum Association of America referred to the administration of the escape clause between 1943 and the conclusion of GATT and stated that "repeated appeals for relief under the Mexican agreement were ignored entirely." The association ascribed responsibility for escape-clause procedures during this period to the State Department. U.S. Congress, Senate Committee on Finance, *Hearings* on H.R. 1612, 82nd Cong., 1st Sess., 1951, Pt. 1, p. 861.

4. The bill was introduced by Representative Jenkins (R., Ohio), a long-time opponent of the trade-agreements program.

5. *The New York Times*, January 17, 26, and February 5, 1947.

prestige and leadership of the United States and the damage that might result from a postponement of the Geneva negotiations.[6]

As a result of the agreement reached between the two senior Republican senators and the State Department representatives, the President issued an Executive Order relating to the escape clause. This order, dated February 25, 1947, established the first formal governmental procedures for considering and acting upon applications by domestic industries for the use of the escape clause on their behalf. It also provided for the inclusion of an escape clause in future agreements, requiring that all future trade agreements entered into by the United States must permit the withdrawal or modification of concessions "if, as a result of unforeseen developments and of the concession granted by the United States on any article in the trade agreement, such article is being imported in such increased quantities and under such conditions as to cause, or threaten, serious injury to domestic producers of like or similar articles. . . ."[7] This language, based on the escape clause in the trade agreement with Mexico, was also substantially identical with that to which the United States later agreed in Article XIX of the GATT.

In prescribing the procedures for investigation of injury, the order designated the Tariff Commission as the agency for conducting the investigations. The commission was to recommend action to the President "for his consideration in the light of the public interest."[8]

In signing the new Executive Order, President Truman commented upon the extension of bipartisanship to the international economic field and said that he was "very happy that Senators Vandenberg and Millikin agree that we should go forward with the Geneva negotiations."[9]

The compromise, however, did not go far toward creating lasting bipartisan support for the trade-agreements program. Senator Millikin, one of the authors of the compromise plan, criticized the administration of the escape clause the following year and argued strongly for further legislative restrictions upon the authority of the President.

Had the Executive Order not been issued and had a partisan struggle

6. See article by James Reston, *The New York Times*, February 5, 1947. See also the statement issued by Senators Vandenberg and Millikin on the result of their talks, printed in U.S. *Congressional Record*, 80th Cong., 1st Sess., Vol. XCIII, Pt. 1 (February 10, 1947), p. 912.

7. Executive Order 9832 (February 25, 1947), 12 Federal Register 1363.

8. *Ibid.* Executive Order 9832 was superseded by 10082 (October 5, 1949), 14 Federal Register 6105 as amended in 15 Federal Register 6901.

9. Statement of President Truman, February 25, 1947, upon signing Executive Order 9832, printed in U.S. *Congressional Record*, 80th Cong., 1st Sess., Vol. XCIII, Pt. 2 (February 26, 1947), p. 1412.

on, the tariff issue taken place in the United States, the international prestige of the United States and its position as a leader in international
economic affairs would undoubtedly have been seriously damaged. The
Geneva negotiations, which resulted in the GATT, were at the time a
key test of the postwar foreign economic policy of the United States.
Even if the Congressional resolution preventing the Geneva Conference
had been defeated, the demonstration of a serious split within the government would have materially weakened the United States position internationally. Widespread doubts as to the stability of United States
trade policy would have been created, and many countries would have
been encouraged to reconsider their decisions to work with the United
States toward the development of a multilateral trading system.

From 1947 to 1951, during the period when the escape clause was
administered in accordance with the new Executive Order, twenty-one
applications to increase tariffs under the escape clause were filed with
the Tariff Commission. One application was withdrawn by the applicant, sixteen applications were dismissed after preliminary investigation,[10]
a finding of no injury was made in one case (spring clothespins), and
action was recommended to the President in three. President Truman
increased the tariff in two of these cases (women's fur felt hats and hat
bodies, hatters' fur) and declined to act upon the commission's recommendations in the third (watches).

THE TRADE AGREEMENTS EXTENSION ACT OF 1951

A clear demonstration of the growing strength of protectionist sentiment and the importance attached to the escape clause by opponents
of the trade-agreements program was provided during Congressional
consideration in 1951 of legislation to renew the trade-agreements authority. Worried by the GATT negotiations at Geneva in 1947, at Annecy in 1949, and at Torquay in 1951, protectionist groups urged that
the trade-agreements authority be severely restricted or preferably terminated. They received support from many members of Congess in
an atmosphere in which the Congress as a whole was becoming increasingly disposed to limit the powers of the Executive branch, especially in
the field of foreign affairs. At this time, also, there was little organized
active support for the trade-agreements program, largely because the
general public, especially those forces in public opinion supporting

10. The U.S. Tariff Commission's publication, *Investigations Under the Escape Clause
of Trade Agreements,* 14th edition, April, 1961, states that fourteen investigations were
dismissed after preliminary inquiry. The reason for this is that in two investigations more
than one application was received.

international co-operation, was fully preoccupied with the Marshall Plan, Point 4, and other means of international economic co-operation.

Protectionist groups concentrated their efforts upon revision of the escape-clause procedures. They criticized the administration of the escape clause under the Executive Order. Thousands of rates had been reduced in trade agreements, they argued, and yet tariffs had been increased to provide relief for a domestic industry in only one case (women's fur felt hats and hat bodies). Even if a complaint resulted in escape action, domestic producers had to wait for a long investigation before getting a decision. The Congress, they maintained, had already shown its lack of confidence in escape-clause procedures by legislating import quotas on cheese and other dairy products contrary to United States commitments under GATT.[11] All this was attributed to the "lack of any standards established by the Congress for the President's guidance in determining when relief should be granted."[12] The protectionist groups demanded precise rules to replace the "looseness and ambiguity" of escape-clause language so that domestic producers could more readily obtain relief.[13] Their arguments reflected the notion repeatedly expressed by the high-tariff proponents, that there is some objective "formula" that can be used to test the extent to which a tariff should be modified.[14]

The 1951 attack on the administration of the escape clause was coupled with pressure for the re-enactment of the peril-point provision of 1948.[15] This provision required the Tariff Commission to determine in advance of a negotiation a precise tariff rate that could be safely agreed to without threat of injury. Peril-point procedures were first provided for in the trade-agreements legislation of 1948 but had been repealed in 1949. In 1951 they again became a part of the law.

The peril-point provision has required the President to furnish to the Tariff Commission a list of all products on which the United States was considering negotiating concessions. The commission was required to hold hearings and to report to the President within a stipulated time the limit to which concessions could be made on each product without causing or threatening serious injury to a domestic industry. The com-

11. Chap. IV, pp. 210-16.

12. U.S. Congress, House Committee on Ways and Means, *Report* to accompany H.R. 1612, 82nd Cong., 1st Sess., Rep. No. 14, January 29, 1951, p. 23.

13. *Ibid.* See also *The New York Times,* January 31, 1951.

14. As, for example, the cost-equalization formula provided for in Section 336 of the Tariff Act of 1930. See Chap. I, pp. 14-24.

15. Those who led the fight for peril points were essentially those who opposed the trade-agreements program. See the statement by Representative Doughton (D., N.C.) in U.S. *Congressional Record,* 82nd Cong., 1st Sess., Vol. XCVII, Pt. 1 (February 7, 1951), p. 1046.

mission was also required to report any increased protection deemed necessary to avoid serious injury. If a concession below the peril point certified by the commission was nevertheless agreed to, the law required the President to report his action and the reason for it to the House Ways and Means Committee and the Senate Finance Committee. The commission then had to send to the two committees a copy of the portions of its report to the President relating to the products on which the peril points had not been complied with.[16] The intended effect was to put the President in a defensive position if peril-point determinations of the commission were disregarded.

Before the adoption of the peril-point amendment a basic concept governing the administration of the Trade Agreements Act was that on all questions presented there should be a balanced judgment taking all aspects into account. This balanced approach was sought through interagency collaboration in the trade-agreements organization so that the various government agencies, each with its special competence and responsibility in relation to a particular aspect of the national interest, should have a voice in the formulation of recommendations for duty changes.[17] The peril-point amendment upset this balanced approach by making the Tariff Commission the guardian of protected interests and giving it a dominant voice in the tariff-adjusting process. The minority members of the House Ways and Means Committee when the 1948 bill was reported pointed out that

. . . the Tariff Commission . . . would be required to consider only the interests of domestic producers, without regard for, and representation of, the broad interests of American industry, labor, farmers, and consumers, and American financial and foreign policy.

*   *   *   *   *   *   *   *   *   *   *   *   *   *

Of even more serious nature is the fact that other governmental agencies with responsibilities with regard to the effect of tariffs on domestic industry and national security are subordinated to the Tariff Commission. The Tariff Commission's judgment should not prevail over that of the Department of Agriculture in the field of agriculture. The Tariff Commission is not qualified to make determinations regarding the national defense.[18]

16. In one respect, the provisions of the 1951 law were an improvement over 1948. The 1948 legislation had required publication of the entire peril-point report covering all products included in the agreement involved. In order to protect the future bargaining position of the United States, this provision was changed in the 1951 law to require publication of only those portions of the peril-point report that related to the product in question.

17. See Chap. II, pp. 99-103.

18. U.S. Congress, House Committee on Ways and Means, *Report* to accompany H.R. 6556, 80th Cong., 2nd Sess., Rep. No. 2009, May 24, 1948, pp. 5 and 10.

Using the same arguments as in 1948, peril-point advocates in 1951 insisted that under a peril-point procedure "proper" rates would be set by the Tariff Commission on an "economic basis."[19] Since the Administration had admitted that it never consciously granted a tariff concession the probable effect of which would be to injure seriously a domestic industry, it seemed only logical, according to opponents of the program, to insert peril-point requirements in the legislation. They argued that peril-point procedures would double-check the escape clause and develop more confidence in trade agreements since the peril-point procedure applied *before* an agreement was concluded. Furthermore, negotiators would not be bound by the peril-point findings, the President having the authority to disregard them as long as his action and the reasons for it were made public.

Those opposing peril-point provisions tried to point out the subtle effect of a Tariff Commission finding upon the attitude of administrators of the program, argued that the peril-point procedure was unnecessary, and attacked the theory that tariffs could be scientifically determined upon application of a special formula by the Tariff Commission.[20] Arguments against the peril-point requirements were presented most forcefully during the consideration of the trade-agreements legislation in 1948 and 1949. In testifying before the Senate Finance Committee in 1949, the chairman of the Tariff Commission, Oscar B. Ryder, said: "Frequently it has been found that the ability to conclude an agreement will depend upon the difference between, say, a 30-percent and a 35-percent duty on some given product. I do not believe anyone can determine in advance with any degree of assurance the differences in the effects of a duty of 30 and 35 percent. It cannot be done that finely."[21]

There is no precise "peril point" that can be established in advance of a tariff reduction, Administration spokesmen argued. Therefore, the extent of reduction of a particular rate must be determined by weighing the degree of protection given to the industry involved with other considerations, such as the benefits to be gained from the concessions received and general foreign policy considerations. These considerations must be weighed against the risk of possible injury to domestic industry, the policy always being to stop short of the point where probable injury to the domestic industry would be caused. "Calculated risks" might be necessary but should the negotiators err and serious injury result, the

19. *Ibid.*, p. 2.

20. See, for example, U.S. Congress, House *Report* to accompany H.R. 6556, pp. 8 and 9.

21. U.S. Congress, Senate Committee on Finance, *Hearings* on H.R. 1211, 81st Cong., 1st Sess., 1949, Pt. 1, p. 20.

remedy lay in the escape clause. In a statement to the Senate Finance Committee in 1948, Undersecretary of State Clayton said:

. . . There is no living body in the world that can determine in advance whether a certain action in the reduction of a tariff will or will not injure an American producer. There is nobody who can tell that. . . . You may have opinions about it, but that is all you have got. My point simply is this, that in order to accomplish certain purposes which I have named, you may have to take some calculated risk. You will not know until you determine by actual practice whether an American industry will be injured or not.[22]

Under the trade-agreements program, rates have been reduced to the levels that administrators of the program have considered *not likely* to cause serious injury. The requirement of a public certification that a particular rate reduction *will not* produce serious injury, it was pointed out, was a very different thing. The requirement of virtual certainty must inevitably result in a "peril point" higher than the rate of duty probably necessary to prevent serious injury.

Neither the peril-point nor the escape-clause provisions were included in the bill for renewal of the trade-agreements legislation submitted to Congress by the Administration in 1951. President Truman asked the Congress to renew the trade-agreements authority in the form in which it had been approved in 1949. Although the bill was reported out of the House Ways and Means Committee in this form, the minority on the committee recommended a series of changes. When the legislation was discussed on the floor of the House, the peril-point and escape-clause provisions urged by the minority of the Ways and Means Committee were added. The peril-point amendment was adopted by a vote of 225 to 168. The escape-clause amendment, offered by Representative Bailey (D., W.Va.), was accepted by a standing vote of 191 to 89.[23]

The escape-clause provisions of the House bill were very restrictive. The bill provided for a Tariff Commission determination of serious injury not only to a "domestic industry" but also to a "segment of such industry." It provided further that "in arriving at a determination in the foregoing procedure, the Tariff Commission shall deem a downward trend of production, employment and wages in the domestic industry concerned, or a decline in sales and a higher or growing inventory at-

22. U.S. Congress, Senate Committee on Finance, *Hearings* on H.R. 6566, 80th Cong., 2nd Sess., 1948, p. 30.

23. Representative Curtis (R., Mo.) had earlier offered an escape-clause amendment. When Representative Bailey, anxious to protect the coal industry of his state from imported petroleum, offered a substitute, it was accepted and the Curtis amendment was withdrawn. The escape-clause vote was reported by *The New York Times,* February 8, 1951, but was not recorded.

tributable in part to import competition, to be evidence of serious injury or a threat thereof."[24] Under these provisions increased tariffs would be virtually automatic with every slight decline in domestic economic activity.

The House action showed clearly the seriousness of the developing divergence of views between the Administration and the Congress and the inability of the Administration to provide legislative leadership. *The New York Times* commented that "the distorted form in which this bill has passed the House indicates the degree to which the Administration has lost effective influence on Capitol Hill."[25]

In view of this situation, the Administration was forced to re-examine its position. Outright opposition to the amendments would probably have been useless in the face of the strong Congressional sentiment in favor of the changes and the close political division in the Senate.[26] There was also the danger that the amendments might pass the Senate in the same form as they had passed the House. The Administration therefore decided to concentrate upon the revision of some of the most objectionable features of the amendments rather than upon the defeat of the amendments themselves. Secretary of State Acheson told the Senate Finance Committee:

These amendments [peril point and escape clause] are unnecessary. . . . They are undesirable and the second [escape clause] is unworkable in its present form. . . .

There appears, however, to be a considerable feeling that some form of peril-point procedure and some form of escape-clause procedure should be written into the act, rather than be dealt with by Executive action. If that is the desire of the Congress, despite the views which have been expressed by the administration and by many witnesses appearing in support of the program, I believe that amendments could be worked out on these two subjects which would permit the program to continue in a workable form.[27]

Most of the changes desired by the Administration were incorporated in the Senate bill and became a part of the final legislation.[28] The law, as enacted, provided that no reduction in or binding of a tariff rate shall remain in effect if "any product, upon which a concession has been

24. U.S. Congress, Senate *Hearings* on H.R. 1612, Pt. 1, p. 3.

25. *The New York Times,* editorial, February 9, 1951.

26. In the Senate there were 49 Democrats to 47 Republicans; in the House the Democrats had 234 seats, the Republicans 199.

27. U.S. Congress, Senate *Hearings* on H.R. 1612, Pt. 1, p. 8.

28. See U.S. Congress, Senate Committee on Finance, *Report* to accompany H.R. 1612, 82nd Cong., 1st Sess., Rep. No. 299, April 27, 1951, pp. 5-6.

granted under a trade agreement is, as a result, in whole or in part, of the duty or other customs treatment reflecting such concession, being imported into the United States in such increased quantities, either actual or relative, as to cause or threaten serious injury to the domestic industry producing like or directly competitive products." The Tariff Commission was required to "promptly make an investigation and make a report thereon" within one year. Investigations could be instituted by the commission upon its own motion and had to be instituted upon the request of the President, upon resolution of either House of the Congress or of the Finance or Ways and Means Committees, or upon the application of any interested party. The commission was required to hold public hearings if it found evidence of injury[29] and to submit its report with recommendations for action to the President. If the President did not act upon the recommendation of the commission, the legislation required him to report to the two committees of the Congress the reasons for his decision not to accept the recommendations of the commission.

Instead of defining injury as the House bill had attempted to do, the law specified certain factors, which, along with others, had to be taken into account in making a determination of serious injury. It provided that the Tariff Commission "without excluding other factors, shall take into consideration a downward trend of production, employment, prices, profits, or wages in the domestic industry concerned, or a decline in sales, an increase in imports, either actual or relative to domestic production, a higher or growing inventory, or a decline in the proportion of the domestic market supplied by domestic producers."

In addition, the President was directed to include an escape clause in existing trade agreements when practicable and to report progress in this respect to the Congress.[30]

A special escape-clause provision on perishable agricultural products was also included. This provision developed from an amendment, proposed by Senator Holland (D., Fla.), that provided for import quotas to keep the price of fruits and vegetables at or above parity.[31] Senator Holland's proposal was not related to the escape clause since it had nothing to do with injury in the usual sense. But in an effort to avoid legislative import quotas on perishables, which would have forced the

29. Although the law left this to the discretion of the commission, a hearing was usually held in each case.

30. The President reported to the Congress periodically under this provision. The reports disclosed steps that were taken to incorporate escape clauses in all trade agreements with the exception of those with El Salvador, Guatemala, and Honduras.

31. See U.S. Congress, Senate *Hearings* on H.R. 1612, Pt. 1, pp. 443-46 and 472-93.

United States into a violation of its commitments under the GATT,[32] the Administration offered a compromise. It authorized the President to take immediate action on perishable commodities under the escape clause or under Section 22 of the Agricultural Adjustment Act of 1933[33] prior to a report of the Tariff Commission if he believed that the emergency required such action. In any case the report of the Tariff Commission and the decision of the President had to be made within twenty-five days after the case had been first submitted to the commission.

The wording of the escape-clause provisions of the 1951 law differed in certain respects from that of the Executive Order of 1947 and of the GATT. Since the differences led to some controversy or doubt as to whether the 1951 law required the United States to apply a policy distinct from that which it had agreed to in Article XIX of the GATT, and which was reflected in the Executive Order of 1947, these are examined briefly:

1. The Executive Order of 1947, and GATT, said nothing about the factors that should be considered in making a determination of serious injury. The selection of factors was left entirely to the Executive. The 1951 Act, in contrast, listed certain factors that should be looked at (a "downward trend in domestic production," etc.), but it did not make them determinative on the Tariff Commission, or the President, as to the finding that should be made. Obviously, there was no necessary inconsistency of policy here between domestic law and international obligation. The escape-clause language of GATT did not attempt to go beyond saying that "serious injury" to a domestic industry could be the occasion for a member nation to withdraw or change the trade-agreement concession that caused it. It was left to each member to apply the clause in good faith, adopting such domestic criteria and procedures as it saw fit. Therefore, as long as the United States was not required by law to apply a test of "serious injury" from trade concessions that offended common sense, the GATT did not stand in the way. Moreover, since the elements listed in the 1951 Act were all factors that any intelligent investigation would encompass, and since these factors were not made exclusive or mandatory in the sense that they would compel indefensible escape-clause actions in concrete cases, there can be no real question as to the compatibility between GATT and the 1951 Act on this score.

2. The Executive Order, and GATT, said that in order to apply

32. The GATT permits import quotas on imports when they are commensurate with domestic restrictions on home production or marketing. The Holland amendment would have called for import restrictions without the necessity of any domestic restrictions.

33. Section 22 of The Agricultural Adjustment Act provides for import fees or quotas in cases where imports interfere with domestic farm programs. See Chap. IV.

the escape clause the increased imports causing the serious injury must
be the result not only of the concession but also of "unforeseen developments"; and this qualifying phrase "unforeseen developments" was
omitted from the 1951 Act. Seemingly the change meant (1) that
GATT precluded escape-clause action if the increased imports were
the result of "foreseen developments," whereas (2) the policy of the
1951 Act required escape action in such cases. Although abstract, the
point is not academic. In 1950 the United States invoked the GATT
escape clause to raise the tariff on women's fur felt hats and hat bodies,
which were mainly imported from Czechoslovakia. Czechoslovakia
complained about the matter to the GATT contracting parties. At that
time one of the difficulties facing the United States hat industry was the
increasing practice of going without hats. Czechoslovakia and other countries argued that this trend, as well as the increase in imports presump-
tively resulting from the tariff concession, could reasonably have been
foreseen and hence that the escape clause was not applicable. The answer
to this argument is simple: under United States trade-agreements procedures, whatever may be the practices of other countries, trade-agreements concessions are not made if future developments such as to cause
injury to flow from the concession are in fact foreseen. Therefore, the
reference to "unforeseen developments" in GATT was meaningless as
far as United States obligations were concerned, and omission of the
phrase from the 1951 Act raised no problem of inconsistency.[34]

3. The Executive Order, and GATT, required that imports must
be entering in "increased quantities" before the escape clause could
apply. The escape-clause language of the Act of 1951 speaks of "increased quantities, either actual or relative." In other words, the Act of
1951 makes it clear that even though imports may have declined absolutely, the escape clause can apply if they are larger, relative to domestic
output, than they were before—say in circumstances in which total
consumption, domestic output, and imports have all declined but imports
have fallen less than domestic output. Again there is no real discrepancy
between the two, for the reason that the GATT wording had from the
beginning of GATT been interpreted by common consent of the contracting parties to embrace both absolute and relative increases.

4. Still another point has been raised by the phraseology of the escape

34. One may wonder why, if the phrase is meaningless, it was inserted in the escape
clause in the first place. The best explanation seems to be that the administrators of the
trade-agreements program who were responsible for originating the clause in 1942 were
fearful that omission of the phrase might lead Congress to believe that injury from tariff
concessions was anticipated. In short, the words were a form of semantic window dressing.

clause in the Act of 1951, which provided that increased imports must be the result of "the duty or other customs treatment reflecting . . . [the] concession." Under the GATT phraseology one cause for the increased imports must be "the effect of the . . . tariff concessions" or of other obligations. The wording of the 1951 Act, which was the handiwork of Senator Millikin, may have been intended by him to create a difference of substance, but it did not in reality do so. The change was apparently occasioned by a widespread misunderstanding as to what constitutes a "concession" in a trade agreement. A "concession" was considered by many to be the amount by which a duty rate was reduced. Senator Millikin was probably concerned with the possibility that escape-clause relief would not be available in a case where the duty was merely bound against increase in a trade agreement and where hence the "concession" in such a case might not be regarded as a possible cause of the increased imports. However, a tariff "concession" is in reality a legal undertaking by a government not to impose a higher duty on an article than that specified in a trade agreement. That duty may be a reduction from a previously higher duty or merely a continuation of a previous duty.

For these various reasons the President took the position that the escape clause in the GATT, which was modeled on the Executive Order of 1947, was "substantially equivalent" to the provisions of the Act of 1951, despite the differences in wording.[35] His position is supported on the record by the criteria that had been developed earlier by the Tariff Commission for the conduct of investigations under the Executive Order.[36] There is much also in the history of the GATT escape-clause provision that bears out the interpretations contended for by the Administration.[37]

Apart from these changes of wording in the escape clause, there were several procedural provisions included in the Act of 1951. One that proved important was the requirement that the Tariff Commission act on all applications submitted to it by domestic industries. Although the law allowed the commission to decide when a public hearing was necessary, the commission had to conduct a formal investigation and issue a

35. U.S. Congress, House *Report on Trade-Agreement Escape-Clauses,* Message from the President of the United States, 82nd Cong., 2nd Sess., Doc. No. 328, January, 1952, p. 4.

36. See U.S. Tariff Commission, *Procedure and Criteria With Respect to the Administradition of the "Escape Clause" in Trade Agreements,* February, 1948 (Revised February, 1950).

37. See GATT, *Analytical Index of the General Agreement* (Geneva: February, 1953), pp. 61-63. See also testimony of Oscar B. Ryder, chairman of the Tariff Commission, U.S. Congress, Senate *Hearings* on H.R. 1612, Pt. 2, pp. 1390-94.

report in every case. It could no longer dismiss applications which it judged, after preliminary investigation, to be without prima facie merit.[38]

Another provision of the 1951 Act required that escape action once taken was to remain in effect only "for the time necessary to prevent or remedy" the injury. This provision was consistent with the GATT escape-clause language, although a comparable provision did not appear in the Executive Order of 1947. In order to implement this provision, the President issued a special Executive Order directing the Tariff Commission to make periodic reports to him concerning developments with regard to the products on which escape action had been taken.[39]

THE TRADE AGREEMENTS EXTENSION ACT OF 1955

The 1953 and 1954 trade-agreements legislation did not make significant changes in the escape clause.[40] When the Trade Agreements Act came up for renewal in 1955, however, protectionist groups, encouraged by the increasing popularity of their arguments with many members of Congress, sought changes designed to make escape action easier. Now, moreover, they could count upon support from a group of Southern Democrats who were gradually emerging as a protectionist bloc in the Democratic party as well as from traditionally high-tariff elements within the Republican party. Protectionist arguments were becoming more and more popular with many domestic producers who were beginning to feel the effect of increased competition from imports as postwar economic recovery abroad enabled foreign countries to increase their exports to the United States. The atmosphere in which the 1955 bill was considered, therefore, was encouraging to proponents of restrictive amendments, and it seemed clear from the start that a concerted effort by the Administra-

38. As indicated earlier, under the Executive Order of 1947 the Tariff Commission dismissed sixteen of the twenty-one applications submitted to it as not being of sufficient merit to warrant a full investigation.

39. Executive Order 10401, 17 Federal Register 9125. The order provided for the Tariff Commission to institute a formal investigation, whenever it believed conditions warranted, to determine whether and to what extent the escape-clause action needed to be continued to prevent or remedy serious injury. The commission was directed to report to the President in each case not more than two years after the original action and thereafter at intervals of one year.

40. The 1953 Trade Agreements Extension Act, however, contained several procedural changes. The Tariff Commission was required to complete its reports in nine months rather than the one year previously allowed it. Cases in which the commission was evenly split, instead of being dismissed, were to be sent to the President. The President could adopt the views of either side as the decision of the commission. This meant in several cases that domestic producers had an opportunity to be considered for escape action by the President even though their case could not command the support of a majority of the commission.

tion and supporting groups would be required to obtain passage of the bill without amendment.

When the 1955 bill was considered in committee, Administration spokesmen testified in favor of the escape-clause and peril-point provisions of the old law. Secretary of State John Foster Dulles told the House Ways and Means Committee that the two provisions were necessary not only to protect individual concerns but also to protect the broader interests of the country as a whole. The escape-clause and peril-point provisions were important, he said, because "we have to maintain here a certain, what we call mobilization base, and we need to have in this country a certain minimum of productive capacity and a certain minimum of skills which are required on an emergency basis as against the possibility that the hazards of war, loss of allies, and the like, might make us more dependent upon ourselves and less able to depend upon others."[41] The escape clause, he continued, provides useful protection to United States producers just by being in the law. Foreign businessmen, knowing that their success in selling to the United States market might bring escape action, tend to keep their exports to the United States within "reasonable bounds."[42]

Although the bill included both escape-clause and peril-point provisions and was presented by the Administration as a major part of its legislative program, attempts in the House to add restrictive amendments were almost successful. Passage of the bill in the House without amendment was due largely to strong appeals by Speaker Sam Rayburn and other members of the House Democratic leadership.[43]

Encouraged by their near success in the House, protectionist groups intensified their efforts to obtain restrictive amendments in the Senate Finance Committee. President Eisenhower, recognizing the seriousness of the situation, spoke out against "crippling amendments" in urging passage of the trade bill.[44] A few days later, however, the Senate Finance Committee reported an amended bill to the Senate.[45] Among the changes were some relating to the escape-clause provision which were intended to facilitate escape-clause action (1) to protect small segments of an industry even if the industry as a whole were not injured, (2) to restrict imports of manufactured goods in order to assist domestic producers of

41. U.S. Congress, House Committee on Ways and Means, *Hearings* on H.R. 1, 84th Cong., 1st Sess., 1955, Pt. 1, p. 64.
42. *Ibid.*, p. 68.
43. See *The New York Times*, April 24, 1955.
44. *Ibid.*, April 26, 1955.
45. *Ibid.*, April 27, and 30, 1955.

the raw-material components, and (3) to restrict imports even when imports were not the primary cause of the injury to the domestic industry.[46]

The amended bill was passed by the Senate and sent to conference. Supporters of the trade-agreements program were anxious to have the amendments removed in conference, and the House Democratic members of the Conference Committee announced their intention to work toward their elimination. Before any action could be taken, however, the Administration endorsed the bill in almost the form approved by the Finance Committee.[47] With this Presidential backing all hope for retaining the House version in conference was lost. The raw-material amendment, to which the Administration had objected, was deleted, but apart from this one major omission and a few clarifying changes the Conference Committee accepted the Senate version.

The Act of 1955, as finally passed, substantively amended the escape clause in two important respects:

1. A new paragraph was added stating that "increased imports, either actual or relative, shall be considered as the cause or threat of serious injury to the domestic industry producing like or directly competitive products when the Commission finds that such increased imports have contributed substantially towards causing or threatening serious injury to such industry." Under this new provision the Tariff Commission presumably could no longer avoid a finding of injury to domestic industry from increased imports in cases in which the chief cause of injury lay elsewhere so long as the larger imports could be shown to be contributing "substantially" to the difficulty. This was an important change, since the major part of the economic difficulties of many import-competing industries stems from domestic causes, especially from an economic environment of increasing productivity in more dynamic industries.[48]

2. The other change in the escape clause was in the definition of the domestic industry. The Trade Agreements Extension Act of 1955 defined the domestic industry as follows:

. . . that portion or subdivision of the producing organizations manufacturing, assembling, processing, extracting, growing, or otherwise producing like or directly competitive products or articles in commercial quantities. In

46. See U.S. Congress, Senate Committee on Finance, *Report* to accompany H.R. 1, 84th Cong., 1st Sess., Rep. No. 232, April 28, 1955.

47. Letter from Gerald D. Morgan, special counsel to the President, to the chairman of the House Ways and Means Committee and the Senate Finance Committee, published in *The New York Times,* May 17, 1955. The letter stated only one objection to the Senate version of the bill—the amendment relating to raw materials, which had been introduced by Senator Morse.

48. See Don D. Humphrey, *American Imports* (New York: The Twentieth Century Fund, 1955), pp. 364-65.

applying the preceding sentence, the Commission shall (so far as practicable) distinguish or separate the operations of the producing organizations involving the like or directly competitive products or articles referred to in such sentence from the operations of such organizations involving other products or articles.

In effect, this required the Tariff Commission to confine its investigation to that portion of the operations of domestic producers which made the like or directly competitive article. The commission was required to disregard market conditions, profits, labor costs, and other factors involving other products made by the same company. Thus if a company producing both circular and square post-hole diggers was in a generally prosperous condition, was making excellent profits on the 90 per cent of its output that consisted of circular diggers but was losing money on the 10 per cent accounted for by square diggers, then imports of square diggers could be restricted under the escape clause.[49]

Apart from the changes that the 1955 Act introduced in the escape clause itself, the Act added a special exception for national-security reasons which is indirectly related to the escape clause. The 1954 legislation had added a new provision prohibiting any duty reduction "if the President finds that such reduction would threaten domestic production needed for projected national defense requirements." In the Act of 1955 this provision was continued. But, in addition, the 1955 Act provided that in cases involving national security the Director of the Office of Defense Mobilization, whenever he had reason to believe that an article was "being imported into the United States in such quantities as to threaten to impair the national security," he would so advise the President. The President, if he agreed that there was reason for such belief, would cause an immediate investigation to determine the facts. If, on the basis of such an investigation, the President found the article was being imported in such quantities as to impair the national security, he would take such action as was "necessary to adjust the imports of such article to a level that will not threaten to impair the national security."

The inclusion of the national-security provision in the law meant that domestic industries affected by import competition had two courses of

49. Other changes in escape-clause procedure brought about by the 1955 Act include elimination of the requirement for semi-annual reports from the President to the Congress on the progress achieved in including the escape clause in trade agreements and addition of a requirement that the Tariff Commission immediately make public its findings and recommendations to the President and publish summaries of its report in the Federal Register. Previously, the Tariff Commission had not made its findings and recommendations public until sixty days after it had made its report to the President, or sooner if the President had acted on the commission's recommendations. The purpose of this change was to enable domestic producers to make their views known to the President while he had an escape action before him for consideration.

action open to them. They could apply to the Tariff Commission for relief under the escape clause and could also petition the Office of Defense Mobilization for action under the national-security exception.

The amendments included in the 1955 Act originated for the most part with opponents of the trade-agreements program and were not desired by the Administration. The promptness, however, with which the Administration accepted the amendments in the Senate after standing firm in the House, is hard to explain unless the Administration had become convinced either that the Senate would not recede, leading to possible deadlock, or that a strong fight would seriously split the Administration and the Republican Congressional leadership.

THE TRADE AGREEMENTS EXTENSION ACT OF 1958

The Trade Agreements Extension Act of 1958 substantively amended the escape-clause legislation in two ways. It provided for the imposition of higher duties and allowed Congress to override decisions of the President.

Duty increases up to 50 per cent above the rates in effect on July 1, 1934, were permitted. Specific duties could be converted to their 1934 ad valorem equivalent before such increases were imposed. Products on the free list could have a duty of up to 50 per cent ad valorem imposed upon them. Before these amendments, duty increases had been limited to 50 per cent above the rates existing on January 1, 1945, and no product could have been transferred from the free to the dutiable list. The effect of these amendments was to make possible much higher duties in escape-clause actions. Because tariff rates in 1945 were generally lower than in 1934, the change to a 1934 base to which increases could be applied enabled the imposition of higher duties than formerly. Because prices in 1934 were generally much lower, the ad valorem equivalent of specific rates of duty were much higher in 1934 than in recent years. Therefore, the conversion of specific duties to their 1934 ad valorem equivalents before application of duty increases enabled very much higher duties to be imposed. Duty-free articles, exempt from escape-clause action until this amendment, could now have duties up to 50 per cent ad valorem imposed on them.

Whenever the President disapproved a recommendation of the Tariff Commission for escape-clause action, within sixty days he could be overruled by the Congress by a concurrent resolution receiving a two-thirds vote of each House. Such a resolution was to be given privileged status. Before this amendment, the President made the final decision in escape-clause cases.

The 1958 Act also amended the national-security clause by extending its scope.[50] The Act listed various criteria that the director of the renamed Office of Defense and Civilian Mobilization and the President should consider in determining whether imports were threatening to impair the national security. It then added this provision:

. . . In the administration of this section, the Director and the President shall further recognize the close relation of the economic welfare of the Nation to our national security, and shall take into consideration the impact of foreign competition on the economic welfare of individual domestic industries; and any substantial unemployment, decrease in revenues of government, loss of skills or investment, or other serious effects resulting from the displacement of any domestic products by excessive imports shall be considered, without excluding other factors, in determining whether such weakening of our internal economy may impair the national security.

In other words, *any* domestic industry, whether related to national security or not, could obtain protection from foreign competition if it were determined that such competition were weakening the internal economy and thereby impairing national security.[51]

2. ADMINISTRATION OF THE ESCAPE-CLAUSE AND PERIL-POINT PROVISIONS

PERIL POINTS

The first trade agreement to which the peril-point procedure was fully applied was one with Venezuela, which was negotiated in accordance with the peril-point provision of the Trade Agreements Extension Act of 1951.[52] The key product in the negotiations, as far as imports into

50. The 1958 Act also simplified procedures under the national-security clause by eliminating the necessity for the director of the Office of Defense and Civilian Mobilization (ODCM) first to advise the President that he believed that imports were threatening to impair the national security before an investigation was made and by designating ODCM as the investigating agency.

51. In practice, however, the national-security clause has had very limited use. For a discussion of this provision and its use, see Willard L. Thorp, "Trade Barriers and National Security," *The American Economic Review*, L (May, 1960), pp. 433-42.

52. The initial preparations for the Annecy negotiations of 1948-1949 were governed by the peril-point provisions of the 1948 Act, but the Trade Agreements Extension Act of 1949 repealed them and, consequently, the President was not required to follow the procedures in concluding the agreements reached at Annecy. The chairman of the Tariff Commission, Oscar B. Ryder, told the Senate Finance Committee in 1949 that the Tariff Commissioners had reached unanimous agreements as to the peril points on 90 per cent of the articles involved in the Annecy negotiations. The 10 per cent on which they disagreed, however, included the most important items in the negotiations and covered much larger total imports than did the other 90 per cent. Mr. Ryder divided the commodities on which unanimous agreement was reached into six groups: (1) items not produced in the United States; (2) items imported in negligible quantities; (3) items exported in greater quantities than they are imported; (4) items not directly competitive with those produced in the United States; (5) items on which information shows that a lowering of duties would not appreciably increase imports; and (6) items on the free list. U.S. Congress, Senate *Hearings* on H.R. 1211, pp. 803-4.

the United States were concerned, was petroleum. At the time the United States tariff on petroleum was 10½ cents per barrel on a yearly quantity of imports equal to 5 per cent of the amount of crude petroleum processed in United States refineries during the preceding year, any imports above this level being dutiable at 21 cents per barrel.[53]   In considering the peril point on petroleum the members of the Tariff Commission split three to three, one group finding that the peril point was the existing tariff quota and the other finding that extension of the 10½ cents per barrel rate to all imports, without quantitative limitation, would not cause or threaten serious injury to the domestic petroleum industry.   Under the trade-agreements authority the President could have agreed to a rate as low as 5½ cents per barrel, without limitation.

The President accepted neither of the Tariff Commission's findings. Instead, he introduced an entirely different rate structure, which could be said to have equally satisfied the criterion of no serious injury.   In the Venezuelan agreement he agreed to a rate of 5¼ cents per barrel on imports testing less than twenty-five degrees API (American Petroleum Institute rating) and 10½ cents per barrel on imports of twenty-five degrees API or higher.   In his peril-point report to the Congress he cited the benefits to be obtained from the new agreement and pointed out (1) that most of the domestic production and most of the United States imports are of twenty-five degrees API or higher, and (2) that the rate of 5¼ cents would apply mainly to residual fuel oil used in power plants and manufacturing industries.   He also emphasized that the majority of representatives of private business at the hearings before the Tariff Commission and the Committee on Reciprocity Information had urged that the rate of 5¼ cents for all imports be established.[54]

The peril-point procedures were also followed in preparing for tariff negotiations at Geneva in 1955 and 1956.   No reductions were

53. The statutory duty on petroleum, established in 1932 in the form of an "import tax," was 21 cents per barrel.   The original trade agreement with Venezuela, concluded in 1939, provided for the tariff quota of 10½ cents per barrel, described above.   In the trade agreement with Mexico of 1942 the 10½ cent rate was applied to all imports, without tariff quota, but when the Mexican agreement was terminated in 1950 the rate structure reverted to the tariff quota arrangement in the original Venezuelan agreement.   At the time of the negotiations with Venezuela that involved the peril-point problem the government of Venezuela was extremely anxious to obtain not only the quota-free tariff treatment that had prevailed from 1942 to 1950 by reason of the Mexican agreement but a more favorable arrangement that would enable future expansion of the Venezuelan oil industry.

54. Letter from the President to the Congress, August 29, 1952, released to the press on the same day, and U.S. Dept. of State, Press Release No. 681, August 29, 1952.   Because the Tariff Commission had divided evenly in its peril-point report on petroleum, there was some doubt that it had made a legal finding and that the President was required legally to make a report to the Congress.

agreed to in these negotiations, which went below the peril points established by the Tariff Commission. However, the peril-point report of the commission on the 1956 negotiations recommended increases in duties for certain tungsten alloys and for violins and violas. These increases were not negotiated at Geneva, the President taking the position that the advantages of obtaining the increases were outweighed by the disadvantages.[55]

The restrictive effect of peril-point determinations on United States negotiating ability was made dramatically clear in the 1960-1962 Geneva negotiations with the European Economic Community (EEC) and other GATT countries. Until these negotiations the effect of peril points had not been extensive because the United States had not engaged in really significant multilateral tariff negotiations since 1951.[56]

The 1960-1962 Geneva tariff negotiations almost failed because of the inability of the United States to offer concessions of equal value to the Europeans. The EEC offer to reduce its common external tariff on industrial goods by 20 per cent directly affected United States trade of $846 million (based on 1958 trade) and was responsive to about 60 per cent of United States requests to the EEC for tariff concessions. In contrast, the United States offered duty reductions requested by the EEC on $90 million of trade (about 20 per cent of EEC requests); duty reductions not requested by the EEC on $396 million of trade; and duty bindings at existing levels on $41 million of trade.

Before the negotiations, the EEC had requested concessions from the United States on products having a trade value in 1958 of $451 million. Peril-point determinations by the Tariff Commission eliminated $220 million of these products from the negotiating list. This was after $128 million of these products had already been eliminated in the interagency screening process that preceded peril pointing by the commission. Thus, trade coverage of the EEC request list was reduced to $103 million or by more than three-fourths. In peril-point determinations the commission also eliminated products having a trade value of $113 million that were not on the EEC request list but that had been submitted in order to strengthen the United States bargaining position.

The response of the EEC to the United States offer was to withdraw and to reconsider its 20 per cent proposal. At stake, however, was the

55. The President explained that increasing the tariff on tungsten alloys would have created problems in classification and that his failure to negotiate an increase for the items cited by the commission did not constitute a bar to action under the escape clause. See U.S. Dept. of State, Press Release No. 297, June 6, 1956, p. 6.

56. The following discussion is taken from William B. Kelly, Jr., Chap. 11, in Don D. Humphrey, *The United States and the Common Market,* a background study (New York: Frederick A. Praeger, 1962).

much broader issue of whether the EEC would follow a protectionist or an outward-looking foreign trade policy. After months of negotiation, the deadlock was broken only when the United States offered new concessions at rates below peril-point findings on trade valued at $76 million (in 1958).[57] The EEC agreed to complete the negotiations on this basis even though it was recognized that the United States offer was still not equivalent to that of the EEC.

ESCAPE CLAUSE

From 1947 to July 1, 1962, 134 escape-clause investigations were instituted by the Tariff Commission. Forty-eight investigations related to only 20 products, because these products have been the subject of more than one investigation.[58] In all, therefore, the 134 investigations covered 106 products.

The Tariff Commission has completed 112 investigations.[59] In 71 of them, no injury was found by the commission and no recommendation for escape-clause action was made to the President.[60] A majority of the commission found injury in 33 cases, the President accepting the finding in 15 cases and declining to accept it in 18. In addition, 8 cases in which the commission was evenly divided were sent to the President for action. In all 8 the President accepted as the commission's view the finding of the commissioners that recommended against escape-clause action.[61]

Each escape-clause investigation has differed from the others in significant respects. The Tariff Commission has not agreed on any standards to be applied to all cases, and there have been a number of dissenting statements issued with the reports. Only a little more than half of the decisions have been unanimous. Nevertheless, general conclusions can be reached from the reports on such matters as the nature of the applicants, the procedures used by the commission in the conduct

57. Additional concessions below peril-point findings were also made in negotiations with the United Kingdom on trade valued at $7 million (in 1958).

58. Two investigations have been made on 14 products: knitted berets, watches, fluorspar, safety pins, garlic, lead and zinc, scissors and shears, handmade blown glassware, hardwood plywood, red fescue seed, alsike clover seed, carpets and rugs, umbrella frames, and creeping red fescue seed. Four have been made on three products: bicycles, groundfish fillets, straight pins, and hatters' fur. Four have been made on two products: wood screws and spring clothespins.

59. Nine investigations were terminated without a formal finding; nine were dismissed at the applicant's request; and four were pending.

60. Under the Executive Order of 1947 the Tariff Commission dismissed 14 applications after preliminary investigation. Under the Act of 1951, as amended, the commission decided against escape action in 57 investigations.

61. For a listing of all escape-clause cases and their outcome or current status, see the appendix to this chapter, pp. 169-73.

of investigations, and the views of the commissioners on the problems involved in determining serious injury.

The following discussion relates primarily to escape-clause actions before the important legislative changes made in the escape clause in 1955 and 1958.[62] Escape-clause cases since these changes have been thoroughly discussed elsewhere.[63] Many of the characteristics of these earlier cases, however, are applicable to more recent ones.

NATURE OF THE APPLICANTS

Normally, it would be expected that complaints would have been restricted to products on which the tariff rate was low. This has not been the case with requests for escape-clause investigations, however. For some of the products involved, tariffs remained quite high even after trade-agreement reductions. Duties on products involved in escape-clause actions have ranged all the way from free to 95 per cent. The following table gives some examples:

RATES OF DUTY ON SELECTED ESCAPE-CLAUSE PRODUCTS*

Scissors, shears, and nippers	40 to 95%
Watch bracelets	65%
Women's fur felt hats and hat bodies	29 to 55%
Hand-blown glassware	15 to 50%
Glacé cherries	36%
Household china tableware	30 to 35%
Watch movements	33%
Screen-printed silk scarves	33%
Chalk whiting	27%
Spring clothespins	21%
Dried figs	16%
Hatters' fur	15%
Rosaries	15%

* The rates of duty shown are those given in escape-clause reports and reflect trade-agreement concessions. Where the rate of duty is specific, e.g., in cents per pound, the ad valorem equivalent, as given in the reports, is used. Where the report shows an ad valorem equivalent as an average for the rates applying to a group of tariff classifications, that average is used; otherwise the lowest and highest rates are noted. Where the report has stated that, for the purposes of the investigation, only one rate or average is important, only that rate is given.

62. Early escape-clause cases are also discussed by Irving B. Kravis, "The Trade Agreements Escape Clause," *The American Economic Review,* XLIV (June, 1954), 319-38; and by Humphrey, *American Imports,* Chap. 19.

63. See William B. Kelly, Jr., "The 'Expanded' Trade-Agreements Escape Clause, 1955-61," *The Journal of Political Economy,* LXX (February, 1962), 37-63. See also George Bronz, "The Tariff Commission as a Regulatory Agency," *Columbia Law Review,* LXI (March, 1961), 468-77.

Motorcycles and parts .... 10 to 15%
Bonito, canned in oil .... 15 to 22%
Tuna, canned, not in oil 13%
Bonito, canned, not in oil .... 10 to 13%
Bicycles .... 8 to 15%
Wood screws of iron and steel 13%
Groundfish fillets 12%
Garlic 11%
Alsike clover seed 10%
Unmanufactured lead and zinc .... 8 to 9%
Pregnant mares' urine and estrogens .... free to 5%

Another interesting point on the nature of the applicants for escape-clause relief has been that the number of workers involved in the industries covered in the investigations was surprisingly small. The following examples are taken from escape-clause reports issued by the Tariff Commission:

EMPLOYMENT IN SELECTED INDUSTRIES THAT APPLIED FOR ESCAPE-CLAUSE ACTION

INDUSTRY	NUMBER OF WORKERS EMPLOYED
Rosaries	225
Wood-wind instruments	900
Briar pipes	1,300
Hatters' fur	1,700
Scissors, shears, and nippers	1,826
China tableware	2,100
Hand-blown glassware	3,100
Watch bracelets	5,000
Women's fur felt hats	3,340
Wood screws	under 6,000
Watches	8,715
Lead and zinc	41,743
Acid grade fluorspar	1,087
Linen toweling	80
Violins and violas	30
Clinical thermometers	773

PROCEDURES IN ADMINISTERING THE ESCAPE CLAUSE

The commission has not placed the burden on the applicant to prove injury. Nor has the applicant been required to demonstrate that the trade-agreement concession of which he complained was the cause of injury. The applicant has presented his case, but the commission has gone beyond the presentation to gather its own information. Chairman

Ryder stated the commission's position clearly on this point in 1949 before the Senate Finance Committee: "The Commission does not require that they [the domestic industry] have to prove anything. They present their case, all the facts they can. We get all the facts we can, in addition to what they have presented, and we make the best finding we can."[64]

Although the Tariff Commission has not relied entirely on the information submitted by the applicant, it has not made any exhaustive examination of the case presented by the adversaries—the importing interests and others who would be adversely affected by escape-clause action. Indeed, the interests of the adversaries, diffused as they are among consumers, importers, and processors, probably could not be effectively presented to the commission. Nevertheless, the commission has not established any procedures to insure its receiving information from those groups that would be adversely affected by a proposed escape action. It should be noted, however, that the sole question that the legislation directed the commission to decide was that of serious injury to the domestic producers involved. The law did not provide for Tariff Commission consideration of the adverse effects of escape action on importers, consumers, exporters, or other domestic economic interests.

Although undoubtedly a well-balanced decision to raise the tariff should include a careful examination of interests other than the domestic industry, the Tariff Commission cannot be criticized for failing to consider this as long as the law provided otherwise.

PROBLEMS IN APPLYING THE ESCAPE CLAUSE

Although the Tariff Commission has gone beyond the data submitted by the applicants to obtain information on conditions in the domestic industry, the commission's reports show that it has encountered serious difficulty both in obtaining sufficient information and in interpreting it. Determining the relationship between imports, the tariff concession, and the condition of the domestic industry involves such problems as the interpretation of financial data and the choice of a base period against which to judge changing developments. Other problems are raised by the measurement of "serious" injury, the definition of the domestic industry, the importance to be attributed to changes in the shares of the market supplied by domestic producers and foreign suppliers, and the ease or difficulty with which domestic producers can shift productive facilities to other products. Yet another problem arises when the commission has to determine what the effect of a tariff increase would be on

64. U.S. Congress, Senate *Hearings* on H.R. 1612, Pt. 2, p. 1350.

the condition of the industry. On all of these matters the commission has been plagued by inadequate information, differences of interpretation or judgment, or all three.

Financial data.—In most of the investigations the Tariff Commission has been unable to obtain complete financial information on the domestic industry involved in an investigation.[65] At times, this lack of data has been due to the difficulties of allocating costs between products in plants where more than one product is produced,[66] or the segregation of data between manufacturing and importing where both operations were engaged in.[67] A principal obstacle, however, has been that the commission has not been able to obtain from all interested parties, not even from all applicants, the information requested. As a result, the commission has often had to generalize on the basis of data covering only a segment of the industry.[68] Such generalizations are of doubtful validity, since a bad profit experience of one or a few firms, whose difficulties might be due to causes other than imports,[69] can disproportionately influence figures on the financial position of the industry as a whole. In the second groundfish fillet investigation, for example, information was supplied by fewer than one-fifth of the vessel owners and only about one-tenth of the processors.[70]

Base Period.—Even when adequate data have been obtained, however, there has been considerable disagreement within the Tariff Commission over the importance or the meaning to be attributed to the figures. These

65. In the first spring clothespins report, the commission commented on this problem as follows: "We have no information as to how indirect labor and overhead costs were distributed between the various articles produced. . . . Moreover, different companies have different methods of computing unit costs of production. . . . Costs submitted by producers are often substantially higher than the costs obtained by the accountants of the Tariff Commission." U.S. Tariff Commission, *Spring Clothespins*, Report to the President, Rep. No. 168, 2nd Ser., 1950, p. 2.

66. See U.S. Tariff Commission, *Motorcycles and Parts*, Report on the Escape-Clause Investigation, Rep. No. 180, 2nd Ser., 1953, pp. 4-5.

67. U.S. Tariff Commission, *Watches, Watch Movements, Watch Parts, and Watchcases*, Report to the President on the Escape-Clause Investigation, Rep. No. 176, 2nd Ser., 1953, pp. 16-17.

68. See U.S. Tariff Commission, *Scissors and Shears, and Manicure and Pedicure Nippers, and Parts Thereof*, Report to the President on Investigation No. 24 Under Section 7 of the Trade Agreements Extension Act of 1951, 1954, p. 26. Commissioners Ryder and Edminster questioned whether the financial data could be considered a representative sample. See also White House Press Release, May 11, 1954, in which the President cited the problem of inadequate financial data in explaining his reasons for refusing to increase the tariff on scissors and shears.

69. A case in point is the condition of the Harley-Davidson Company. See U.S. Tariff Commission, *Motorcycles and Parts*, pp. 4-5.

70. See U.S. Tariff Commission, *Groundfish Fillets*, Report to the President on Escape Clause Investigation No. 25 Under the Provisions of Section 7 of the Trade Agreements Extension Act of 1951, 1954, pp. 34-35.

differences in interpretation have often involved the determination of a base year to be used for purposes of comparison. Abnormal conditions existed in a number of domestic industries and in international trade in the early postwar years. The slow return of imports, which were cut off during the war, together with the deferred demand of the war years caused many domestic industries to expand production to an unusually large degree in the early postwar years. Later, when imports more fully recovered and perhaps even expanded their markets as compared with prewar sales, the domestic producers with over-expanded production facilities were faced with the threat of a downward trend in production. The inflationary effect of the Korean war and the consequent short-term spurt in consumption further complicated the situation. In such cases, the choice of a "normal" period for purposes of comparison could easily determine the outcome of the investigation.[71]

Some members of the Tariff Commission frequently took a prewar period as most representative of normal conditions for the industry, but others consistently placed emphasis upon comparisons with the years immediately following the war. The finding of a threat of serious injury in the scissors case, for example, depended to a considerable extent upon the choice of a base year. Commissioners Brossard, Talbot, Schreiber, and McGill, in the majority report, emphasized the deterioration in conditions in the domestic industry since 1948. Commissioners Ryder and Edminster, however, in dissenting from the majority finding, were of the opinion that the period from 1948 to 1950 was too abnormal to qualify as representative. They felt that the years immediately preceding the war constituted a much more appropriate base period.[72] In the investigation on hand-blown glassware, Commissioners Ryder, Edminster, and McGill considered the prewar period from 1935 to 1938 most representative, while Brossard, Talbot, and Schreiber selected the postwar year of 1946. The first group of commissioners said that "the escape clause legislation was never intended to protect United States industries from receiving more severe foreign competition than they received when few foreign producers had access to the United States market—

71. In the investigation on motorcycles, Commissioners Brossard and Gregg emphasized changes since 1948 while the majority considered 1948 an abnormal peak year for the domestic industry. See U.S. Tariff Commission, *Motorcycles and Parts*, pp. 9 and 4. Brossard and Gregg in the glacé cherries investigation emphasized 1951 as a year of deterioration for the domestic industry, whereas the majority considered that 1951 was an abnormal year when domestic production decreased because of a short cherry crop and imports, consequently, were very large. See U.S. Tariff Commission, *Glacé Cherries, Report on the Escape-Clause Investigation*, Rep. No. 185, 2nd Ser., pp. 8-9 and 5-7.

72. U.S. Tariff Commission, *Scissors and Shears*, p. 24. The view of the dissenting commissioners on this point was concurred in by President Eisenhower. See White House Press Release, May 11, 1954. A similar problem arose in the 1955 investigation on bicycles.

such as during the war—or when the major foreign producers were only beginning to reestablish themselves in the years immediately following the war."[73]

Share Doctrine.—Even when the base year has been chosen, however, the problem of determining the significance of changes in consumption, production, and imports remains. The extent of the increase in imports, and particularly the trend in the relative shares of imports and domestic production in supplying the United States market, has received considerable attention in escape-clause reports. Some commissioners placed so much emphasis upon changes in the relative position of imports and domestic production that what amounts to a "share doctrine" emerged. According to this view, a domestic industry sustains "serious injury" if domestic producers get a smaller share of the market relative to imports than in a previous representative period, even though their absolute volume of sales may not have declined.

Probably the most significant use of the "share doctrine" occurred in the first report on watches, when Commissioners Brossard, Durand, and Gregg based their finding of injury largely upon the fact that the share of the market supplied by domestic producers had declined.[74] The other commissioners argued that a decline in the share of the market supplied by domestic producers was not sufficient proof of injury if employment and production in the domestic industry continued at a high level.[75] President Truman, in explaining his reasons for rejecting the commission's recommendation for an increase in the tariff on watches, said: "In fact, it [the share doctrine] finds that serious injury exists when the domestic industry fails to gain something it never had, even though the industry may be prospering by all of the customary standards of levels of production, profits, wages and employment. This is the doctrine on which the claim of injury by three Commissioners appears to be based."[76]

In cases in which there has been a majority finding of serious injury by the Tariff Commission, however, domestic output almost invariably had decreased while imports increased. When domestic production as

73. See U.S. Tariff Commission, *Hand-Blown Glassware,* Report to the President on Investigation No. 22 Under Section 7 of the Trade Agreements Extension Act of 1951, as Amended, 1953, pp. 52-53. See also pp. 61-62 and 36.

74. The share of the market supplied by domestic watch producers fell from 80 per cent in the period 1936-40 to 51 per cent in 1951. See U.S. Tariff Commission, *Watches,* p. 9. The share doctrine also figured prominently in the 1954 investigation on watches.

75. Commissioner Edminster voted for the escape-clause action not on the ground of the share doctrine, which he opposed, but on the reasoning that there was a "threat" of injury in the future.

76. U.S. Tariff Commission, *Watches,* p. 78.

well as imports and domestic consumption have risen, a majority of the commission has found no cause for action under the escape clause, even though domestic production has not increased as much as imports.

Shifts in the Pattern of Domestic Production.—Disagreements within the Tariff Commission over the importance of the share doctrine has demonstrated rather clearly the view of certain commissioners that domestic production should be protected under the serious injury concept in the sense that it should not in any way be displaced or changed by imports. Commissioner Brossard, in particular, and Commissioner Gregg consistently held the view that the function of the escape clause was to protect the existing pattern of domestic production. A shift from the production of one article to the manufacture of another, even if already produced by the domestic firms concerned, or a shift from manufacturing to importing, no matter how profitable these shifts may be, were considered positive evidence of serious injury by these commissioners:

More important, however, . . . in our judgment, is the fallacy involved in the theory that producers of a particular product cannot be found to be seriously injured because of the possibility that they might cease the production of the item in question, and undertake increased production of other items or convert their operations to importing, thus retaining their markets but abandoning their functions as producers of the product in question. We believe that any such interpretation will defeat the purpose of the escape-clause legislation. An interpretation of the escape clause which results in the elimination of many small industries on the uncertain ground that producers in those industries could shift to other lines of production, leaving to foreign producers the market in the United States for the particular products under consideration, surely does violence to the intent of Congress.[77]

The ability to shift to the production of other commodities was especially important in the case of garlic. Garlic is grown on farms engaged in general truck farming and normally constitutes a small percentage of the total crop on the farms on which it is grown. President Truman, in his letter rejecting the Tariff Commission recommendation for increased duties on garlic, said that "farmers who were dissatisfied with their financial return from garlic had ample opportunity to increase their production of other crops. The report also indicates that these other crops enjoyed good markets. Thus, I cannot understand how these farmers can be suffering 'serious injury' from imports."[78] The same point was

77. U.S. Tariff Commission, *Glacé Cherries*, pp. 10-11. See also the dissenting statement of Commissioner Brossard, U.S. Tariff Commission, *Wood Screws of Iron or Steel*, Reports on the Escape-Clause Investigations, Rep. No. 189, 2nd Ser., 1953, pp. 39-40.

78. U.S. Tariff Commission, *Garlic*, Report to the President on the Escape-Clause Investigation, Rep. No. 177, 2nd Ser., 1953, p. 27. See also pp. 6-8.

involved in the first investigation on watches, which showed that domestic producers had shifted from the production of watches with seventeen jewels or less to watches with more than seventeen jewels. The rates on higher jeweled watches had not been reduced, and they were, therefore, subject to higher duties.[79]

Definition of the Domestic Industry.—The extent to which domestic industry may avoid serious injury from imports by shifting production to other articles is closely related to another problem in interpreting the escape clause—the definition of the domestic industry. From 1947 to 1955 the escape clause provided for action when serious injury was caused to or threatened the "domestic industry producing like or directly competitive products." Until the Trade Agreements Extension Act of 1955, decisions as to what constituted the "domestic industry" in the case of concerns producing several items were left to the Tariff Commission or the President.

There was considerable discussion of the scope that should be given to the term "domestic industry" in the public hearing on the escape-clause investigation of straight pins. The straight-pin manufacturers, eight firms, filed an application for escape action, but refused to submit voluntarily any information with regard to other products produced by their firms. All of the firms, with one exception, manufactured products other than pins. The industry representative maintained that the other products did not constitute a part of the domestic industry. "By no stretch of the imagination could it be contended that the inquiry should extend into the manufacture of plumbing hardware . . . simply because the manufacturer of pins also happens to make plumbing hardware in some other division of its corporate organization, and it is no more logical to extend the inquiry into the sales and profits of the applicants arising from their production of other products."[80]

Because of the unwillingness of the applicants to submit this information, the Tariff Commission terminated the investigation without formal findings on the merits. The report emphasized the importance to the

79. In commenting upon the shift to the production of twenty-one jewel watches President Truman said: "It is difficult to see how any serious injury is evidenced by a shift from the production of one product to the production of another which can be produced with equal or greater profit by the same labor and equipment." U.S. Tariff Commission, *Watches*, p. 78. See also U.S. Tariff Commission, *Screen-Printed Silk Scarves*, Supplementary Report to the President on Escape Clause Investigation No. 19 Under the Provisions of Section 7 of the Trade Agreements Extension Act of 1951, 1954. This report (p. 6) indicates that firms previously engaged in manager-jobber activities had shifted to importing.

80. Statement of Alexander M. Heron, counsel for applicant, published in *Congressional Record*, 83rd Cong., 2nd Sess., Vol. C, Pt. 6 (May 26, 1954), p. 7174.

commission in discharging its investigatory responsibilities of obtaining all information that might be pertinent. The report emphasized, however, that the action taken "does not constitute a decision of the Commission as to the scope of the domestic industries concerned."[81] The commission, therefore, was unanimous in protecting its power to obtain information, but it did not settle the conflict over the scope of the domestic industry.

Before the 1955 legislative changes, some of the tariff commissioners, Brossard in particular, argued that when more than one commodity is produced by the domestic firms making a product like or directly competitive with imports, all commodities produced by the domestic firms other than that one product should be disregarded entirely.[82] Even if that one product constituted only a very small part of the domestic manufacturer's business, it should receive escape action if that small segment of the business was injured. Profits from other portions of the business should be entirely disregarded. The fact that several products were already produced in the same plants was in his view immaterial to the determination of serious injury.

In the 1954 report on wood screws, Republican Commissioners Brossard, Talbot, and Schreiber stated:

Were this phrase "domestic industry" to be interpreted as including the profits on all other products such as nonferrous wood screws, machine screws, tapping screws, builders' hardware, etc., that might be produced by these same concerns that produce wood screws of iron or steel, as long as the companies, though losing money on wood screws of iron or steel, were making such other products at a profit and the company was making an over-all profit or could find some other alternative products to manufacture other than wood screws of iron or steel, that would show an over-all profit, few claims of injury would be allowed as a result of "escape-clause" investigations.[83]

The Democratic commissioners, in general, disagreed with this view. While there is not sufficient information in the reports to indicate the development on their part of a definition of "domestic industry" which they consistently applied to all cases, the Democratic commissioners

81. U.S. Tariff Commission, Report on Escape-Clause Investigations No. 28 (*Straight Pins*) and No. 29 (*Safety Pins*) Under the Provisions of Section 7 of the Trade Agreements Extension Act of 1951, 1954, p. 14.

82. See, for example, U.S. Tariff Commission, *Wood Screws*, p. 39.

83. U.S. Tariff Commission, *Wood Screws of Iron or Steel*, Report to the President on Escape-Clause Investigation No. 34 Under Section 7 of the Trade Agreements Extension Act of 1951, 1954, pp. 10-11.

clearly acted upon certain principles. They maintained the need for information regarding the total production of each company investigated and the range of articles produced by it. They considered this information basic to a determination of the scope of operations covered by the investigation as well as necessary for judging the validity of the methods used in distributing overhead costs to the various operations.

The Democratic commissioners consistently maintained, in opposition to their Republican colleagues, that when two or more commodities were produced in the same plant with largely the same equipment and labor, the "domestic industry" within the meaning of the escape clause be defined broadly enough to include all of these products. In the investigation on glacé cherries, for example, the Democratic commissioners considered that the domestic industry included not only the production of glacé cherries (the "like" domestic product) but also the production of maraschino cherries and other glacé fruits.[84] The report shows that there probably was no domestic firm producing glacé cherries whose production of glacé cherries accounted for as much as 40 per cent of the value of the total business of the firm.[85]

The same position was maintained by the Democratic commissioners in the 1954 report on wood screws in which they held that the "domestic industry" constituted the productive facilities used to manufacture all screws (i.e., machine screws as well as wood screws) produced by the applicants.[86]

A further point of disagreement within the commission over the definition of the domestic industry was whether there was properly a "domestic industry" if the domestic article in question accounted for a very small part of the productive facilities of the applicants. Democratic Commissioners Ryder, Edminster, and McGill maintained that when, as in the case of garlic, the domestic product constituted a negligible, or almost negligible, part of the output of the domestic producers, it not be considered a separate industry for the purposes of an escape-clause investigation. In the garlic case, the value of the crop affected by competition from imports was very small relative to the total business of the farms producing garlic. In addition, only a very small number of farms concentrated in only a few counties in only one state was involved.

84. U.S. Tariff Commission, *Glacé Cherries*, p. 6.
85. *Ibid.*, pp. 5-6.
86. However, this point was not a decisive one, because the Democratic commissioners held that no serious injury could be found even if the domestic industry was confined to wood screws of iron or steel. The Democratic commissioners in this case were Ryder, Edminster, and Sutton. See, U.S. Tariff Commission, *Wood Screws*, Report to the President on Escape-Clause Investigation No. 34, pp. 40-41.

These factors prompted Commissioners Ryder and Edminster to question whether there was such a thing as a domestic garlic industry.[87]

A third principle followed by the Democratic commissioners in defining the domestic industry involved substitute products. When the imported product under investigation was found to be directly competitive not only with the "like" domestic product produced by the applicants but also with some other domestic article or articles not produced by the applicants, the Democratic commissioners held that the domestic industry should be defined so as to include both domestic products. In the investigation on imports of chalk whiting, for example, they held that the domestic industry consisted not only of the one domestic firm producing chalk whiting (a calcium carbonate pigment made by grinding chalk) but also of other domestic firms producing limestone whiting and precipitated calcium carbonate. The latter products, they felt, were substitutes for chalk whiting, the article subject to the escape-clause investigation, and were directly competitive with it. They argued that curtailing imports of chalk whiting would not aid the domestic producer of chalk whiting since his problem was competition from domestic substitutes for chalk whiting more than from imports of chalk whiting itself. Since the producers of limestone whiting and calcium carbonates were not suffering difficulties, and must be considered a part of the domestic industry, the claim of injury could not be sustained. Commissioner Brossard argued the contrary, saying that the production of chalk whiting constituted a domestic industry separate and distinct from the industry producing substitutes for chalk whiting. The sole domestic producer of chalk whiting constituted the domestic industry for the purposes of the investigation, and this producer was being seriously injured from competition with imports.[88]

The importance of the 1955 change in the legislative definition of the domestic industry can be readily seen. The domestic industry was defined as "that portion or subdivision of the producing organizations" producing the like articles, and these operations were to be separated from the operations of such firms involving other products. The Tariff Commission, therefore, was required to define the industry as narrowly as possible. The legislative definition was in accord with the view of Commissioner

87. See U.S. Tariff Commission, *Garlic*, pp. 6-7. The same point was made in the investigation on mustard seeds. See, U.S. Tariff Commission, *Mustard Seeds (Whole)*, Report on Escape-Clause Investigation No. 23 Under Section 7 of the Trade Agreements Extension Act of 1951, 1953, p. 25. The decision against the escape-clause action in the case of mustard seeds, however, was made on other grounds.

88. See U.S. Tariff Commission, *Chalk Whiting*, Report on Escape-Clause Investigation No. 15 Under Section 7 of the Trade Agreements Extension Act of 1951, 1953, pp. 15 and 16-21.

Brossard on multi-product firms. The 1955 change appeared to rule out the position earlier taken by the Democratic commissioners that the industry be defined to include products other than the one under investigation when produced in the same plants with largely the same labor and equipment.

The 1955 law also required that the domestic industry produce the product under investigation "in commercial quantities." It would appear that any product actually marketed commercially would be considered to have been produced in commercial quantities. This would seem to rule out the position taken by the Democratic commissioners in questioning whether the production of garlic could be considered a separate domestic industry.

Remedial effects of a tariff increase.—Another difficult problem on which the commissioners have disagreed involves the causal relationship between increased imports and injury. When the effect of a tariff concession was not clear, as is the case in most instances, there was disagreement over the probable effect of remedial action.[89] Will or will not a tariff increase cure the problems of an industry? President Eisenhower raised this point in his letter on silk scarves when he asked whether a tariff increase might not have the effect merely of raising the price to consumers without giving actual benefit to the industry.[90]

The same question has come up in other cases. Usually, it has arisen with respect to those industries whose main difficulties clearly were due to factors other than imports. In the case of a declining industry whose total market is shrinking, a tariff increase will do little toward solving the basic problems confronting the domestic producers and by raising prices will usually cause the market to shrink further. Temporary relief in the form of increased duties was granted the women's fur felt hat industry. Tariff rates were modified from the concession rates of 40 to 55 per cent by increasing them to 62 to 80 per cent, but changes in consumer preference from plain felts to velours, together with the increasing practice among both men and women, but particularly among men, of going without hats, remained the greatest problems facing the industry. In fact, the increase in the duty may have the result in the long run of intensifying the problems of this industry. Apparently, the duty

89. For example, in the first follow-up report under Executive Order 10401 after the escape-clause was invoked in regard to women's fur felt hats and hat bodies, the commission said that imports had declined after the duty had been increased, but that a substantial part of the decline was in imports from Czechoslovakia and was due to causes other than the change in duty treatment. See U.S. Tariff Commission, *Women's Fur Felt Hats and Hat Bodies,* Report to the President (1952) Under Executive Order 10401, 1952, p. 1.

90. White House Press Release, June 10, 1953, p. 3.

increase encouraged the industry to shift some of its resources from the production of men's hats to the production of women's hats. After the change in duty treatment, the percentage of facilities devoted to the production of women's hats increased over men's hats, even though the long-term trend in domestic consumption of women's hats was downward.[91] The industry's rate of decline may have been temporarily checked by capturing that portion of the market formerly supplied by imports. However, because the domestic market for women's hats is declining, the shift toward greater production of women's hats could, in the long run, merely intensify the problems facing the industry.

The same problem of a shift in consumer preference was responsible for the deteriorating condition of the briar pipe industry—in this case from pipes to cigarettes and cigars, with the resultant sharp decrease in domestic consumption of pipes. President Eisenhower refused to increase the tariff on pipes, saying: "I am not persuaded that the industry's difficulty is due primarily to increased imports under the existing trade agreement rates nor that the application of the Tariff Commission's recommendations under the "escape clause" procedure would remedy such deterioration as has taken place in the domestic industry."[92]

Loss of markets to the domestic industry because of technological developments was an important factor in the cases of chalk whiting and hand-blown glassware. In the former, the majority of the commissioners felt that the predominant factor influencing the domestic production of chalk whiting had been competition from substitute pigments produced domestically, not competition from imports.[93] Poor financial conditions in the hand-blown glassware industry, according to the Democratic commissioners, was due primarily to competition from domestic machine-made glassware: "In our view, the escape clause should not be invoked to lessen the degree of foreign competition received by a domestic industry suffering primarily from causes which are not attributable to increased imports."[94] In requesting further information on this case, President Eisenhower asked the Tariff Commission to give consideration to the relative importance of imports as against technological improvements in accounting for the decline in the market for domestic hand-blown glassware.[95]

91. See U.S. Tariff Commission, *Women's Fur Felt Hats and Hat Bodies*, Report to the President (1953) Under Executive Order 10401, 1953, p. 7.
92. White House Press Release, November 10, 1953, p. 2.
93. U.S. Tariff Commission, *Chalk Whiting*, pp. 12-13.
94. U.S. Tariff Commission, *Hand-Blown Glassware*, p. 76.
95. White House Press Release, November 20, 1953, p. 1.

Probably because of cases like these, the Trade Agreements Act of 1955 introduced the new statement of causal relationship between injury and imports, quoted in full earlier, which merely required a showing that imports had "contributed substantially towards causing" the injury. This provision seems to be an attempt by the Congress to prevent a strict construction of causal relationship between imports and injury and to enable the use of higher tariffs to offset disadvantageous factors other than imports, such as technological changes. Increased imports no longer needed to be a primary cause of injury or even a very important one, as long as, in the opinion of the Tariff Commission, they contributed substantially to the injury.

THE ROLE OF THE PRESIDENT

The escape clause has required the Tariff Commission only to make a determination as to injury and to recommend appropriate action to the President. It has neither required the President to accept the determination of the commission as to injury nor to take the action recommended. All that has been required is that the President, if he did not put into effect a recommendation of the commission, must report this fact, together with the reasons for his failure to take action to the House Ways and Means Committee and the Senate Finance Committee. The law has not limited the discretion of the President in these actions.

When the Tariff Commission found no more than a threat of injury as a basis for escape action, Presidents Truman, Eisenhower, and Kennedy indicated their reluctance to disturb existing tariff rates. In rejecting the recommendation of the commission in the 1954 investigation on scissors, for example, President Eisenhower said that when escape action was recommended on the basis of a threat of serious injury he believed that "the evidence brought forth to substantiate the judgment of threat must be of such a character as to leave no doubt that actual injury is imminent."[96]

In other cases in which the Tariff Commission decided that actual injury existed and recommended escape action, the President often questioned the commission's views directly or by implication.

President Truman used the escape clause to increase trade-agreement rates in three cases—hatters' fur (first), women's fur felt hats and hat

96. White House Press Release, May 11, 1954, pp. 2-3. Commissioners Ryder and Edminster, in dissenting from the majority finding in this scissors investigation, stated that a finding of a threat of serious injury in their view required that (a) the industry must at the present time be injured by imports subject to a concession, and that (b) the injury shortly will become serious. See U.S. Tariff Commission, *Scissors and Shears*, p. 22.

bodies, and dried figs—but refused to take the action recommended by the Tariff Commission in two cases—watches (first) and garlic (first).

President Eisenhower invoked the escape clause in ten cases—alsike clover seed (first), watches (second), bicycles (second), linen toweling, spring clothespins (fourth), safety pins (second), clinical thermometers, lead and zinc (second), stainless-steel table flatware, and typewriter-ribbon cloth. He rejected the majority recommendations of the Tariff Commission for escape action in thirteen cases,[97] and in five divided cases he accepted the recommendation of the commissioners who were against escape action.[98]

President Kennedy has raised duties under the escape clause in two cases—carpets and rugs (second) and sheet glass. He did not accept the majority recommendations of the Tariff Commission for escape action in three cases,[99] nor did he invoke the escape clause in three divided cases.[100]

Each of the Presidential rejections was based upon a variety of factors. In all of them, however, the President was not convinced that serious injury due to imports had been conclusively proved. Presidential statements on the cases also indicate the conviction that the President, as leader of the nation, must make his determination upon a broader base than that of the concept of serious injury alone. The original Executive Order of 1947 referred to the President's "consideration in the light of the public interest."[101] The phrase does not appear in the later legislation that superseded the original Executive Order. Nevertheless, the President has clearly been guided in part by consideration of national interest or public policy.

President Truman referred to the serious foreign policy implications involved in imposing escape-clause restrictions on garlic. He said that increased protection to the domestic producers of garlic must be weighed against the effect of the restriction upon the Italian economy and the importance of a strong Italy to the security of the United States.[102] In his letter on watches, Truman commented upon the importance of trade

97. These cases were tobacco pipes and bowls, scissors and shears (first), groundfish fillets (second), lead and zinc (first), screen-printed silk scarves, ferrocerium (lighter flints), groundfish fillets (third), velveteen fabrics, straight pins (second), violins and violas, umbrella frames (first) tartaric acid, and cream of tartar.

98. These cases were handmade blown glassware (first), spring clothespins (third), wood screws (third), fluorspar (second), and para-aminosalicylic acid.

99. These cases were baseball and softball gloves, ceramic mosaic tile, and straight pins (third).

100. These cases were binding twines, hard-fiber cords and twines (second), and alsike clover seed (second).

101. Executive Order 9832, 12 Federal Register, 1363.

102. U.S. Tariff Commission, *Garlic,* pp. 27-28.

with Switzerland to United States export interests.[103]   President Eisenhower stated the Presidential role more clearly. In rejecting the recommendation of the Tariff Commission for increased tariffs on briar pipes,
he said: "The law, however, lays upon the President the responsibility of weighing these recommendations and of making a final determination on the basis of them. Reasons of public policy or national
interest which lie beyond the scope of the Tariff Commission's field of
inquiry may, from time to time, enter into this final judgment of the
Commission's findings. . . ."[104]

The President, therefore, in addition to considering the issue of serious
injury, has considered a variety of other elements that affected the relationship of the proposed escape action to the national or public interest.
The effect upon foreign relations, and in particular upon the objectives
of the mutual security program,[105] the danger of provoking retaliatory
action or stimulating anti-United States propaganda abroad as well as
such economic considerations as the importance of the product in question
to domestic consumers and the effect of the action on United States exports—all of these factors have entered into Presidential decisions.

In no case, however, has the President declined to accept a majority
recommendation of the Tariff Commission for escape action on the
grounds of public policy or national interest alone. In all cases, the
President has listed, as well, several reasons for his disagreement with
the determination of injury made by the Tariff Commission or, where he
has agreed with the determination, has argued that the cause of the
injury was due to factors other than to imports.

ADJUSTMENT AID

For more than a decade there has been discussion of the possibility
of governmental aid to ease necessary adjustments in industries genuinely
and seriously injured by trade-agreements concessions (or even to compensate them for losses).[106] Such government assistance in most instances
would be in lieu of the escape clause and peril points.

The first reference by government officials to a possible program of
adjustment aid arose in connection with the Economic Cooperation Administration (ECA) legislation in 1950. Both Secretary of State Acheson

103. U.S. Tariff Commission, *Watches,* pp. 79-80.
104. White House Press Release, November 10, 1953, p. 2.
105. See, for example, the reference to the international implications of escape-clause
actions in President Eisenhower's rejection of the Tariff Commission's recommendation
for an increase in duty in the silk scarf investigation, White House Press Release, June 10,
1953, p. 2.
106. For a critical discussion of the idea of compensation, see Clair Wilcox, "Relief for
Victims of Tariff Cuts," *The American Economic Review,* XL (December, 1950), 884-89.

and ECA Administrator Paul Hoffman stressed the need for a substantial increase in imports by the United States and spoke of the possibility of direct assistance to domestic industries in the event of serious injury as a result of increased imports. Their statements indicated quite clearly, however, that no official study of the problem had been made and that there was no Administration position on the issue. Hoffman, while emphasizing his belief that imports could be absorbed without injury in almost all cases, talked of direct relief to workers in the few industries that might be injured.[107] In a later clarification of his position, he wrote:

. . . if this new competition, slight though it might be, should result in a loss of employment, I suggest it might be a good thing as a matter of public policy to develop programs for the retraining and relocation of workers, such as we had during the war. This is the kind of relief, if needed, that I had in mind. I repeat it is my belief that failures due to increased imports would be so utterly insignificant that I consider this question of relocation and retraining of workers academic rather than factual.[108]

The State Department's view of adjustment aid was somewhat broader than that presented by Hoffman.[109] Secretary Acheson spoke of governmental responsibilities to management and investors as well as workers. In discussing the need for increased imports to the United States before the House Foreign Affairs Committee, he said: "The steps we will have to take will be very substantial steps. As we take those, they will cause difficulty and hardships of one sort or another to some groups in the United States. That would seem to me as this matter is studied, to be a problem of concern to the Government. . . . I should think it would be a matter of governmental concern to see that there is help in the adjustments to these new situations."[110] Acheson said that he did not have a specific adjustment aid plan in mind but felt that the entire problem should be carefully studied: "It is not enough to say, if there is a difficulty in some industry which becomes marginal, then the fate of management and the investors and the workers is of no concern to all of us. It is of concern to all of us. Now, what we should do about it, I do not know. . . ."[111]

The Bell Report suggested government loans for new capital requirements, extended unemployment insurance, job retraining, and co-opera-

107. See U.S. Congress, Senate Committee on Foreign Relations, *Hearings* on S. 3101, 81st Cong., 2nd Sess., 1950, pp. 7 and 88-90; and U.S. Congress, House Committee on Foreign Affairs, *Hearings* on H.R. 7378, 81st Cong., 2nd Sess., 1950, Pt. 1, pp. 93-94.

108. Letter from Paul Hoffman to Senator H. Alexander Smith, March 21, 1950.

109. See article by James Reston in *The New York Times*, February 22, 1950.

110. U.S. Congress, House *Hearings* on H.R. 7378, Pt. 1, p. 23.

111. *Ibid.*

tion between the federal, state, and local governments on problems involved in the diversification of industry.[112]

A similar plan for adjustment aid in cases of injury was submitted to the Randall Commission by one of its members. David J. McDonald, one of the presidential appointees to the commission, said that he doubted that any President would reduce tariffs below the limits set by the Tariff Commission in the peril-point procedure unless a plan for sharing the burdens of adjustment were established. He suggested a program of adjustment assistance which would include the use of federal funds to provide technical assistance and governmental loans to affected industries. He also suggested accelerated tax amortization on new plants and equipment to encourage management to shift their facilities to new products, special unemployment compensation financed from federal funds for workers in the affected industries as well as intensive counseling and placement programs, special training and moving allowances, and increased benefits under the Social Security system for older unemployable workers.[113]

The other sixteen members of the Randall Commission were unable to accept McDonald's plan:

. . . for the reason that no matter how great our sympathy may be for the problems of a displaced worker, or those of a business with a shrinking volume, this is but one phase of a much broader problem.

*   *   *   *   *   *   *   *   *   *   *   *   *   *

In a free economy, some displacement of workers and some injury to institutions is unavoidable. It may come about through technological change, alterations in consumer preferences, exhaustion of a mineral resource, new inventions, new taxes, or many other causes. Since it has never been seriously proposed that the burden of all such injury arising in a free economy should be assumed by the Government, the Commission felt that it was not appropriate to propose such a plan in the tariff area only.[114]

The commission nevertheless felt that the McDonald plan should be presented to the public and, therefore, appended it to the report.

In subsequent years, many bills were introduced in Congress to provide for governmental assistance where it was needed to adjust to tariff reductions. Most of them were designed to provide assistance to industries in cases where the President, acting in the national interest,

---

112. Public Advisory Board for Mutual Security, *A Trade and Tariff Policy in the National Interest* (Washington: February, 1953), pp. 66-67.

113. Commission on Foreign Economic Policy, *Report to the President and the Congress* (Washington: January, 1954), pp. 53-58.

114. *Ibid.*, p. 54. Several comments on the McDonald plan by individual members of the commission were appended to the report. See *ibid.*, pp. 59-61.

might refuse to take escape action recommended by the Tariff Commission. The bills included such plans as increased unemployment benefits, government counseling and placement services for displaced workers, training allowances, and tax benefits for the establishment of new industry.[115] The adjustment assistance provisions of the Trade Expansion Act of 1962 is the only one of these proposals to have been enacted.[116]

3. ASSESSMENT

Investigations under the escape clause have been carried out by the Tariff Commission since 1947. From that time to July 1, 1962, forty-one cases have been sent to the President for action. The escape clause has been invoked in fifteen cases. The record, therefore, indicates that increased trade restrictions pursuant to escape-clause action have been few in number.

A numerical or even a quantitative analysis,[117] however, does not adequately reflect the effects of the escape clause on imports. Apart from the immediate impact on trade, invocation of the escape clause has had international policy effects. Confidence in the stability of trade-agreements concessions granted by the United States has been weakened. Since foreign exporters have been faced constantly with the possibility of an increase in the tariff, they have been discouraged from enlarging their productive facilities and developing marketing outlets required for expanding sales in the United States.[118] A substantial increase in sales to the United States might easily have precipitated tariff or other restrictive action against the imported product. Moreover, the fact that an escape-clause request for a particular product was denied in the past provided no assurance of stable tariff treatment in the future, since the domestic industry had only to file another application to obtain a new investigation.[119] Foreign businessmen, consequently, have been reluctant to invest their energies and resources in building up markets in the United

115. For a discussion of various legislative proposals, see Bruce E. Clubb and Otto R. Reischer, "The Trade Adjustment Bills: Their Purpose and Efficacy," *Columbia Law Review*, LXI (March, 1961), 490-503. See also U.S. Congress, Joint Economic Committee, Subcommittee on Foreign Economic Policy, *Trade Adjustment in Theory and Practice*, by Otto R. Reischer, 87th Cong., 1st Sess., 1961.

116. See Chap. II, p. 121.

117. For a quantitative analysis of escape-clause actions, see Kelly, "Trade-Agreements Escape Clause," *Political Economy*, pp. 55-57.

118. Secretary Dulles cited this psychological factor as an example of the usefulness of the escape clause as a preventive measure. See U.S. Congress, *Hearings* on H.R. 1, Pt. I, p. 68.

119. A good example of this is the escape action taken on imported bicycles in August, 1955, after the first request had been turned down in 1952. See *The New York Times*, August 28, 1955, for an account of the protests from affected Western European countries.

States which may easily be withdrawn from them if they are successful in bringing about a substantial increase in sales.

Experience in administering the escape clause demonstrates that the avoidance of serious injury to domestic industry is not an objective or scientific principle of tariff making. The record shows that the judgment as to the existence or nonexistence of serious injury due to imports in a particular case depends in large part upon the general attitude or philosophy toward the tariff on the part of the administrators making the decision. For example, the following table shows some of the extremes of interpretations on key points that can be attributed to disagreeing groups within the Tariff Commission, or to the President.

ESCAPE CLAUSE—SCOPE FOR INTERPRETATION[120]

A. *Those who believe that the tariff is basically harmful to the country as a whole and, therefore, should be used only in special cases of serious social distress that cannot be relieved by other methods:*

1. Production, employment, and income in domestic industry must decline absolutely relative to a base period. Mere failure to maintain a given percentage of the market would not be enough to sustain a finding of injury.

2. The base period must not be one where domestic output was stimulated by isolation from foreign competition due to non-trade agreement factors (e.g., immediate postwar).

3. The domestic industry should include operations of firms involving products other than the "like" domestic product when (a) other articles are produced in the same plant with largely the same equipment and labor, (b) the imported product is found to be directly competitive with other domestically produced substitute articles, or (c) the domestic product in question constitutes a negligible part of the output of the domestic producer.

4. An industry, using the same plant, capital, and labor, that has already shifted from production of the article affected by import competition to another article or that has demonstrated an ability to do so, should not be deemed to have suffered serious injury from imports.

5. A decline in domestic output, employment, etc. must be *primarily* attributable to increased imports in order for a determination of

120. This table is based upon escape-clause cases decided under the criteria prior to the 1955 legislative changes. These changes, however, narrowed only a little the scope of interpretation. A similar table could be derived from escape-clause cases decided under the changed criteria.

injury to be sustained. It would still be possible, however, for a domestic industry to be injured if (a) total consumption declined and (b) domestic output declined much more than imports. In this case, however, the ability of imports to command a larger share of a declining market would have to be a more important factor than the decline in the total market before imports could be considered as a primary factor.

6. The qualification "serious" contained in the wording of the escape clause should be strictly construed. Whenever there is doubt as to serious injury, restrictive action should not be recommended.

7. A tariff increase should not be adopted if it will not solve the basic problem of the industry or if its effect will be slight.

8. Considerations bearing on the importance of the domestic industry to national defense are entirely outside the scope of escape-clause investigations.

B. *Those who think the tariff is basically good for the country and, therefore, should be kept at a level (including increases when necessary) that will preserve present patterns of production and should not be reduced except when the effects of reduction are small or negligible.*

1. Domestic industry is entitled to the tariff protection necessary to preserve its "share" of the domestic market.

2. The share of domestic industry should be determined on the basis of that previous period when the domestic share was highest.

3. "Domestic industry" should be defined as that portion of domestic capital and labor devoted to producing the particular article that enters into direct competition with the imported article. The condition of capital and labor devoted to other articles but associated in the same firm or group of firms should be ignored, except when it is not good and strengthens the case for relief.

4. Successful shifts or demonstrated ability to shift from production of an article subject to increased import competition to others that are not should be ignored in determining injury to domestic industry.

5. The tariff should be increased even though the primary cause of distress to the domestic industry is not attributable to import competition, so long as a part of the injury is due to that cause and the tariff increase can ameliorate if not cure the condition.

6. Any injury is serious, and there is a presumption of injury if domestic production declines or if it loses any part of its market.

7. The tariff should be increased even if it helps a little and even if it

causes a further decline in domestic consumption, so long as the effect is to increase domestic output or to prevent a decline in domestic output.

8. Considerations bearing on the importance of an industry to national defense fall within the scope of escape-clause investigations.

The notion that the Tariff Commission in discharging its responsibilities relating to the escape clause has been engaged in an objective fact-finding activity is erroneous because the findings of the commission have been based in large degree upon differing interpretations of the law and on subjective judgments as to the implications of the facts. This is necessarily so since the functions assigned to the commission—finding serious injury and recommending remedial action—are essentially policy functions rather than fact-finding functions. It should not be supposed, therefore, that the escape-clause judgments of the commission are entitled to greater intellectual respect than those of the Executive on the theory that the judgments of the commission have been more thoroughly grounded in fact or scientific principle.

Adherence to the principle that tariff concessions must not seriously injure any domestic industry, particularly when carried to the extreme of a formalized peril-point and escape-clause system, raises a question about the value of such concessions. It may be conceded that tariff reduction does some good even if its effect is confined to the elimination of excessive profits and the reduction of prices, thus presumably expanding consumption and stimulating a greater absolute volume of imports than would otherwise take place. But the main purpose of international trade, and the major justification for reducing the governmental barriers that limit it, is to enable greater international specialization. If these purposes are to be achieved, industrial adjustments must be allowed to take place. For social reasons, it may be argued that adjustments should be gradual or that adjustments should not go so far as under a system of complete free trade. But to the extent that the application of the no-serious-injury rule prevents adjustment, then to that extent it inevitably defeats the major economic purpose of any program for the reduction of trade barriers.

It should also be recognized that prevention of adjustment by import-competing industries through the retention of tariffs or the raising of tariffs simply forces downward adjustments on other industries, particularly those engaged in export, or acts as a brake on the growth of such industries.

The Trade Expansion Act of 1962 shifts the emphasis of protection to domestic producers from no serious injury to adjustment assistance along the lines of the McDonald proposal in the Randall Commission report. However, it retains the escape clause as an alternative to adjustment assistance under certain conditions and also retains certain vestiges of the peril-point provision.[121] Whether significant tariff reductions and internal adjustments along more productive lines result from these legislative changes will depend largely on how the law is administered.

APPENDIX

Outcome or Current Status of Escape-Clause Investigations Instituted by the United States Tariff Commission as of July 1, 1962[122]

Investigations instituted by the commission 134

    Investigations dismissed by the commission at applicant's request.... 9

        Knit gloves and mittens, wool (6-0) (July 11, 1951)
        Hard-fiber cords and twines (4-0) (Jan. 14, 1953)
        Fluorspar (1st investigation) (6-0) (Nov. 23, 1953)
        Wood screws (4th investigation) (4-0) (Apr. 9, 1956)
        Cotton blouses (5-0) (June 22, 1956)
        Certain cotton cloth (gingham) (5-0) (Jan. 29, 1957)
        Creeping red fescue seed (6-0) (June 1, 1961)
        Umbrella frames (2d investigation) (3-0) (Sept. 21, 1961)
        Umbrellas (3-0) (Sept. 21, 1961)

    Investigations terminated by the commission without
        formal findings 9

        Straight pins (1st investigation) (6-0) (June 22, 1954)
        Safety pins (1st investigation) (6-0) (June 22, 1954)
        Leather handbags (6-0) (Mar. 14, 1956)
        Toyo cloth caps (4-0) (June 21, 1957)
        Fine-mesh wire cloth (3-2) (July 14, 1958)
        Nails, spikes, tacks, brads, and staples (6-0) (Mar. 12, 1959)
        Galvanized fencing wire and galvanized wire fencing (6-0)
          (Mar. 12, 1959)
        Broadwoven silk fabrics (5-0) (June 26, 1959)
        Tennis rackets (4-2) (Apr. 19, 1961)

    Investigations in which decisions by the commission are pending..... 4
        Vanillin
        Household china tableware and kitchenware
        Earthenware table and kitchen articles
        Hatters' fur (3d investigation)

Investigations completed by the commission.........................112

121. See Chap. II, pp. 119-21.

122. The vote of the commission (where applicable) and the date of the particular action are shown in parentheses.

Investigations in which the commission dismissed the applications
    after preliminary inquiry under procedure provided
    for in Executive orders (no reports issued)................ 14

    Marrons (4-0) (Aug. 27, 1948)
    Whiskies and spirits (5-0) (Jan. 3, 1949)
    Crude petroleum and petroleum products (4-2) (May 3, 1949)
    Hops (4-2) (May 11, 1949)
    Knitted berets (1st investigation) (3-3) (July 8, 1949)
    Sponges (3-3) (July 22, 1949)
    Narcissus bulbs (6-0) (Jan. 13, 1950)
    Knitted berets (2d investigation) (5-1) (Jan. 13, 1950)
    Reeds (5-0) (Feb. 17, 1950)
    Beef and veal (3-3) (June 30, 1950)
    Silk woven fabrics (5-0) (Sept. 21, 1950)
    Aluminum and alloys (6-0) (Nov. 21, 1950)
    Lead (5-0) (Jan. 25, 1951)
    Stencil silk, dyed or colored (6-0) (June 7, 1951)

Investigations in which the commission decided against escape
    action (no reports sent to the President)................. 57

    Spring clothespins (1st investigation) (5-1) (Dec. 20, 1949)
    Wood screws (1st investigation) (4-2) (Dec. 29, 1951)
    Blue-mold cheese (5-1) (June 12, 1952)
    Motorcycles and parts (4-2) (June 16, 1952)
    Spring clothespins (2d investigation) (3-2) (Aug. 21, 1952)
    Groundfish fillets (1st investigation) (3-2) (Sept. 4, 1952)
    Bicycles and parts (1st investigation) (5-0) (Oct. 9, 1952)
    Glacé cherries (3-2) (Oct. 17, 1952)
    Bonito and tuna, not in oil (3-2) (Nov. 26, 1952)
    Household china tableware (4-0) (Feb. 6, 1953)
    Wood screws (2d investigation) (3-1) (Mar. 27, 1953)
    Pregnant mares' urine (4-0) (Apr. 2, 1953)
    Chalk whiting (3-1) (Apr. 9, 1953)
    Wood-wind musical instruments (5-0) (Apr. 28, 1953)
    Cotton-carding machinery (5-0) (July 29, 1953)
    Metal watch bracelets and parts (6-0) (Aug. 20, 1953)
    Rosaries (6-0) (Aug. 21, 1953)
    Mustard seeds (6-0) (Dec. 10, 1953)
    Ground chicory (5-0) (Sept. 7, 1954)
    Coconuts (6-0) (Oct. 25, 1954)
    Wool gloves and mittens (5-1) (Dec. 28, 1954)
    Glue of animal origin (6-0) (Jan. 7, 1955)
    Hardwood plywood (1st investigation) (5-0) (June 2, 1955)
    Red fescue seed (1st investigation) (4-0) (June 22, 1955)
    Dressed rabbit furs (6-0) (Feb. 29, 1956)

Cotton pillowcases (3-2) (Nov. 21, 1956)
Certain jute fabrics (5-0) (May 15, 1957)
Bicycles (3d investigation) (6-0) (Aug. 19, 1957)
Wool felts, non-woven (5-0) (Jan. 6, 1958)
Garlic (2d investigation) (5-0) (Feb. 19, 1958)
Barium chloride (6-0) (Oct. 10, 1958)
Certain carpets and rugs (1st investigation) (3-2) (Jan. 12, 1959)
Scissors and shears (2d investigation) (6-0) (Feb. 25, 1959)
Handmade glassware (2d investigation) (6-0) (May 21, 1959)
Axes and ax heads (5-0) (May 21, 1959)
Calf and kip leather (5-0) (May 29, 1959)
Hardwood plywood (2d investigation) (4-2) (June 22, 1959)
Mink skins (6-0) (Sept. 17, 1959)
Red fescue seed (2d investigation) (5-0) (Oct. 28, 1959)
Zinc sheet (3-2) (Jan. 14, 1960)
Women's and children's leather gloves (5-0) (Mar. 21, 1960)
Typewriters (6-0) (May 10, 1960)
Lamb, mutton, sheep, and lambs (4-2) (June 1, 1960)
Barbed wire (4-0) (Aug. 3, 1960)
Cast-iron soil-pipe fittings (6-0) (Aug. 23, 1960)
Crude horseradish (6-0) (Sept. 15, 1960)
Hatters' fur (2d investigation) (6-0) (Oct. 7, 1960)
Iron ore (5-0) (Dec. 30, 1960)
Ultramarine blue (6-0) (Mar. 16, 1961)
Plastic raincoats (4-2) (Mar. 29, 1961)
Cantaloups (6-0) (Mar. 30, 1961)
Cellulose filaments (rayon staple fiber) (4-2) (Apr. 10, 1961)
Watermelons (6-0) (Apr. 20, 1961)
Rolled glass (3-2-1)[123] (May 25, 1961)
Procaine and salts and compounds thereof (3-0) (Nov. 2, 1961)
Standard clothespins (5-0) (Feb. 14, 1962)
Creeping red fescue seed (2d investigation) (3-2) (May 21, 1962)

Investigations in which the vote of the commission was evenly
divided (reports sent to the President).................... 8
Handmade blown glassware (1st investigation) (3-3)
(Sept. 22, 1953)
Spring clothespins (3d investigation) (3-3) (Oct. 6, 1954)
Wood screws (3d investigation) (3-3) (Oct. 27, 1954)
Fluorspar (2d investigation) (3-3) (Jan. 18, 1956)
Para-aminosalicylic acid (3-3) (June 14, 1956)
Binding twines (2-2) (Dec. 9, 1960)

123. Three commissioners found no injury; two commissioners found injury; one commissioner found a threat of injury.

Alsike clover seed (1st investigation) (June 30, 1954)
Watches (2d investigation) (July 27, 1954)
Bicycles (2d investigation) (Aug. 18, 1955)
Toweling, of flax, hemp, or ramie (June 25, 1956)
Spring clothespins (4th investigation) (Nov. 9, 1957)
Safety pins (2d investigation) (Nov. 29, 1957)
Clinical thermometers (Apr. 21, 1958)
Lead and zinc (2d investigation) (Sept. 22, 1958)
Stainless-steel table flatware (Oct. 20, 1959)
Cotton typewriter-ribbon cloth (Aug. 23, 1960)
Sheet glass (Mar. 19, 1962)
Certain carpets and rugs (2d investigation) (Mar. 19, 1962)

President declined to invoke the escape clause.................... 26

Garlic (1st investigation) (July 21, 1952)
Watches (1st investigation) (Aug. 14, 1952)
Tobacco pipes and bowls (Nov. 10, 1953)
Scissors and shears (1st investigation) (May 11, 1954)
Groundfish fillets (2d investigation) (July 2, 1954)
Lead and zinc (1st investigation) (Aug. 20, 1954)
Handmade blown glassware (1st investigation) (Sept. 9, 1954)
Spring clothespins (3d investigation) (Nov. 20, 1954)
Screen-printed silk scarves (Dec. 23, 1954)
Wood screws (3d investigation) (Dec. 23, 1954)
Fluorspar (2d investigation) (Mar. 20, 1956)
Para-aminosalicylic acid (Aug. 10, 1956)
Ferrocerium (lighter flints) (Nov. 13, 1956)
Groundfish fillets (3d investigation) (Dec. 10, 1956)
Velveteen fabrics (Jan. 22, 1957)
Straight pins (2d investigation) (Mar. 29, 1957)
Violins and violas (Mar. 30, 1957)
Umbrella frames (1st investigation) (Sept. 30, 1958)
Tartaric acid (Mar. 14, 1959)
Cream of tartar (Mar. 14, 1959)
Binding twines (Feb. 7, 1961)
Hard-fiber cords and twines (2d investigation) (Feb. 7, 1961)
Alsike clover seed (2d investigation) (Oct. 1, 1961)
Baseball and softball gloves (Mar. 19, 1962)
Ceramic mosaic tile (Mar. 19, 1962)
Straight pins (3d investigation) (April 28, 1962)

Source: United States Tariff Commission

CHAPTER IV

United States Commercial Policy and the Domestic Farm Program

The United States has encountered one of the most stubborn problems of governmental policy in attempting to reconcile its domestic farm programs with its declared purpose of promoting expanding opportunities for international trade. The trade and the farm programs were born together in the midst of the depression of the 1930's and have grown up side by side. Under the farm program the government has attempted to stabilize farm income through measures of governmental intervention in the market—measures that in recent years have increasingly led to the use of import restrictions, export subsidies, and increased tariff protection in the form of import fees.

Under the trade-agreements program the government has sought to stimulate the freer flow of international trade, principally by seeking agreement with other countries to reduce or remove governmental barriers of the same type employed in connection with the domestic farm program. This chapter is concerned with this conflict between the two programs and deals with (1) the beginnings of the conflict prior to World War II; (2) the broadening of the agricultural and trade programs during and after the war; and (3) the widening of the conflict since 1948.

1. BEGINNINGS OF CONFLICT BETWEEN TRADE POLICY AND AGRICULTURAL PROGRAMS

It would be easier to convey an idea of the conflict between the agricultural and trade-agreements programs if one could impute to each the extreme objective that might be deduced by carrying some of its underlying principles to their full, logical conclusion. For example, assume (1) that the trade-agreements program had aimed at establishing complete freedom of trade, without material governmental influence over the economic processes that determine the location of industry between or within nations; and also (2) that the agricultural program had aimed at establishing thoroughgoing governmental control of agriculture so as to create an arbitrary pattern of national farm output, prices, and income wholly unrelated to the pattern that could be expected to result from a free market. Then it would be obvious that these two programs could not be carried out side by side, at least insofar as agricultural products are concerned.

But of course these simplifying assumptions are denied us. As is so often the case in the area of public policy, the trade and agricultural programs have been halfway houses. Neither has been designed to produce an extreme solution. Each of them, the one oriented toward freer trade with less governmental intervention, the other toward greater state responsibility for farm income, has contained some of the elements of the other. Thus, while the trade-agreements program has sought to limit or prohibit the more extreme forms of trade barriers, such as high tariffs, absolute quotas, and discriminatory internal regulations, it has not attempted to remove moderate tariffs, to reduce all tariffs, to eliminate all quotas under all circumstances, or to prevent direct governmental payments or domestic subsidies to producers. Similarly, from the opposite end of the spectrum, the agricultural program has not sought to establish complete governmental control of agriculture: farm-aid operations have tended to be selective as between commodities, although less so after World War II; prices have been "supported" by floors of varying significance for international and domestic trade rather than "fixed" by government fiat; direct payments have been used to some extent in lieu of import quotas and tighter controls over supply; and a substantial although contracting area of normal competition between foreign and domestic agricultural products, and between domestic agricultural products, has continued to exist.

Conversely, it is sometimes suggested that there is no conflict between the goals of the trade and agricultural programs since both share the common aim of raising farm income; and the conflict is only one of methods. But this is only a partial truth. The farm program has also had in view changing the distribution of income between farm and non-farm producers. This aspect of the ultimate goal of the farm program has no counterpart in the trade program, which, if anything, is biased against the forced alteration of the distribution of income as compared with the distribution determined by competitive processes.

Rather than to view the conflict, therefore, as a clash at all points between inherently incompatible systems based on flatly contradictory goals, or merely as a conflict of methods rather than objectives, it is more accurate to conceive of it as a historical pattern of growing inconsistency between two mixed systems pointed in different directions. This makes the issue more difficult to grasp because attention must be given to an accumulation of detail rather than to a simple contrast between opposing principles. Nevertheless, the issue is not less important for that reason. For, as will be seen, what started as a relatively small policy gap twenty-five years ago has by a process akin to erosion widened into a gulf that it now seems much more difficult to bridge.

BASIC AGRICULTURAL LEGISLATION

To begin examining the course of this growing conflict between trade and agriculture, it is necessary to look first at the basic agricultural legislation. Five laws, enacted in the 1930's, have since determined, with two important exceptions,[1] the general framework of government aid to agriculture:

The Agricultural Adjustment Act (AAA) of 1933, approved May 12, authorized the Secretary of Agriculture to enter into voluntary agreements with producers of seven designated "basic" commodities—wheat, cotton, corn, rice, tobacco, hogs, and milk and milk products[2]—to reduce the acreage planted to these commodities, or their production for market, or both, for the purpose of raising market prices in accordance with the policy of Congress "to reestablish prices to farmers at a level that will give agricultural commodities a purchasing power with respect to articles that farmers buy, equivalent to the purchasing power of agricultural commodities in the base period." The base period for the basic commodities, except tobacco,[3] was fixed in the law as the five years between August, 1909, and July, 1914.[4] This was considered to be a period favorable to agriculture. In order to induce voluntary farmer acceptance of the restrictive agreements, the Secretary was further authorized to make benefit payments to co-operating producers on that part of production required for domestic consumption. Revenue for financing the benefit payments was to be derived from a tax on the "first domestic processing" of the commodity concerned, payable by handlers or processors such as cotton manufacturers and flour millers. The tax was made equal to the difference between the current market price of the com-

1. These exceptions relate to sugar and wool. Wool is discussed briefly on pp. 218-19. For a discussion of sugar, see Harold A. Wolf, "Sugar: Excise Taxes, Tariffs, Quotas, and Program Payments," *The Southern Economic Journal,* XXV (April, 1959).

2. Certain other products were added to the basic list in 1934 and 1935 but were later relegated to the category of "non-basics." Hogs were dropped, milk was treated separately, peanuts were added, so that the "basics" have ordinarily comprised six commodities: wheat, cotton, corn, rice, tobacco, and peanuts.

3. Parity for tobacco was calculated on the basis of the period from 1919 to 1929. Later, parities for certain fruits and vegetables were also calculated on this alternative base.

4. The base period was changed later to January, 1910, to December, 1914 (Title II of Agricultural Act of 1948).

modity and its "fair exchange value," that is, the parity price aimed at in the Congressional declaration of policy.[5]

However, the processing-tax device for raising farm income was not fully tested. The constitutionality of the legislation was immediately challenged in hundreds of cases brought before the federal courts and in January, 1936, it was held unconstitutional by the Supreme Court in *U.S.* v. *Butler.*[6]

The Soil Conservation and Domestic Allotment Act of 1936, approved on February 29 after the Supreme Court's decision in *U.S.* v. *Butler,* sought to cure the constitutional defect of the original AAA by relating the control of agricultural supply to the purpose of soil conservation, a matter clearly within the federal power, and by providing direct Congressional appropriations for benefit payments in lieu of the processing tax. Benefit payments were geared to the notion of soil conservation by making them payable to farmers in return for undertakings to shift production away from surplus (equated with soil-depleting) crops such as wheat, corn, cotton, and tobacco, and into soil-conserving crops such as alfalfa and clover. The Act reaffirmed the broad objective of "parity," but in addition to referring to parity prices, the Congressional declaration of policy spoke of "parity of income" between agricultural and non-agricultural producers as being the desirable objective.[7]

The Agricultural Marketing Agreement Act of 1937, approved on June 3, continued the grant of authority to the Department of Agriculture, originally embodied in the AAA of 1933, to enforce what are in effect private restrictive agreements among producers in the name of maintaining "orderly marketing conditions." Such agreements have not in practice usually involved direct price-fixing, except for milk, or

5. For a technical discussion of the terms "parity price," "parity income," and "parity ratio," see Commission on Foreign Economic Policy, *Staff Papers* (Washington: February, 1954), pp. 213-16.

6. 297 U.S. 1 (1936). The court held that the tax was unconstitutional on the ground that it was not a tax for the support of the government but an exaction instrumental to the control of agricultural production, a matter beyond the powers delegated to the federal government. The court's decision also had the effect of causing Congress, at the President's request, to repeal the Bankhead Cotton Act (1934), the Kerr-Smith Tobacco Control Act (1934), and the Warren Potato Act (1935). These laws, providing coercive measures for the restriction of output, had been passed after cotton, tobacco, and potato producers had refused to co-operate in restriction programs under the voluntary system of the AAA.

7. However, actual price-support operations have continued to be geared to parity prices rather than income parity, which is quite a different concept. Income parity would have to take account of amounts produced and sold as well as with prices received. Generally speaking, price-support operations based on income parity would result in lower parity prices in years of high production and higher parity prices in years of low or controlled production.

benefit payments; but market prices are affected by the controls that the agreements impose over quality, quantity, and rate of shipment to market. The law makes it clear that these arrangements are not to be considered "combinations in restraint of trade" such as would be forbidden by anti-trust legislation. Marketing agreements under the Act of 1937 have been largely confined to milk, fruits, vegetables, and nuts.

The Agricultural Adjustment Act of 1938, approved on February 16, was designed to reinforce the relatively weak compliance features of the Soil Conservation and Domestic Allotment Act. It authorized the government to establish mandatory acreage allotments, without the approval of producers, and marketing quotas (with the approval of two-thirds of the producers) for the "basics"—corn, wheat, cotton, rice, tobacco, and peanuts. It should be observed that acreage allotments do not necessarily determine output, since farmers may, and often do, cultivate more intensively if acreage is limited than if it is not. Also, acreage limitations on a given product, say cotton, may lead producers to raise additional amounts of another product, say livestock, thus reducing surpluses of cotton but creating surpluses of milk and meat. Marketing quotas tend to limit directly the amounts reaching the market since penalties are provided for over-quota sales; but, again, they do not necessarily limit production if storage is available. The Act of 1938 did not itself provide for benefits or other payments to producers but relied for a sweetener on the payments under the Soil Conservation and Domestic Allotment Act and on price-support help from the Commodity Credit Corporation, both of which were made conditional on producer cooperation in controlling supply.

The Commodity Credit Corporation (CCC), established by Executive Order of October, 1933,[8] under powers stemming from the Reconstruction Finance Corporation (1932), was authorized to buy, hold, lend upon, or deal in any agricultural commodities designated by the President. From the demise of the processing-tax scheme to the present it has been through the instrumentality of the CCC that the government has exerted its major impact on the supply and market prices of agricultural commodities. The CCC not only exerts a direct influence on current market prices through its dealings in the market, but its preparedness to engage in price-support operations for any given commodity through purchase agreements with, or price-support loans[9] to, particular producers is an

---

8. The charter of the CCC was placed on a statutory basis in 1949, but its powers have remained substantially the same.

9. Such loans are made without recourse on the basis of estimated prices. If prices go up, the producer sells the commodity and repays the loan. If they go down, he simply turns over the commodity to the government instead of repaying the loan.

important factor in bringing about the compliance of producers with the acreage or marketing controls for that commodity provided for under other agricultural legislation.

The agricultural laws outlined above have continued since the 1930's to provide the basic source of federal regulatory power over agricultural output and price. Various agricultural acts have from time to time made alterations of detail—some of them of great importance—such as in the commodity scope of the program, in the methods of calculating parity, and in the percentages of parity that CCC or other operations are expected to support. But the fundamental legal and philosophical framework of the 1930's continues to govern the domestic agricultural programs today.

To summarize, basic agricultural legislation in the United States has provided five general methods for governmental intervention on behalf of agriculture: (1) the establishment of limitations on acreage; (2) the establishment of limitations on amounts permitted to be marketed without penalty; (3) the enforcement of producer agreements regulating marketing; (4) subsidization through direct payments; and (5) direct governmental support of market prices by means of CCC purchases or non-recourse loans. These five methods have been used in various combinations, and with varying practical effect, to lift the income of farmers toward "parity" with non-farm incomes. Apart from these general methods, special programs have been in effect for sugar (substantially complete governmental regulation) and for wool (direct subsidization).

IMPORT QUOTAS AND EXPORT SUBSIDIES—SECTIONS 22 AND 32.

In the planning stages of the agricultural-support program and the reciprocal-trade program the Administration had given little thought to the precise means by which the two were to be fitted together. Unlike the National Industrial Recovery Act of June 16, 1933,[10] whose Section 3(e) authorized import quotas or fees to prevent foreign competition from interfering with NRA codes, the AAA of 1933 said nothing about imports or exports of commodities to which the support program was to be applied. And the Trade Agreements Act of 1934 gave no clue as to how such commodities might be treated under trade agreements.[11]

10. The National Industrial Recovery Act was held unconstitutional by the Supreme Court in *Schechter* v. *United States*, 295 U.S. 495 (1935), on grounds similar to those later applied to the agricultural-processing taxes, i.e., that the NRA codes regulated local affairs reserved to the states and not within the federal power. Neither of these cases can be regarded as reflecting the modern judicial view of the scope of the federal power, which has changed since these cases were decided.

11. However, an early administration draft of the Trade Agreements Act contained a disputed section that provided that "In administering this [Act] the President shall have

There was, of course, an awareness among Administration officials that the ideologies of the two programs did not precisely jibe. More than once Secretary Cordell Hull privately voiced his concern over the probable intrusion of restrictive New Deal planning into the trade arrangements he had in mind. But the confusion of the times did not make for nice consistencies. The crisis of the depression called for emergency treatment and bold experiment rather than for cautious long-term planning. If conflicts developed, they would have to be taken care of later. The one thing that was beginning to be clear in 1933 was that the domestic program would have to come first. Although Secretary Hull had wanted to obtain Congressional action on the trade program in 1933—a move that would have strengthened the position of the United States at the pending World Economic Conference—the Administration laid it aside in order to avoid any distracting element in Congressional consideration of the domestic features of the National Recovery Program.

It was not long before the area of potential conflict between the agricultural and trade programs was more clearly perceived and remedies were provided by the Congress at the request of the Administration. In August, 1935, little more than a year after the passage of the Trade Agreements Act, Congress amended the AAA of 1933 in two significant respects. By the addition of Section 22 it established the principle that imports ought not to be allowed to "render ineffective, tend to render ineffective, or materially interfere with" AAA programs. To this end it authorized the President, after a finding of facts and submission of recommendations by the Tariff Commission, to prevent such interference by establishing import quotas[12] on the commodities concerned which could cut imports to as little as 50 per cent of their level in the period July 1, 1928–June 30, 1933.[13] By the addition of Section 32 to the AAA, it established the principle of export subsidies for farm products and authorized the setting aside of 30 per cent of annual customs revenues to be used by the Secretary of Agriculture for this and certain other purposes.

However much one may quarrel with the decision of the United States in 1935 to enact new trade-restricting legislation at the very time it was trying to lead the nations of the world in an opposite direction,

---

due regard for the policies of other parts of the National Recovery Program, particularly as embodied in the National Industrial Recovery Act and the Agricultural Adjustment Act." This hortatory language was omitted from the final version of the bill worked out within the Executive branch undoubtedly because it might have invited Congress to curtail some of the President's discretionary power under the proposed legislation.

12. Authority to impose import fees was added later. See below, pp. 190 and 200.

13. This period was changed later to January 1, 1929–December 31, 1933 (less favorable to imports); and changed still later to a "previous representative period."

it must be recognized that there was logic to Sections 22 and 32. The agricultural programs were designed to raise the price of agricultural commodities by controlling supply and providing governmental price-support. It was possible that these activities might lift prices within the United States for some commodities above the comparable world price, after figuring transportation costs and the tariff. If this should occur, it might have consequential results for both imports and exports: imports, attracted by the artificially higher United States price, might enter in such quantities as to undermine the domestic program; and exports would tend to fall off or even cease to flow as long as world prices were below the domestic. The domestic price-support program might become a world price-support program financed by the United States. Obviously, the only offset to these effects would be to limit the imports and subsidize the exports.

It can be argued that the original AAA programs, involving the use of processing taxes, except in unusual circumstances would have been unlikely to have created abnormal incentives for imports or disincentives for exports. Under these programs the processing tax applied to both imports and domestic production on a nondiscriminatory basis, but did not apply to exports.[14] Hence market prices in the United States (less the tax) and the world price would continue to bear their normal relationship so that no special restrictions would be needed to prevent "abnormal" imports, nor would an export subsidy be necessary to enable United States output to compete in the export market. And while it was true that money benefits were to be paid to domestic producers, and that processing taxes would tend to reduce domestic consumption and indirectly induce exportation, the effect that this might otherwise have in stimulating domestic output at the expense of foreign production could have been offset by the restrictions on domestic production or marketing provided for under the voluntary agreements between the Secretary of Agriculture and domestic producers. No benefit payments were made to farmers on amounts produced for export.

The only likely circumstance under the original AAA in which import quotas might be needed (but not export subsidies) would have been for those commodities of which the United States is normally a substantial net importer and whose domestic output was made subject to control. In this case, the effect of the control might well have been to raise domestic prices above the world price plus processing taxes, and abnormal

14. This treatment of international trade for internal tax purposes was in conformity with the principle of "national treatment" long accepted as a fair principle by other countries as well as the United States and provided for in commercial treaties and trade agreements.

imports might have been stimulated. But for most of the commodities under AAA programs, including all of the seven "basics," the United States has regularly been a heavy net exporter.

In short, the technical features of the original AAA plan were such that they might have permitted a fairly high degree of reconciliation with the objectives of the trade-agreements program to reduce barriers to international trade. The processing taxes conformed to the national-treatment principle, and such import quotas as might have been required would have squared with the equally defensible principle that when domestic output is restricted, proportionate restrictions may be placed on imports which do not alter previous competitive relationships between domestic and foreign suppliers.

But in 1935 the processing tax was already under attack in the courts. In addition, some provision had to be made for those commodities of which the United States was a net importer and which might be placed under production control or restrictive marketing agreements among producers.[15] These considerations, plus perhaps some uncertainty as to the precise effects of the domestic programs on imports and exports, appear to have been what led the Administration to ask Congress for discretionary and precautionary power to restrict imports and subsidize exports.

It should be emphasized that Sections 22 and 32 were not originally intended to provide extra protection to the United States farmer against foreign competition. The thought behind these two provisions of the law was not the same as that motivating the usual import tariff or quota, or the usual export subsidy—to take markets away from other countries. On the contrary, their purpose was to keep the effects of governmental aid to agricultural products from spilling over into the international market to such an extent as to transfer markets in the opposite direction, i.e., from the domestic to the foreign farmer.

Yet there were deficiencies in the language of Sections 22 and 32 which failed to make this purpose entirely clear and left these provisions open to protectionist interpretations. Section 22 could be used to impose a rigid limit on imports on the ground that they were "materially interfering" with an agricultural program. But the law required no showing that there must be an increase in imports, or excessive imports in relation to lowered domestic output, or that the imports complained of must in some way be attributable to the program. In short, no cause and effect relationship was spelled out. Thus it could theoretically be argued that

15. Congress had added cattle, rye, flax, barley, and peanuts—all imported products—to the list of "basic" commodities in March, 1934, although they were later dropped.

any imports at all would "interfere" with a domestic program if they took place at a time when the CCC was engaged in purchasing the like domestic product in conjunction with acreage allotments regardless of how much domestic output increased under such allotments. Also, Section 22 did not provide, as a purely non-protectionist law should have, that import quotas should not reduce the proportion of imports to domestic production as compared with past levels. It only said that they should not be cut to less than half of what they had been in absolute quantities. Thus, even though domestic production might have increased, imports could have been forcibly reduced.

The safeguards against these potential abuses were entirely administrative. The power to initiate, as well as finally approve, Section 22 action was reserved to the President, who would presumably apply it in a reasonable way and without the protectionist bias or the excessive zeal for conserving CCC funds that might have influenced the Department of Agriculture. And the Tariff Commission, rather than the Department of Agriculture, was given the authority to develop findings of facts and recommendations for the President's consideration as to the degree of interference which imports might create for domestic programs. The various ambiguities in the law later gave room to Congressional and other critics to allege that the Administration was not applying Section 22 forcefully enough, that it was not being used to curtail agricultural imports to the extent the law allowed.

With respect to the export-subsidy authorization in Section 32, here the potentialities for abuse were, if anything, greater and the safeguards almost nonexistent. The authority to pay export subsidies was limited only by the amount of funds available from 30 per cent of the customs revenue;[16] no requirement was made that they should not be used except in cases in which the domestic price had been raised above the world price by some other program of the Department of Agriculture; and no inhibitions were provided against the use of subsidies as a fighting weapon to take over the normal markets of other countries. The decision to grant export subsidies was vested exclusively in the Secretary of Agriculture. Neither the President nor the Tariff Commission was given a statutory role in this decision-making process.

BILATERAL TRADE-AGREEMENTS PROVISIONS RELATED TO FARM PROGRAMS

Those in the government concerned with commercial policy could do little or nothing to influence the future course of the farm programs,

16. These were substantial, amounting to $60 million annually during the period from 1935 to 1939; they have run at $150 million annually during the postwar period.

which were of key importance to the New Deal. The legislative policies established by Sections 22 and 32 were regarded as untouchable. Accordingly, the trade-agreements program was made to conform. In the bilateral agreements concluded up to 1943, the "standard" clause prohibiting import quotas on products subject to tariff concessions was qualified by a special exception, of which the following is a sample:

The [prohibition against import quotas on products subject to tariff concessions] shall not apply to quantitative regulations in whatever form which may hereafter be imposed by the Government of either country on the importation or sale of any article the growth, produce or manufacture of the other, *in conjunction with governmental measures or measures under governmental authority (a) operating to regulate or control the production, market supply, quality or price of the like article of domestic growth, production or manufacture;*

* * * * * * * * * * * * *

Provided . . . that such quantitative regulation is necessary to secure the effective operation of such measures. . . .[17]

An open-end exception of this sort was not always easy to negotiate, especially with countries like Canada which have an important agricultural export trade with the United States. Use of the exception for a given product might easily nullify any tariff concession provided for the product in the agreement. Since the agreements were reciprocal, United States negotiators also had to take into account the possibility that the other party to the agreement might use the exception to restrict United States agricultural exports. In an attempt to keep the exception from being resorted to by either side unless really necessary, it was customary to provide in the agreements that the exception could not be used by either party without advance consultation with the other. If the two governments could not agree, and the quota was imposed anyhow, then the other party could terminate the whole agreement on short notice. This was of doubtful efficacy as a restraint; and as a remedy it was none at all. But little more could be done in the light of Section 22.

The bilateral trade agreements of the prewar variety contained no special provisions relating to export subsidies such as those authorized by Section 32. The reason for this was not that foreign governments were unconcerned about United States export subsidization. It was that, un-

17. Italics added. U.S. *Executive Agreement Series,* No. 149, Reciprocal Trade Agreement between the United States and Canada, signed November 17, 1938, Article X, paragraph 2. The reference to manufactures was not dropped from the bilateral trade agreements despite the junking of NRA. No comparable provision with regard to manufactures was made in the postwar multilateral trade arrangements.

like the multilateral arrangements of the postwar period, the scope of the bilateral trade agreement was confined to trade between the two countries and did not attempt to cover their export relationships to third countries. To cite a typical case: the trade agreement with Brazil set forth the rules governing Brazil's imports from the United States and imports into the United States from Brazil. But it did not extend to the conditions under which Brazilian cotton and United States cotton would be exported in competition with each other to a third country, say Germany. The only provision of the bilateral agreements bearing on the problem of export subsidies was one that authorized each country to impose a countervailing duty on imports of any product of the other country which was produced or exported with benefit of subsidy. This provision, of course, dealt with only a minor aspect of the problem of export subsidization since, as a policy issue between any two governments, export subsidies are primarily of importance in third-country trade.

USE OF SECTIONS 22 AND 32 BEFORE WORLD WAR II

Relatively little use was actually made of Sections 22 and 32 before the war. There were several reasons for this. During most of the 1930's price-support programs were mainly confined to the "basic" commodities for which import competition was not an important factor. For these commodities the parity goals were established at modest levels as compared with later price objectives. Usually parity was set within the range of 50 to 75 per cent in contrast to the goals of 90 per cent and more which prevailed after the war. Also, during much of the period, notably from 1935 to 1937, the farm-surplus problem temporarily disappeared because of droughts in 1934 and again in 1936. Substantial amounts of foreign corn, wheat, barley, oats, hay, butter, and canned beef were imported during some of these years to eke out domestic shortages.[18] Another factor may have been the greater degree of internal governmental co-ordination of the farm and trade programs which appears to have prevailed in the prewar as compared with much of the postwar period.[19]

18. Actually, although imports were largely judged by past levels, they were small in relation to the shortages. For example, it was estimated that the drought of 1934 created a domestic shortage of fifty million tons of food and feedstuffs, whereas increased imports of the short commodities amounted to only three or four million tons.

19. In at least one important case Section 22 action was avoided because of this co-ordination. In 1940 a proposal by the Department of Agriculture to impose Section 22 quotas on fats and oils was reviewed by the interdepartmental Executive Committee on Commercial Policy *before* reaching the stage where the President would have had to ask the Tariff Commission for a public investigation. The advice of the committee was adverse, because it appeared that the proposed restrictions were intended primarily to

For these various reasons Sections 22 and 32 were brought into play on only two occasions before the war: import quotas and export subsidies were applied to cotton in 1939 and to wheat in 1941. These actions, although perhaps of greater psychological than of practical importance for international trade, are nevertheless of interest in any study of the conflict between trade policy and agriculture. They are good illustrations both of the legitimate application of the concept of offsetting the international effects of domestic farm programs and of the administrative temptations to apply these offsets to a greater degree than necessary.

In 1937 the United States had a record crop of cotton—nineteen million bales—and there were large crops elsewhere. The Department of Agriculture, in an attempt to prevent the domestic price from falling too far, established a loan rate on cotton of 9 cents per pound in 1937 and 8.3 cents in 1938. This was somewhat above the price at which foreign suppliers were willing to sell cotton on the world market so that United States exports began to fall. By the middle of 1939 exports were running at half the level of the previous year, and CCC stocks jumped from seven million bales in the fall of 1938 to eleven million bales in the spring of 1939. Secretary Wallace complained that the trouble was that cotton from competing countries was sold at a price just under our loan level.[20]

Discontinuance of the loan on cotton, it was estimated, would have meant a drop in the domestic price of cotton of from 2 to 3 cents per pound and a loss of income to the growers of around $200 million. But if the loan were continued, and nothing done to equalize the higher domestic price with the lower world price, exports would probably fall below three million bales (six million would have been "normal"); cotton acreage would have to be cut from twenty-seven million acres to twenty million; and CCC stocks would go up from eleven million bales

raise prices rather than to prevent interference with existing domestic programs, and because this proposed action would not square with commitments under the Philippine Independence Act and in trade agreements with the United Kingdom, the Netherlands, and Brazil. After Section 22 was amended in 1950 to give the Secretary of Agriculture statutory authority to take the first public step of initiating Section 22 action, the degree of interdepartmental review was much less, and there was no *formal* review by an interdepartmental committee.

20. The same complaint seems to have been voiced by the Department of Agriculture in 1955 when it sought, unsuccessfully, to establish an export subsidy program for 1955-1956. See *The Washington Post*, July 30, 1955. The implication of foreign finagling in these statements, however, has little to support it. The problem is created initially by the establishment within the United States of a price-support level above the world market, not by market rigging abroad. Naturally, the world market will tend to approach the United States price as far as it can, and hence the United States support tends to benefit foreign producers in the absence of an export subsidy.

to fourteen million. Faced with this situation, the Department of Agriculture inaugurated an export subsidy program on cotton of $1\frac{1}{2}$ cents per pound, effective July, 1939. The stated purpose was to restore normal price relationships and to maintain the customary United States percentage of the world's cotton trade.

The cotton subsidy shortly led to a curious and apparently unforeseen predicament. The world cotton price fell so far below the domestic that it became profitable for traders not only to move foreign cotton into the United States market to replace United States exports but to reimport United States cotton that had been shipped with benefit of the subsidy and pay the transportation cost both ways. Hence, if the subsidy program was to be continued, import quotas were necessary. Section 22 was promptly invoked and quotas proclaimed, effective September 20, 1939, on various classes of cotton and cotton waste.[21]

The export subsidy program was therefore inevitable, once the decision was taken to maintain price support at the 8 to 9 cent level in lieu of helping growers by means of direct money payments for which Congressional appropriations would have been required. The cost to the country, of course, would have been roughly the same either way; under the course that was followed, consumers of cotton made up the difference instead of taxpayers. And, once the export subsidy was in effect, import quotas under Section 22 were also inevitable. To have refrained from them would have brought the collapse of the whole program.

As in the case of cotton, the wheat loan of 60 cents per bushel (52 per cent of parity) during 1938-1939 proved to be higher than the comparable world market price, and rather than cut the loan rate the Department of Agriculture inaugurated an export subsidy of 26 cents per bushel in August, 1938. The declared purpose was to enable the United States to supply its "normal" share, then estimated at one hundred million bushels annually, of world wheat imports. At the same time the United States attempted to revive interest in replacing the international commodity agreement on wheat which had broken down soon after its negotiation in 1933-1934. Despite the subsidy, exports fell off as war closed important European markets.

The effect on imports of the difference between the price of wheat in the United States and the lower price of foreign wheat was for a time offset by the tariff of 42 cents per bushel provided in the Tariff Act of 1930. But in the spring of 1941 Congress raised the loan rate to 85 per

21. Separate quotas were established for short-staple cotton (less than $1\frac{1}{8}$ inches), for long-staple cotton ($1\frac{1}{8}$ inches or more), and for cotton waste. In 1940 quotas were removed on highly specialized imports of the very longest staples (over $1\frac{11}{16}$ inches).

cent of parity (97 cents per bushel), and by May the prices of United States and Canadian wheat widened to the point where it would soon pay Canadian shippers to send large amounts into the United States market over the rather substantial tariff wall. The Tariff Commission stated that, if this should happen, acreage allotments for wheat under the Soil Conservation and Domestic Allotment Act would automatically have to be reduced, and hence there would be import interference with a domestic agricultural program. Accordingly, import quotas of eight hundred thousand bushels of wheat and four million pounds of flour and other wheat products, almost exclusively affecting imports from Canada, were proclaimed under Section 22, effective May 29, 1941. These amounts were fairly generous in the light of historical imports.

The wheat import quota has been of trivial significance. Wheat imports are very largely limited to sporadic shipments from Canada through Buffalo. However, like the basic quotas on long-staple cotton, those on wheat have remained in force, unchanged in quantity throughout periods of alternating surplus and scarcity and despite all of the large shifts that have occurred over the years in the domestic program, export payments, and world prices. The ordinary tariff of 42 cents per bushel has not been reduced so that a considerable cushion between United States and foreign wheat prices would continue to exist even in the absence of a quota. At various times, also, world trade in wheat has been affected, although not fully regulated, by an intergovernmental commodity agreement. The continuing relationship, if any, of the wheat quotas to the problem of "interference" with the domestic program is therefore not at all clear, although from a policy point of view the practical significance of the trade is so small that the matter perhaps may be dismissed as being de minimis.

In the case of both the cotton and wheat actions, the export subsidies caused a greater disturbance to foreign relations than the import quotas. This was natural because the export subsidies posed a far greater economic threat to foreign producers of cotton and wheat than the limits placed on the fairly small outlets for their products within the United States. It could of course be explained, as Secretary Wallace often did, that the United States was only trying to preserve its "fair" share of world trade. But the unilateral character of the programs, the apprehension that they would be pressed too far, and the circumstance that export subsidization, no matter what the justification, had traditionally been regarded as an unfair method of competition,[22] all combined

22. United States laws and those of many other countries authorized countervailing and antidumping duties to offset foreign subsidization of exports or export sales by a foreign country below its own market prices.

to create foreign distrust of United States motives and disillusionment with United States commercial policy.

The policy issue of export subsidies versus trade agreements came to a head in the middle of 1939, shortly after the President had publicly announced the proposed export plan for cotton, but before it had been instituted. The following statement was issued by Secretary Wallace against the background of disagreement between himself and Secretary Hull:

Numerous questions have arisen in regard to the relationship between the reciprocal trade agreements program, administered by the Department of State, and certain programs, current and proposed, administered by the Department of Agriculture in the field of foreign trade. After consultation with the Department of State, I believe it appropriate, therefore, to indicate the position of the two departments with reference to these questions.

Both departments, I believe, are agreed that the trade agreements program represents the soundest long-term approach to the solution of the foreign trade relations of the United States, including, particularly, the problem of disposition of our agricultural export surpluses. This program recognizes concretely the fundamental principle that a nation must buy if it expects to sell.

Both departments, I believe, recognize, however that other programs of a strictly agricultural character, involving conservation of our soil resources, are necessary to the advancement of agricultural welfare in the United States and that these programs contribute to the solution of the export surplus problem and the welfare of the entire nation.

With regard to an export subsidy on cotton, I am informed that Secretary Hull still stands on his statement of March 28, 1939, as follows: "The Secretary of State when asked to comment upon the President's statement of today on cotton exports, said that of course the attitude of the Department of State in support of our program for general economic restoration is well known. Secretary Hull said that we are earnestly carrying it forward and shall continue to do so. He said, further, that naturally if and when the President and Secretary of Agriculture reach a decision to the effect that an emergency treatment in their judgment is necessary, he would cheerfully recognize and acquiesce in such a decision."

There is no question in my mind that emergency conditions do exist with respect to agricultural surpluses, arising to a large extent from present unsettled world conditions and, in the case of cotton, from the enormous production of 19 million bales in 1937. Such a situation may require emergency action. Such action may include the strictly temporary use of export subsidies to enable the United States to maintain during these unsettled times its fair share of the export market. But undoubtedly a sounder approach to this problem of agricultural surpluses, which, it must be recognized, is not confined to the United States, is to be found in international collaboration looking toward an adjustment in basic maladjustments between the supply of these products in the exporting countries and the demand in the importing countries.

With certain foreign countries now taking from the United States only a small fraction of their former imports of specific agricultural products, it is obvious that those departments of government which have power to deal with this situation in one way or another should give the problem the most careful consideration.[23]

Following the experience with the cotton and wheat subsidies, the Administration asked Congress to amend Section 22, presumably to make it entirely clear that import limitations could be used to offset the effect of export subsidies or other Section 32 payments even if used independently of any other agricultural program. Until then Section 22 was applicable only to prevent interference with programs authorized by the Agricultural Adjustment Act, the Soil Conservation and Domestic Allotment Act of 1936, and the Agricultural Marketing Act of 1937, all of which contemplated at least some element of limitation over domestic output or marketing.

After the new amendment, effective early in 1940, Section 22 could be used to prevent interference with Section 32 programs as well. For example, the mere payment of an export subsidy on an agricultural commodity, or the mere act of distributing small amounts of surplus products to low-income groups at cut-rate prices by using Section 32 funds, could be sufficient warrant for the legal application of Section 22. Suppose that the Department of Agriculture had a program to distribute 500,000 pounds of lard to domestic relief agencies at below-market prices. Then, conceivably, the new Section 22 could be used to control millions of pounds of imports of coconut oil, copra, and palm kernel oil on the theory that this was necessary to ensure the price-raising effects of the relief program for lard.[24]

Along with this significant change, the 1940 amendment broadened Section 22 to authorize the use of import fees of not more than 50 per cent ad valorem over the regular tariff, as well as import quotas.

To summarize the trade-agriculture conflict in the prewar period: The legal framework for conflict was set as early as 1935 by the adoption of Sections 22 (import quotas) and 32 (export subsidies) to the Agri-

23. U.S. Dept. of Agriculture, Press Release, Washington, D.C., June 21, 1939.

24. See above, footnote 19, for a reference to the (unsuccessful) efforts of the Department of Agriculture to use the new law in 1940 to restrict imports of fats and oils. The domestic production of marketing of fats and oils, such as lard, was not subject to any limitation, but there were small programs in effect for relief distribution at special prices to low-income groups.

cultural Adjustment Act, enacted at a time when the United States was attempting to exercise world leadership toward lower trade barriers. The likelihood of conflict at some point along the line was greatly enhanced when the Department of Agriculture was forced by the Supreme Court to abandon the processing-tax-plus-benefit-payment technique of supporting farm income and to replace it by the direct support of market prices through CCC purchases and loans.

For various reasons, including the droughts of 1934 and 1936 and the relatively low parity goals of the period, a direct clash was avoided until 1939, when it centered on the use of export subsidies for cotton, and later wheat. The import quotas that were adopted along with the export subsidies under the emergency circumstances surrounding these commodities at that time have continued to be applied to the present despite changed conditions. Throughout, the provisions of bilateral trade agreements in the prewar period were subordinated to the requirements of the domestic farm program, although there appeared to be somewhat closer interdepartmental co-ordination of the trade and agricultural programs than has existed at various later times.

When the issue of basic philosophy was joined in the debate about export subsidies between Secretaries Wallace and Hull, the views of Secretary Wallace prevailed. Although the debate concerned export subsidies, the real problem lay in the techniques of the domestic price-support program and in the level of price support which it sought to promote in relation to existing world prices. A further widening of the conflict between agriculture and trade policy was foreshadowed by the 1940 amendments to Section 22, which authorized high import fees as well as quotas and which extended the potential use of these devices to several additional programs of the Department of Agriculture under Section 32, even though they might be of small importance and even though they might not involve limitations on domestic output or marketing. These changes gave to Section 22 a more protectionist flavor and undoubtedly helped pave the way for still more significant changes later and for the heavy pressures for the use of Section 22 which came from Congress and the agricultural community in the postwar period.

2. Broadening the Agricultural and Trade Programs—1942-1948

THE AGRICULTURAL PROGRAM

It might have been thought that with the entry of the United States into World War II the depression-born farm programs would have lost some of their appeal. Farm surpluses were no longer the immediate problem, which was rather one of encouraging a great expansion of output to meet rising domestic requirements and to supply the growing needs of allied nations. Prices for farm commodities rapidly mounted and for many of them exceeded 100 per cent of parity for the first time in more than two decades.[25]

But, paradoxically enough, it was during the wartime period of farm prosperity that the notion of government responsibility for assuring parity of income for the farmer became more firmly embedded in the law. In a series of legislative enactments beginning in 1941 and culminating in 1948, the Congress (1) lifted parity goals from the prewar range of 50 to 75 per cent to 90 per cent and upward; (2) made parity price-support mandatory not only for the basic commodities but for many others as well; (3) authorized the Department of Agriculture to engage in comparable price-support operations for a large number of still other farm commodities; and (4) assured continuance of an important part of these expanded programs well into the postwar period. The rationale of these decisions was that farmers should not be asked to submit to war-time price ceilings[26] and also to increase output to meet war demand unless assurances could be given them that farm prices would be protected in the postwar period of contraction of output to more normal levels. In addition, there was considerable apprehension that, despite official intentions to promote a high level of employment after the war, a recession might develop, which would once again lead to farm difficulties. The various parts of this enlarged and extended program were:

Basic commodities.—In the Stabilization Act of 1942, Congress made it mandatory to raise price supports up to the level of 90 per cent of parity for the "basics," wheat, cotton, corn, tobacco, rice, and peanuts. In 1944 the parity for cotton was raised to $92\frac{1}{2}$ per cent.

Steagall commodities.—These were the commodities brought under price support by the so-called Steagall Amendment, attached as a rider to the Act of 1941 appropriating funds for the CCC. It required the Secretary of Agriculture to offer price support at 85 per cent of parity for all commodities whose expanded output was needed for the war effort, but authorized him to discontinue support after reasonable notice to allow for readjustment. By the Stabilization Act of 1942, the support level for these commodities was raised to 90 per cent and, as in the case of the

25. The last prewar year in which the parity ratio of farm prices hit 100 was 1919, when it stood at 119. During the 1930's it ranged between 58 in 1932 to 93 in 1937. In 1942 it rose to 105, in 1945 to a wartime peak of 116, and in 1947 to a postwar peak of 115.

26. The Office of Price Administration was prevented by law from imposing price ceilings on any agricultural commodity whose price had not reached 110 per cent of parity. In the Stabilization Act of 1942 this prohibition was repealed simultaneously with the enactment of postwar price supports.

basic commodities, the Secretary of Agriculture was required to continue this support level for two years after the war.[27]

Other commodities.—In addition to providing special treatment for the Steagall commodities, the Act of 1941 declared it to be the policy of the Congress that the loan and purchase operations of the Department of Agriculture should be carried out so as to bring up the prices of all other agricultural commodities—some 140 in number—into a fair parity relationship with the basic and Steagall commodities, to the extent that funds for this purpose were available.[28]

Additional aids to export.—Before the war, techniques for export subsidization were largely limited to the use of Section 32 funds for the payment of direct export subsidies. In the Surplus Property Act of 1944, a new technique was added: the CCC, normally prohibited from selling surplus commodities below the parity or market price (whichever was higher), was authorized to do so for export in order to meet competitive world prices. This authority was reaffirmed in the Act of 1945 extending the life and increasing the borrowing power of the CCC and became an important precedent for the foreign disposal programs in the later postwar period. In this way an additional and important method of financing, ultimately dependent, of course, upon Congressional appropriations, was opened up for the purpose of export subsidization.

The Agricultural Act of 1948.—The government's pledge to the farmers for mandatory price support at high levels was scheduled to expire at the end of 1948, two full years after the end of the year in which hostilities were officially terminated (1946). But little had been done toward readjustment. During 1946 and 1947 food shortages still existed. By 1948, when surpluses might otherwise have begun to appear on the horizon, the prospect of high foreign demand for United States agricultural products was renewed by the enactment of the Marshall Plan program for massive economic aid to Europe. In the Agricultural Act of 1948, Congress continued for the time being the wartime price supports for the basic commodities and mandatory support for the Steagall commodities (although at a somewhat lower range), but also provided for a long-run program of downward adjustment in price-support levels. The Act of 1948 also provided a larger fund for payment of export subsidies. Whereas, previously, Section 32 funds unexpended in any one year had

27. By the end of the war the list of Steagall commodities included: hogs, eggs, chickens, turkeys, milk and butterfat, dry peas, dry edible beans, soybeans for oil, peanuts for oil, flaxseed for oil, American-Egyptian cotton, potatoes, and sweet potatoes.

28. Price supports actually instituted for these other commodities, ranging from 90 to 160 per cent of parity, included wool, naval stores, hemp, certain fruits and vegetables, barley, rye, grain sorghums, Sea Island cotton, and some seeds.

to be returned to the Treasury, the new law authorized the Department of Agriculture to accumulate these up to a level of $300 million.[29]

In the Agricultural Act of 1949 Congress removed most of the flexibility from the long-run program envisaged in the Act of 1948. It was not until 1955 that a program of flexible support was actually made effective under the Agricultural Act of 1954.

THE TRADE PROGRAM

While Congress was widening the postwar base of the domestic farm programs, the Administration was at work in another arena on the postwar framework for international trade, including trade in agricultural products. The general nature of these efforts culminated in the GATT in 1947 and in the abortive International Trade Organization (ITO) Charter in 1948. For present purposes, three aspects of these arrangements need to be recalled:

First, experience plus the practical negotiating facts of the period from 1942 to 1947 dictated that any workable postwar trade agreement would have to be multilateral, establishing common trading rules applicable equally to a large number of countries. Bilateral trade agreements of the prewar type were considered inadequate to the problems of the postwar period and, in any case, were unacceptable to the governments of foreign countries of major importance in world trade. Since agricultural products make up a heavy proportion of the exports of some countries and a sizable part of total world trade, rules of general application would have to be developed for agricultural products as well as manufactures and minerals.

Moreover, the rules for agricultural products would have to be directed, as were other rules, toward the reduction of trade barriers and high protection if the purposes of over-all expansion in international trade were to be achieved and if agreement were to be reached between countries on the one hand mainly exporting industrial products and importing raw materials, and on the other hand, those mainly exporting raw materials and importing industrial products. This objective was in accord with the agricultural interests as well as the over-all interests of the United States, since the structure of the agricultural economy of the United States is such that it has much more to gain from reducing barriers to agricultural exports than from retaining its freedom of action to restrict agricultural imports.

Second, lying at the core of the postwar trade plans was the objective of eliminating absolute import and export quotas as devices for giving

29. Little use was in fact made of this new authority.

protection to domestic industries. The elimination of quotas was of key importance, because without it the reduction of lesser kinds of trade barriers, such as tariffs and discriminations, would be fruitless. Nor could quotas be dealt with selectively, product by product, like tariffs. For whatever might be the amount agreed upon through selective quota negotiations, the upper limits of trade would still be set by restrictive government regulations. These would cut across the market-price mechanism and prevent it from operating to encourage the production of goods in those countries best fitted to produce them and to discourage their production in those least fitted. The choice, therefore, was either to condemn quotas as protective devices and work toward their complete removal for this purpose, or to accept a world of planned governmental control of trade. Obviously for the United States this was not really a matter of choice. The United States had in the past imposed very few absolute quotas on international trade in time of peace. The nature of its economic system and its political traditions committed it to competitive enterprise operating in the main free of government control and with primary reliance on costs and prices to determine how much should be produced of what. The elimination of protective quotas, then, was a compelling international objective of the United States in the light of its own methods of doing business.[30]

Third, success in negotiating a multilateral trade agreement involving commitments to eliminate protective quotas meant that the United States would have to make substantial reductions in its tariff on a broad basis, covering virtually all products—including agricultural products of any export importance to its trading partners. It would not be possible, as it had been under the old bilateral agreements, to avoid painful tariff reductions by failing to negotiate with certain important countries or by making very mild tariff concessions. It would be necessary, for example, to reduce the tariff on such sensitive import products as wool, butter, and meat, as well as other agricultural products, and to make these reductions fairly substantial in order to make possible a multilateral trade agreement with important countries, such as those of the British Commonwealth.[31]

Nevertheless, within these general objectives—for the removal of quotas, for the widespread reduction of tariffs, and for the development of rules covering other trade barriers—room had somehow to be found

30. For a discussion of United States policy in regard to quantitative restrictions, see Chap. I, pp. 53-63.

31. For example, there is no doubt that the negotiations for the GATT would have collapsed in the absence of a 25 per cent tariff reduction by the United States on imports of wool, mainly imported from Australia, New Zealand, and South Africa.

for those restrictive measures that might be necessary to prevent the collapse of the domestic farm programs that Congress had already projected at least some distance into the future. This, of course, was not by any means exclusively a United States problem. For reasons similar to those which gave birth to the United States farm programs of the 1930's, many governments had engaged in extensive aids to domestic agriculture. These, in one way or another, had tended to encourage national self-sufficiency and to discourage imports.

In some countries these aids to agriculture took the form of direct subsidies to the producer; in others, various kinds of state trading were used; in still others, discriminatory internal taxation or "mixing regulations"[32] were applied. Some had relied chiefly on very high tariffs or on import quotas admittedly of a protectionist character. The United States system, however, was distinctive in one respect—it was almost the only important system that depended almost entirely on direct governmental support of domestic market prices, a method that, as we have seen, can at times compel the use of import quotas and export subsidies if the system is not to be abandoned. Therefore, either some accommodation had to be made for this system or Congress would have to be asked to redesign the domestic farm programs completely. Needless to say, this alternative was not seriously considered.

The problem was settled, instead, through a special exception from the rule against import quotas, through an understanding as to the treatment of agricultural import fees, and through the failure to reach any acceptable understanding on the use of subsidies, either domestic or export. A detailed account of the GATT-ITO negotiations on agricultural import quotas and subsidies can be found in *The United States and the Restoration of World Trade*.[33] What follows highlights those aspects of the agreement finally reached which seem to be of relevance to the continuing conflict in United States policy.

32. Mixing regulations are governmental directives to domestic processors that force them to use prescribed proportions of different raw materials, or prescribed proportions of a given raw material that may be drawn from domestic and foreign sources, in making up the processed product. A mixing regulation need not be protective of domestic industry against foreign competition, but it may be. If Urbania, for example, requires that all bread be made of 70 per cent wheat flour and 3 per cent rye flour, and both rye and wheat are produced domestically in substantial quantities, the regulation may protect rye producers versus wheat producers, but neither is necessarily protected against imported rye and wheat. If the regulation says not less than 60 per cent domestic wheat, or not more than 40 per cent foreign, then it is protective. The GATT (Article III, para. 5) does not prevent all mixing regulations, but it does ban protective ones as being discriminatory internal regulations.

33. William Adams Brown, Jr., *The United States and the Restoration of World Trade* (Washington, D.C.: The Brookings Institution, 1950).

Import Quotas.—From the beginning United States negotiators insisted that the general rule of the proposed multilateral trade arrangements prohibiting import quotas should not apply to an import quota on an agricultural product as long as the domestic production or marketing of that product was made subject to comparable restrictions. In addition, quotas might be used to offset purely temporary programs for the domestic disposal of a surplus and to ease the working off of government stocks in a short transition period after the war. This was a considerable advance over the predecessor clauses in the bilateral trade agreements before the war, which, it will be recalled, would have permitted import quotas to bolster price supports even though no restrictions existed on the domestic producer.[34] The new formulation, it was felt, would tend to minimize if not entirely prevent the use of agricultural import quotas for purely protective reasons, i.e., in order to raise home output by cutting down on imports. This limitation, while curtailing freedom of action, was considered important to the United States as an assurance that United States agricultural exports would not be made subject to protective quotas abroad.

Despite this basic safeguard the agricultural exception put forward by the United States was looked upon by other governments as an attempt by the United States to gain special treatment for itself. This view undoubtedly weakened somewhat the influence of the United States in keeping down or limiting other exceptions to the no-quota rule. Nonetheless, it is easy to overstate this factor. Most of the exceptions to the no-quota rule eventually agreed upon were either entirely legitimate, such as the exception permitting quotas to protect monetary reserves,[35] or else, as in the case of development quotas,[36] they were so ardently desired by the governments proposing them that they would have had to be admitted anyway in the interests of reaching agreement.

The final formulation of the agricultural exception did not differ materially from the original ideas of the United States and appeared in the GATT in Articles XI and XX (the same provisions, with slightly improved drafting, were reproduced in the now-defunct ITO Charter). The relevant GATT provisions were as follows:

[Article XI]

2. The provisions of paragraph 1 of this Article [prohibiting quantitative restrictions on imports and exports] shall not extend to the following:

*　*　*　*　*　*　*　*　*　*　*　*　*　*

34. See above, pp. 183-84.
35. Article XII.　　　　　　　　　36. Article XVIII.

(c) Import restrictions on any agricultural or fisheries product, imported in any form, necessary to the enforcement of governmental measures which operate:

(i) to restrict the quantities of the like domestic product permitted to be marketed or produced, or, if there is no substantial domestic production of the like product, of a domestic product for which the imported product can be directly substituted; or

(ii) to remove a temporary surplus of the like domestic product, or, if there is no substantial domestic production of the like product, of a domestic product for which the imported product can be directly substituted, by making the surplus available to certain groups of domestic consumers free of charge or at prices below the current market level; . . . .

*   *   *   *   *   *   *   *   *   *   *   *   *   *   *

Any contracting party applying restrictions on the importation of any product pursuant to sub-paragraph (c) of this paragraph shall give public notice of the total quantity or value of the product permitted to be imported during a specified future period and of any change in such quantity or value. Moreover, any restrictions applied under (i) above shall not be such as will reduce the total of imports relative to the total of domestic production, as compared with the proportion which might reasonably be expected to rule between the two in the absence of restrictions. In determining this proportion, the contracting party shall pay due regard to the proportion prevailing during a previous representative period and to any special factors which may have affected or may be affecting the trade in the product concerned.

[Article XX]

. . . nothing in this Agreement [including the prohibition against quantitative restrictions] shall be construed to prevent the adoption or enforcement by any contracting party of measures:

*   *   *   *   *   *   *   *   *   *   *   *   *   *   *

II. (c) essential to the orderly liquidation of temporary surpluses of stocks owned or controlled by the government of any contracting party . . . *Provided* that such measures shall not be instituted by any contracting party except after consultation with other interested contracting parties with a view to appropriate international action.

Measures instituted or maintained under Part II of this Article which are inconsistent with the other provisions of this Agreement [e.g., the prohibition against quantitative restrictions] shall be removed as soon as the conditions giving rise to them have ceased, and in any event not later than January 1, 1951; *Provided* that this period may, with the concurrence of the

CONTRACTING PARTIES,[37] be extended in respect of the application of any particular measure to any particular product by any particular contracting party for such further periods as the CONTRACTING PARTIES may specify.

Clearly these provisions, broad as they might seem, were something less than would be needed if full scope were given to Section 22 of the Agricultural Adjustment Act as it had been amended in 1940. Price-support programs alone, without restrictions on marketing or output could not be made the basis for import quotas under Section 22 without running afoul of the GATT. And while quotas could be used to protect certain domestic give-away programs,[38] they had to be strictly temporary affairs, such as would not satisfy long-term price-support operations related to a permanent parity concept. Temporary, also, was the right to use quotas as a transitional device for helping to dispose of government-held stocks at the end of the war; and this, too, was unrelated to long-term agricultural programs.

It has sometimes been suggested, in the light of later controversy over Section 22 versus GATT both in the Congress and in the GATT meetings, that there was no inconsistency between the GATT commitments quoted above and United States freedom to do as it wished under Section 22. This theory rests on the argument that the GATT, being a provisional instrument pending acceptance of the ITO Charter, bound its members to apply the rule against quotas (and certain other rules) only "to the fullest extent *not* inconsistent with existing legislation,"[39] i.e., Section 22. Whatever scope for legal dueling this language might give, this argument does not truly reflect what United States (and foreign) officials believed at the time. The true explanation is, first, that Section 22 was considered by both the Department of Agriculture and the Department of State to reserve a very large measure of discretion to the President. Indeed the "mile of latitude" afforded the President under Section 22 had been the subject of frequent complaint by Congressmen interested in its greater use. Under Section 22, therefore, the President was believed to have the authority to avoid applying import quotas unless the GATT requirements were met.

37. "CONTRACTING PARTIES" in capital letters refers to what may be more simply called the GATT organization, i.e., the members acting jointly and reaching decisions by majority vote.

38. The standard illustration given by Department of Agriculture officials to foreign governments was that, if the United States, in order to get rid of a temporary surplus of apples, gave them away through school-lunch programs, a temporary limit could be placed on imports of Canadian apples to keep them at their previous level.

39. Italics added. Protocol of Provisional Application of the General Agreement on Tariffs and Trade, paragraph 1 (b).

Secondly, although Congress, as has been indicated above, greatly broadened price-support operations to which the CCC was committed by law, the Department of Agriculture considered that it had ample legal authority to condition such price supports upon the acceptance by producers of adequate production or marketing controls in conformity with the GATT principle.

Finally, there is little doubt that most officials in the Department of Agriculture, at least those responsible for approving the GATT provisions, believed that the domestic programs would soon be readjusted to postwar needs. For these various reasons, the Department of Agriculture felt safe in reassuring foreign officials, especially the Canadians, that Section 22 could and would be operated in conformity with the GATT requirements.

Import fees.—The authority to use import fees, in lieu of or as a supplement to import quotas under Section 22, had been added to the law in 1940. The question presented in the GATT negotiations was whether, in the case of the many products that were made the subject of tariff concessions (more than 80 per cent of United States tariff rates were involved), the right should be retained to impose agricultural fees on top of the GATT rates under the same circumstances that would justify the use of import quotas. But fees were objectionable because they smacked of permanent tariff protection rather than an offset device. It was also hard to see how an import fee could be equated, as an import quota could, to a restriction on the like domestic product. The chances were that if agricultural fees were permitted—to others as well as the United States—they would tend to be more restrictive than import quotas whose size could be regulated by the reasonably precise standards of Article XI. Accordingly, it was agreed that the commitment as to tariff concessions would be unqualified.[40] Again, it was felt that the President had ample leeway under Section 22 to choose between quotas and fees and, accordingly, to enter into an international commitment not to use fees in preference to or as a supplement to a quota.

Subsidies.—Some of the sharpest of the GATT-ITO negotiating debates concerned the use of subsidies. It was easy enough to gain recognition by the trade experts of the various governments that, in principle, domestic subsidies in the form of direct governmental payments to producers on the whole of their production were usually to be preferred to tariffs or other import restrictions because they do not raise

40. Article II. It should be noted that under the Protocol of Provisional Application Article II was to be applied fully. It was not subject, like the quota prohibition in Article XI, to the qualification that it need be applied only "to the fullest extent not inconsistent with existing legislation."

consumer prices, they do not discriminate between markets, and their budgetary cost is a built-in limitation on their use. Hence, it was reasonable to say that governments should be allowed the safety valve of domestic subsidies at a time when they were attempting to reduce more serious trade barriers such as tariffs and quotas. Everyone seemed to agree (again in principle) that export subsidies were a more dangerous thing than domestic subsidies. By this device a government could keep its home prices high and yet take foreign markets away from its neighbors with a much smaller expenditure of money than a domestic subsidy would require. In short, ease of manipulation and tempting opportunities for trade distortion at little cost were features of the export subsidy which did not apply to the domestic subsidy. Therefore, in the effort to frame sensible rules of world trade, logic was on the side of a rule that forbade export subsidies and at the same time permitted domestic subsidies.

The main difficulty came in trying to fit these admirable principles to the facts of the United States agricultural program and the facts of the agricultural programs of certain foreign governments. There is little doubt, for example, that the United States is a relatively efficient wheat producer and the United Kingdom a relatively inefficient one. Under free trade the United Kingdom would import more of its wheat than it now does, and much of the wheat would come from the United States. Yet, given the nature of the domestic wheat program of the United States, the principles suggested above would at times prevent the United States from keeping its normal share of the world market for wheat, while they would allow the United Kingdom to expand its domestic output of wheat through the producer-payment system that it had instituted to help the British wheat farmer. Also, for countries such as Canada, which exports almost all of its wheat production, the distinction between export and domestic subsidies would be all but meaningless. In these instances it is hard to say that British and Canadian domestic subsidies would be less damaging to trade than a United States export subsidy. And there were other comparable situations involving other products and other countries.

The result was that no effective rules relating to subsidies could be agreed upon. GATT merely said that member governments must notify the GATT organization of their subsidies and, if they cause serious damage to anyone, be prepared to discuss the possibility of limiting them.[41] To be sure, some tortuous language was included in

41. Article XVI. In the 1955 review of GATT this article was amended to provide that export subsidies on primary products would not be used to acquire "more than an equitable share of world export trade."

the ITO Charter that sought to regulate export subsidies. As far as United States agricultural products were concerned, however, this amounted to little more than an undertaking to try to negotiate inter-governmental commodity agreements for surplus products before re-sorting to export subsidies and, in any case, not to use export subsidies to gain more than a fair share of the world export trade.

The multilateral trade rules developed during and immediately after the war, therefore, were designed to provide as full an accommodation as possible for the domestic agricultural policy of the United States short of writing agricultural products out of the multilateral trade arrange-ments entirely. They were somewhat stricter than the provisions com-monly included in the prewar bilateral trade agreements, but they gave leeway to agricultural import restrictions other than those of a flagrantly protectionist character and placed no serious limitations on the use of export subsidies. In short, the international trade policy objective of reducing barriers to world trade once again gave way at the point of conflict to the objectives of the domestic farm program. Failure to reach agreement on subsidies did not of course solve the real problem underly-ing the international controversy. Indeed, as will be seen, the increasing resort by the United States to export subsidization became perhaps an even more persistent cause of international friction in the trade field than its successive applications of import measures in contravention of the GATT principles.

COMPROMISE OF 1948

When in the spring of 1948 it became evident that Congress was determined to continue high price-supports not only for the "basics" but for the Steagall and other commodities brought within the program dur-ing the war, the Department of Agriculture, naturally enough, immedi-ately thought in terms of the possible use of Section 22 import restrictions to protect these additional programs. Although there was freedom under GATT to apply import quotas to these products provided domestic restrictions were imposed or other conditions met, it was discovered that there was no authority in domestic law to apply them. The power of the President under Section 22 was limited to those agricultural programs specifically authorized by the Agricultural Adjustment Act (including marketing agreements), the Soil Conservation and Domestic Allotment Act, and Section 32, but did not extend to the programs for Steagall com-modities such as milk, peanuts, and potatoes or other non-basics such as wool, barley, and rye. With the President's approval, therefore, the Secretary of Agriculture asked for a broadening of Section 22.

But if the commodity coverage of Section 22 was to be broadened, so as to include a number of products of which the United States was a net importer as well as the basic commodities of which it was a net exporter, the danger existed that pressures would develop for the use of Section 22 in ways that did not conform with GATT and for the purpose of raising domestic output at the expense of imports. This would be a more serious matter than the wheat and cotton quotas before the war. With this danger in prospect the Department of State proposed that whatever action affecting imports might be authorized by the new Section 22, it should not conflict with international agreements, such as, GATT, to which the United States is a party.

Congress accepted the proposals of both the Secretary of Agriculture and the Secretary of State. Section 3 of the Agricultural Act of 1948 amended Section 22 to authorize restrictions or fees on imports of any article that materially interfere with *"any loan, purchase, or other program or operation* undertaken by the Department of Agriculture."[42] Then it added a new subsection (f) to Section 22 stating that no action under Section 22 shall be taken in contravention of any treaty or international agreement to which the United States is a party. In addition, the President was given power to determine the base period for calculating the size of import restrictions and the old statutory base of 1929-1933 was repealed. This last change had the advantage that it would facilitate meeting the GATT requirement that import restrictions should at least reflect the proportions between imports and domestic output that prevailed during a previous "representative" period.

Thus, in 1948 a compromise was attempted with respect to agricultural import restrictions, not only between the international commitments of the United States and the plans and intentions of the Department of Agriculture but also between these commitments and the letter of the domestic law.

A flaw in the compromise was that the new law failed to make clear any intelligible principle. It did not state that import quotas were to be applied only when domestic controls were in effect, or to offset temporary and local cut-price programs to dispose of surpluses, or to help siphon off government-held stocks for a short transition period. Instead it repeated the old idea that imports must not "materially interfere" with a domestic program but then seemed to say that such interference would be tolerated if a trade agreement were involved. The new law reflected the issue of conflict rather than that of reconciliation. A layman or a Congressman might be pardoned if he could not

42. Italics added.

tell what the law meant or if he concluded that reasonable aid to the farmer was being hindered by trade agreements. This confusion may help to explain in part why only half the compromise stuck.

3. THE WIDENING CONFLICT

The postwar settlement of 1947-1948, in which, as we have seen, a partially successful attempt was made to reconcile the essential requirements of the domestic farm programs and the minimum standards of commercial behavior needed for a workable system of international trade relationships, lasted for only a short time. Pressures for breaking away from the limitations on United States freedom of action implied in the GATT agricultural arrangements boiled up from several directions. To some extent these pressures for damping imports and subsidizing exports were the natural consequence of the agricultural surpluses that began to build up as farm support programs were kept at inflated levels in relation to the demand for farm products. To be sure, certain elements of flexibility in support levels had been introduced by the Agricultural Act of 1948, and under the Agricultural Act of 1954 the general level of support was somewhat lowered. But most farm economists would have agreed that the support program as a whole since 1948 had been out of keeping with the realities of the demand situation.

To some extent pressures against the GATT were traceable to the cutback in United States agricultural exports after 1951-1952, and to the steady if modest rise in competitive agricultural imports throughout the postwar years. Some decrease in the tremendous outflow of agricultural exports that took place during the peak war and postwar years was to be expected as the postwar recovery of foreign agriculture proceeded with the help of United States aid programs and as the aid programs themselves were tapered off.[43] But when it came the decline was fairly sudden and sharp, its steepness accentuated by the continuation of foreign restrictions against United States exports, some of which were not always justified by the stringency of foreign monetary reserves.

Intermixed with these influences deriving from the domestic farm program and lower foreign demand was that of a revived protectionist movement. This was not confined to agriculture but also found its outlet in restrictive amendments to the Trade Agreements Act and in

43. During the war years agricultural exports, partly financed by Lend-Lease, ranged from $2.0 billions in 1941-1942 (fiscal year beginning July 1) to about $3.0 billions in 1944-1945. In the postwar years 1945-1946 through 1951-1952 they averaged $3.5 billions, partly financed by UNRRA relief, dollars spent under the Anglo-American Loan of 1947, and grant aid under the Marshall Plan. In 1951-1952 they reached a record high of $4.0 billions. In 1952-1953 they fell suddenly by 30 per cent to $2.8 billions.

demands for greater recourse to the "escape clause" in the case of a number of manufactured products as well as a few agricultural ones.[44]

Within a few years after the conclusion of GATT, Congress reversed its 1948 action by authorizing the use of Section 22 in disregard of GATT commitments; Congress itself imposed severe import restrictions on dairy products contrary to United States commitments under GATT. A series of restrictive actions under the revised Section 22 were then set in train, and the United States was ultimately forced by these events to rupture its GATT relationships to the extent of insisting that other member governments waive the GATT rules for any action that the United States might have to take under Section 22. In addition, a large program of cut-rate disposal of United States agricultural products in world markets was inaugurated, which was similar in its effects to export subsidies.

These various actions, and the prospect of more to come, naturally enough had their foreign repercussions. Protests were lodged by foreign governments over what seemed to be a developing determination by the United States to elbow its way into the world of agriculture. Foreign appreciation for the vast help previously given by the United States, much of it in the form of vital supplies of food and agricultural raw materials, was to a degree dissipated by the new and seemingly contradictory United States attitude. The fact that agricultural protectionism had also begun to reappear in the postwar economies of many foreign countries[45] did not help much to justify United States behavior except in a negative sense. Rather it lent point to the need for maintaining, and indeed adding to, the vigor of United States leadership toward freer international markets.

BROADENING THE LEGAL BASE OF SECTION 22

From 1948 on several attempts were made in Congress to "make Section 22 more effective" against competitive imports. Leadership for these efforts was provided by Senators Magnuson (D., Wash.) and Morse (then R., Ore.), and in the House by Representative Andresen (R., Minn.). The movement gathered behind it sufficient bipartisan support so that amendments seriously damaging to the trade program were held off for the time being only by the prospect of Presidential veto. Congressional critics contended that the Executive branch was evading the intent of Section 22 because it had been used only in two cases—wheat

44. The agricultural products involved in escape-clause actions were mostly small specialized products for which Section 22 help could not easily be invoked (e.g., garlic, figs, clover seed, and chicory). See Chap. III, pp. 169-73.

45. For example, the liberalization of intra-European trade under the Organization for European Economic Cooperation (OEEC) was much less successful in the agricultural-products sector than in the sectors of manufactures and non-agricultural raw materials.

and cotton—both dating from prewar days.[46] Charges were also made that the Section 22 procedures were administratively clumsy, were too time consuming, and gave too much latitude to the President and the Tariff Commission and not enough authority to the Secretary of Agriculture. The controversy was also colored by the running battle between the Executive and the Congress over GATT: "Congress adopted section 22. Congress did not adopt article 11 [of GATT], and it should have no part in the agricultural program."[47]

In 1950 Congress moved in the direction of Senator Magnuson's proposals by attaching a rider to the act of that year increasing the borrowing power of the CCC. The legislation that emerged, a compromise between the views of Senator Magnuson and the opposing views of the Administration, revised Section 22 in two respects. It tied the hands of the President in making any future international agreement that would inhibit United States freedom of action under Section 22 beyond the

46. In effect, however, the principles of Section 22 had also been applied in a third case, potatoes, by a special agreement with Canada in 1948. During the war, the government stimulated the expansion of potato output through various measures, including price supports and premium payments to growers. After the war, high support prices were continued for table-stock potatoes in accordance with the Steagall amendment and the Agricultural Act of 1948. Acreage allotments failed to hold production down, so that the CCC acquired tremendous stocks of potatoes which could neither be stored for very long nor sold except for low-grade use. In 1948 alone CCC acquisitions amounted to four million tons and financial losses to more than $200,000,000. The high support price also attracted abnormal imports from Canada. (Although Canadian potatoes normally command a premium over domestic, in December, 1948, the price for Maine potatoes was $2.70 per bushel or 92 cents above the price of $1.82 for Canadian potatoes across the border at Charlottetown, Prince Edward Island). Since Section 22 restrictions on imports of Canadian potatoes in the absence of effective production or marketing controls on the domestic crop would have been considered inconsistent with GATT, the President concluded an executive agreement with Canada under which the Canadian government undertook to limit exports to the United States and the United States agreed not to apply Section 22.

This agreement came before the courts as a result of a case brought by the United States government against a United States importer who had failed to honor his contract with the Canadian government not to divert imported seed potatoes (on which no restrictions were placed) to table use (*U.S.* v. *Guy W. Capps, Inc.*, 204 F. 2d 655 (4th Cir.), *cert granted*, 346 U.S. 884 (1953). The lower court held that the United States-Canadian executive agreement was invalid on the ground that by Section 22 Congress had limited the means open to the President for taking remedial action in the circumstances and that he could not constitutionally resort to the alternative of the executive agreement. The Supreme Court, however, ignored the constitutional issue when the case came before it in the fall of 1954 on appeal by the government, but it held for the importer on other ground not involving the validity of the executive agreement. The potato agreement was terminated in 1949 after support prices had been lowered from 90 to 60 per cent of parity. After 1951 price supports for potatoes were not authorized unless marketing quotas were in effect.

47. U.S. *Congressional Record*, 81st Cong., 2nd Sess., Vol. XCVI, Pt. 7 (June 26, 1950), remarks by Senator Magnuson, p. 9166.

inhibitions already established in GATT. And it vested in the Secretary of Agriculture statutory authority to take the first step in initiating Section 22 investigations. Heretofore, this authority had in fact been exercised by the Secretary, but his power stemmed from a delegation of authority by the President rather than from Congress.

These were seemingly slight changes. The first was not of immediate practical importance because the Administration had no intention of doing what the amendment sought to prohibit, i.e., tightening the international rules of GATT relating to agricultural import restrictions. But the new prohibition, though futile, gave some evidence of the developing temper of Congressional disapproval.

The importance of the second change lay more in a subtle shift of the status of the Secretary of Agriculture as the originator of Section 22 investigations than in any diminution of the President's ultimate authority to control the end result. No doubt it was thought that the President would be less willing to discourage his Secretary from initiating unwelcome action if the latter's legal power to do so stemmed from Congress rather than from the always revocable words of an Executive Order. It may also have been hoped that with his authority transferred from Executive Order to statute the Secretary would be less inclined to consult with other agencies of the government before setting the investigatory machinery in motion. In any event, by these concessions the Administration was able to fight off the more serious changes sought by Senators Magnuson and Morse—to remove the GATT limitation entirely, to reduce sharply the area of Presidential discretion, and, in lieu of investigations by the Tariff Commission, to authorize the Department of Agriculture to investigate its own programs.

The new law did not result in additional Section 22 restrictions. President Truman had asked the Tariff Commission in April, 1950, to conduct an investigation on tree nuts, which were of considerable interest to constituents of both Senators Magnuson (filberts) and Morse (filberts and walnuts). The unanimous report of the commission, submitted to the President in November, 1950, concluded that there was no basis for Section 22 action on the ground of import interference with the programs of the Department of Agriculture on tree nuts under the Marketing Agreement Act.

The bill for renewing the President's authority under the Trade Agreements Act, scheduled to expire in June, 1951, provided another opportunity for attacking Section 22. Heretofore, the amendments sought by Senator Magnuson and his supporters had been proposed in connection with agricultural legislation, to which opponents had brought the objection that since the amendments concerned trade they should be considered in a trade context. This was perhaps an unfortunate transfer of locale from the viewpoint of the trade-agreements program. For 1951 proved to be the year in which the Trade Agreements Act underwent a drastic transformation. In that year the cumulative demands of protected groups to check the process of further tariff reduction, and preferably to restore some tariffs to the higher levels of an earlier period, seemed to have come to a head. Senator Magnuson's proposal, or at least the essence of it, rode through on a wave of restrictive amendments. Some supporters of the trade-agreements program felt that the legislation was so bad that it should have been vetoed. In defense of the President's signature, it could be said that worse amendments were defeated and that a curtailed trade program might be better than none at all.

The basic change made in Section 22 by the Trade Agreements Extension Act of 1951 was simple and sweeping. Paragraph (f) of Section 22, which had previously stated that Section 22 should be applied consistently with trade-agreements commitments, now said that "no trade agreement or other international agreement heretofore or hereafter entered into by the United States shall be applied in a manner inconsistent with the requirements of this section." It seems likely that many members of Congress who voted for this provision did not realize the extent to which international trade commitments had already been fashioned to accommodate the domestic farm programs. But there can be little doubt of the Congressional intent to override international commitments, unilaterally if need be, in any remaining area of conflict found to exist.

The report of the Senate Finance Committee recommending the amendment contained a phrase that was designed to soften the issue but only served to sharpen it: "Where a choice of remedies under Section 22 makes it possible the President will choose a course not incompatible with our foreign commitments."[48] The obvious implication was that where this choice did not exist the commitments would be ignored. During the history of the trade-agreements program, this is the only instance on record of deliberate action by the Congress directing the President to violate trade-agreements commitments.[49]

48. U.S. Congress, Senate Committee on Finance, *Report* to accompany H.R. 1612, 82nd Cong., 1st Sess., Rep. No. 299, April 27, 1951, p. 7. There are only two "remedies" under Section 22: increased tariffs and absolute quotas. The first would be inconsistent with the tariff provisions of GATT applicable to all products, including most of those involved in domestic farm programs on which the United States had granted tariff concessions. The second would be inconsistent with the quota provisions of GATT unless the GATT conditions regarding restriction of domestic production, etc., were complied with.

49. There are other instances in which the Congress has adopted conflicting legislation

In addition to reversing the field on GATT, the 1951 amendments introduced a special provision for dealing with "perishable" products, an elastic description definite enough in the middle of the spectrum but hazy at each end. This revision authorized the President to take immediate action under Section 22 or under the escape clause—without waiting for the Tariff Commission to find out whether the action was necessary—"with regard to any agricultural commodity that due to the perishability of the commodity a condition exists requiring emergency treatment."[50] The language was awkward, but the purpose was clear. Under it the tree-nut interests and the fruit and vegetable growers, who had sponsored the change, could urge the President to act now and think later. The criticism on which this change was based—that the commission took too much time for study in emergency cases—was not borne out by the record. In the cases of cotton and wheat the commission had shown an ability to file its report with great speed where the matter was urgent. Delays were likely only where real urgency was wanting or the wisdom of action doubtful.

The Congressional decisions of 1951—more particularly the decision relating to GATT—might have been enough to open Section 22 to uses more closely akin to ordinary protection than to preventing "interference," rigorously defined[51] and also to lead the United States into the untenable position vis-à-vis the GATT countries in which it later found itself (see below). But Congress was not yet through. In 1953, after the change-over of administration, Section 22 was amended for the

without knowledge of its consequences (see the discussion below of the "cheese amendment"); or had directed the President to modify trade-agreements commitments by negotiation "as soon as practicable." But there is no other instance where Congress has knowingly compelled the violation of a commitment.

50. It was required also that in any event, the Tariff Commission must complete its study and the President must make his decision within twenty-five days after submission of the case to the commission.

51. It should be recalled that there *can* be cases in which abnormal imports are interfering with a domestic program, in the genuine and rigorous sense that the extra imports are induced by the program and are in fact preventing the program from operating with a reasonable level of government expenditure; and that even in such cases import restrictions could be inconsistent with the GATT rules. The best illustration would be that of a program that established domestic prices well above foreign prices but failed to limit domestic output or marketing; and in consequence of the higher domestic price imports increased to such a point that CCC expenditures were becoming unreasonably high. If in these circumstances imports were restricted to their "normal" level, that would be preventing "interference" in the genuine and rigorous sense meant above. But if this price-support-plus-import-quota system were long continued without controlling domestic supply, then the system as a whole would be indistinguishable from ordinary protection, for domestic supply would expand while imports remained static. This, of course, is why the main agricultural rule in GATT requires effective controls over the domestic product as a condition of import restrictions.

fourth time in the postwar period, by extending the "perishable" provisions quoted above to non-perishables as well. This amendment was
enacted as a part of the Trade Agreements Extension Act of 1953, intended to be a stop-gap measure pending the re-examination of United
States foreign economic policy later carried out by the Randall Commission. President Eisenhower accepted this change reluctantly in the
face of fairly clear evidence that the alternative would have been adoption
of another amendment—associated with Senator Cordon (R., Ore.)—
which would have removed the one remaining safeguard left in Section
22, the discretion of the President. The experiences of the new administration with the stiffening Congressional attitude on agricultural imports
evident in both Democratic and Republican quarters paved the way for
the application of Section 22 import quotas and fees to several trade-
agreement products during and after 1953. By 1954 Congress was apparently satisfied that Section 22 was at last being applied in accordance
with its wishes; no further amendments to the law have been seriously
proposed during the debates on subsequent trade-agreement-extension
acts.

THE "CHEESE AMENDMENT"

One of the more colorful episodes in the conflict between trade and
agriculture was the cheese legislation of 1951, which brought under import
control—in order, as the law said, to protect "the security interests of the
United States"—such strategic materials as Danish blue cheese, French
roquefort, and Italian provolone. Unlike most trade controversies this
one attracted wide public interest. It also became something of a *cause
célèbre* internationally.[52]

The circumstances under which this slur on the military significance
of the delicatessen trade managed to get through Congress was not so
much a criticism of the Congressional sense of proportion as it was a
commentary on the procedure through which legislative curiosities can
somtimes arrive on the statute books untested for sanity, relevance to
the public interest, or consistency with other governmental policies.
The history of the case also provides another illustration of the common-
place that once a restriction has been imposed on international trade
ways can usually be found to supply whatever may be missing from the
logic for its continuance.

52. For a good, fully-documented account of the legislative history of the cheese amendment, and the domestic and foreign reaction to it, see Gardner Patterson *et al.*, *Survey of
United States International Finance* (Princeton, N.J.: Princeton University Press) for the
years 1951, 1952, and 1953.

While the Senate Finance Committee was still considering the future of Section 22 in conjunction with the Trade Agreements Extension Act of 1951, the Banking and Currency Committee had before it a vestigial part of the old Second War Powers Act of 1942, a portion of the law whose life had been prolonged beyond its natural span in order to continue import controls—actually embargoes—on butter, peanuts, peanut oil, flaxseed, and rice. The bulk of the wartime trade-control system had been dismantled earlier, in 1949, when the international allocation of commodities in short supply had come to an end. But for these products the United States had continued to apply import controls in the language of GATT, as being "essential" either to the "acquisition or distribution of products in general or local short supply" or "to the orderly liquidation of temporary surpluses of stocks owned or controlled by the government" at the close of the war.[53]

By 1951 the use of this "escape" from the GATT rule against import quotas had worn very thin, and especially so with respect to butter, on which the United States had granted modest but psychologically important tariff concessions to New Zealand and Australia (Geneva, 1947) and Denmark (Annecy, 1949). When this residual segment of the Second War Powers Act came up for Congressional consideration in the spring of 1951, the Administration proposed that it be allowed to lapse, as scheduled, at the end of June.

Meanwhile, however, the Department of Agriculture had secured powers under Section 101 of the original Defense Production Act of 1950, which it felt would authorize import controls on certain of these commodities—notably flaxseed and rice and their products—on the theory that their diversion from United States shores could be justified on defense grounds connected with the new military program generated by the outbreak of the Korean hostilities.[54] As for butter and peanuts, the

53. Article XX, Part II (a) and (c). Originally, measures applied under Article XX, Part II, were subject to a time limit ending January 1, 1951, but this limit was later extended by the GATT members to January 1, 1954.

54. Section 101 authorized import restrictions as a part of the general powers that it granted to the President "to allocate materials and facilities in such manner, upon such conditions, and to such extent as he shall deem necessary or appropriate to promote the national defense." The products actually subject to import controls under Section 101 were flaxseed, flaxseed screenings, linseed oil (derived from flaxseed), and rice and rice products. None of these commodities was subject to United States tariff commitments under GATT. Rice imports have usually been negligible. Imports of flaxseed and linseed oil have come mainly from Argentina (not a GATT member but entitled to tariff concessions on flaxseed under a bilateral trade agreement with the United States), where they have been subject to export restrictions since the war. While some of these products, especially rice, had been in relatively stringent supply internationally in most of the postwar period, the bases for United States import controls under Section 101 of the

Administration contemplated a period of decontrol, to be followed by Section 22 investigations if the reimposition of controls should prove necessary. The new controls could be more liberal toward imports than the old embargoes around which vested interests had become encrusted; and they might, moreover, be made reasonably conformable to the GATT requirements regarding comparable domestic restrictions, domestic surplus disposal programs, and the size of any import quotas that might be established.

The cheese amendment, in the form of a new Section 104 of the Defense Production Act, was adopted on surprise motions from the floor offered in the Senate by Senator Magnuson and in the House by Representative Andresen when the debates were about to conclude on other 1951 amendments to the Act. The record indicates that in the Senate, at least, most members thought they were merely extending the hold-over provisions of the Second War Powers Act which would otherwise have expired. In fact, of course, the amendment not only continued the old import controls on peanuts, butter, rice, etc., but also brought all other dairy products under control, including cheese, and established entirely different and more restrictive criteria for the application of controls. There was little floor discussion and no public hearings or committee consideration. The Administration tried to have the offending section stricken while the bill was in conference, but the situation was then past saving. When identical provisions have been accepted by both Houses, it becomes nearly impossible to obtain their removal in conference, the primary purpose of which is to reconcile differences between the House and Senate versions. Since the 1951 extension of the Defense Production Act also carried with it money urgently required for the defense program, a Presidential veto was out of the question.

Section 104 provided that the Secretary of Agriculture must apply restrictions "necessary for the protection of the essential security interests and economy of the United States in the existing emergency in international relations,"[55] on imports of fats and oils, butter, cheese and other

---

Defense Production Act represented an odd assortment of this and other considerations. These controls were declared by the Secretary of Agriculture to be necessary to prevent diversion to the United States of supplies urgently needed by rearming allies, to encourage domestic output and reduce dependency on foreign sources during a possible war, and to relieve the burden on the rearmament-taxed transportation and distribution systems.

55. This wording was a transparent effort to bring the new restrictions within the security exception of GATT, whose Article XXI excepts from GATT commitments national actions that a country "considers necessary for the protection of its essential security interests . . . taken in time of war or other emergency in international relations." The Administration did not resort to this subterfuge in discussing the Section 104 restrictions at GATT meetings.

dairy products, peanuts, and rice,[56] to the extent that he found such restrictions necessary to prevent imports which would:

(a) impair or reduce the domestic production of any such commodity or product below present production levels, or below such higher levels as the Secretary of Agriculture may deem necessary in view of domestic and international conditions, or

(b) interfere with the orderly domestic storing and marketing of any such commodity or product, or

(c) result in any unnecessary burden or expenditures under any Government price support program.

Under this language the Secretary of Agriculture continued the earlier import embargoes on peanuts, peanut oil, flaxseed and its products, rice and its products, and butter and butter oil; embargoed non-fat dry milk solids; established import quotas, allocated country by country among foreign sources of supply, for each of the several varieties of cheese; and placed an import quota on casein.[57] Since the cheese quotas were small in any case, and since imports from the first of the year were counted against them, they amounted to an embargo on imports for the rest of 1951.

Nine foreign governments, seven of them GATT members and all entitled to trade-agreements concessions on dairy products, made formal representations to the United States regarding the new control measures: Argentina, Australia, Canada, Denmark, France, Italy, the Netherlands, New Zealand, and Switzerland. In some of these countries dairy exports formed a substantial segment of the export trade, and the larger part of domestic production depended upon world markets.[58] In some of them, also, the United States had actively promoted the development of the cheese industry under the Marshall Plan.[59] In one of them, Italy, the

56. The full list read: "fats and oils (including oil-bearing materials, fatty acids, and soap and soap powder, but excluding petroleum and petroleum products and coconuts and coconut products), peanuts, butter, cheese and other dairy products, and rice and rice products."

57. The casein control was quickly dropped (December, 1951). Since almost two-thirds of total United States consumption of casein is imported, it seems probable that industrial consumers (chiefly the textile and cement industries) were responsible for effecting removal of the quota.

58. In 1951 dairy products accounted for 25 per cent of the total exports of New Zealand; 20 per cent of the total exports of Denmark; and 10 per cent of the total exports of the Netherlands. In 1952 New Zealand exported 80 per cent of its butter production and 90 per cent of its cheese; Australia 20 per cent of its butter and 50 per cent of its cheese; Denmark 75 per cent of its butter and 66 per cent of its cheese; and the Netherlands 67 per cent of both.

59. The European Cooperation Administration (ECA) had actively encouraged the expansion of the cheese industry in Denmark and Italy as a part of its efforts to reduce the dollar gap and eliminate dependence on extraordinary assistance from the United States.

cheese industry particularly affected the poorer regions in which Italian democratic elements were attempting, through economic improvement, to combat Communism. And with respect to another, Denmark, the cheese restrictions came at a time when the United States was trying to dissuade the Danish government from certain trade transactions in strategic items with the Soviet Union, which the Danish government partly justified on the need to make up for some of Denmark's shortage of dollar exchange. In comparison with the damaging impact of the cheese restrictions on United States relations with foreign countries, their significance for the United States dairy industry seemed close to trivial: in 1950, immediately before the restrictions, total imports of cheese into the United States— worth about $25 million—amounted to no more than ½ of 1 per cent of domestic cheese production. And the value of cheese production in the United States accounted for no more than 10 per cent of farm income from dairying.

But foreign governments were more concerned over the long-term policy implications of Section 104 than they were about the immediate losses of trade involved. The memorandum presented by the Italian government to the Department of State sounded a note that was echoed by the other governments. After stating that Italy was encouraged by the trend towards "trade-not-aid," whereby it could re-establish normal trade relations with the United States by earning and paying its own way through exports, the Italian memorandum continued:

> There have been, however, indications in recent months that, while the American Government continues to be fully committed to the principle of trade liberalization, renewed recourse is being made to restrictive practices and that the inconsistencies between principle and practice, far from disappearing, are once more increasing. Should this new trend continue unchecked, a very serious situation would result. Much of the progress made through GATT and other agreements would be undone and many of the gains of the Marshall Plan would be wasted. Such a prospect is naturally viewed by the Italian Government with considerable alarm, and it is a matter of major concern, particularly under the current unsettled conditions of the international and European economy.[60]

The restrictions on dairy products under Section 104 were, of course, inconsistent with the GATT commitments. The GATT members decided at their meeting in Geneva in the fall of 1951 that the breach was sufficiently flagrant to warrant retaliation against the United States by the other countries affected.[61] However, they recommended that such

60. U.S. Dept. of State, Press Release No. 286 (April 16, 1952), pp. 5-6.
61. Resolution of October 26, 1951, adopted at the sixth session of the contracting parties. The resolution found that "the import restrictions in question constitute an

action not be taken until the United States had had an opportunity to carry forward its proposal to seek repeal of Section 104 when the further extension of the Defense Production Act came up for consideration in the following session of Congress. Although the Administration's request for outright repeal early in 1952 was backed by a respectable body of support,[62] the strength of the dairy interests was such that Congress would consent to no more than a slight modification of the control system, effected in July, 1952.[63] Consequently, when the GATT members met again in the fall of 1952, they acceded to the request of the Netherlands— the only affected country that chose to exercise its rights—for authority to cut back on Dutch imports of wheat flour from the United States by way of compensation.[64]

infringement of Article XI" of the Agreement; that concessions granted by the United States "have been nullified or impaired within the meaning of Article XXIII" of the Agreement; and that "the circumstances are serious enough to justify recourse to Article XXIII paragraph 2" (authorizing the withdrawal of concessions from an offending party) by the contracting parties affected. GATT, *Basic Instruments and Selected Documents*, Vol. II, May, 1952, p. 16.

62. Along with many other private organizations, the largest of the farm organizations, the American Farm Bureau Federation, strongly advocated repeal of Section 104. Identification of the supporters and opponents of Section 104, and the arguments they used, can be found in U.S. Senate Committee on Banking and Currency, *Hearings* on S. 2594 and S. 2645, 82nd Cong., 2nd Sess., March, 1952, Parts 1 and 2.

63. Certain technical changes were introduced which allowed the Secretary of Agriculture to increase quotas by 15 per cent (if he considered this advisable after "taking into consideration the broad effects upon international relationships and trade"), and which, in the language of the Conference Committee on the Defense Production Act amendments of 1952, directed him to exempt from control "types of cheeses, such as Roquefort and Switzerland Swiss, which, because of their United States selling price, are clearly not competitive with domestically produced cheeses." Lifted from control in July, 1952, were Swiss, Gruyere, Roquefort, and Italian cheese made from sheep's milk (mainly Pecorino). Kept under control with slight quota increases in some cases were Cheddar, Blue-mold, Edam, Gouda, and Italian cheeses made from cow's milk (e.g., Reggiano, Parmesano, Provolone, Provolette, and Sbrinz). The resulting distinction drawn between types of cheeses supplied by different countries led to charges of discrimination against the United States in addition to those based on the purely restrictionist aspect. The butter, peanut, rice, and flaxseed embargoes were not affected, although the Secretary later removed from control some minor rice and flaxseed products.

64. Determination of November 8, 1952, seventh session of the contracting parties, which authorized the Netherlands to reduce imports of United States wheat flour during the calendar year 1953 to sixty thousand metric tons. An accompanying resolution of the same date reaffirmed the earlier GATT resolution regarding the inconsistency of Section 104 restrictions with GATT and recommended that the U.S. continue its efforts to obtain repeal "as the only satisfactory solution of this problem." GATT, *Basic Instruments*, First Supplement, March, 1953, p. 32. This incident illustrates the relative ineffectiveness of actual retaliation—as distinct from the threat of it—as a means of inducing good international behavior in the trade field. It also points up a perplexing problem in this area—the difficulty that governments encounter in choosing retaliatory import restrictions that do not do as much damage to themselves as to the offending party. The Netherlands action was undoubtedly taken despite some harm that it brought to the Dutch economy because of popular resentment against the United States and the matter of principle involved.

Whatever improvement in the international atmosphere may have been accomplished by the relaxations of the cheese quotas in July, 1952, it was more than offset by the action of the out-going Secretary of Agriculture, announced in December, 1952, sharply restricting imports of dried whole milk, dried buttermilk, and dried cream in order to minimize government expenditures under the price-support program for butterfat and milk solids. A fresh wave of protests came from New Zealand, the Netherlands, Denmark, Italy, Australia, Sweden, and Canada. In March, 1953, the new Secretary of Agriculture replaced these import quotas with complete embargoes.

SECTION 22 ACTIONS AFTER 1952

Apart from continuing the prewar wheat and cotton quotas, and negotiating the short-lived potato restriction with Canada,[65] the Administration had applied Section 22 restrictions to only one product in the postwar period up to the end of 1952. In December, 1951, and again in September, 1952, President Truman had accepted Tariff Commission recommendations for Section 22 fees on imports of almonds (on which no trade-agreement concession had been granted), while rejecting its proposal in 1952 for an absolute quota on imports of filberts (which were subject to GATT commitments with respect to both tariffs and quotas).[66]

Until 1953, therefore, the Administration had consistently refrained

65. See above, footnote 46.

66. U.S. Tariff Commission, *Edible Tree Nuts:* Reports to the President Under Section 22, November, 1950; November, 1951; and September, 1952. The President's proclamation of September 27, 1952, imposed, in addition to the ordinary import tariff of 16½ or 18½ cents per pound, a fee of 5 cents per pound, but not more than 50 per cent ad valorem, on shelled almonds imported during October 1, 1952–September 30, 1953, up to a quantity of 7,000,000 pounds, and a fee of 10 cents per pound, but not more than 50 per cent ad valorem, on imports in excess of that quantity. Traditionally the major foreign supplier of almonds to the United States has been Spain, with which the United States does not have a trade agreement; but in recent years the principal share has been supplied by Italy, a GATT member. In accordance with the general practice of the United States of limiting tariff concessions to those products of which the trade-agreement partner is normally a principal supplier, no tariff concession on almonds was granted in GATT, and hence the United States was not precluded by international commitments from applying to almonds the fees recommended by the Tariff Commission. With respect to filberts, the commission recommended the establishment of an absolute quota of 4,500,000 pounds during the period October 1, 1952–September 30, 1953. Filberts are imported chiefly from Turkey and Italy and the United States had granted a tariff concession on this product in the GATT negotiations with these countries at Torquay (1951). Moreover, since the Tariff Commission had recommended an absolute import quota, a question of consistency with the GATT provisions on agricultural import quotas was involved. In rejecting the filbert quota President Truman stated that the threat of interference with the domestic program did not appear serious enough to justify restrictive action. He noted that the burden of the restriction would fall on Turkey, whose trade with the United States had been adversely affected by the recent escape-clause action on figs.

from applying Section 22 in ways contrary to United States commercial policy understandings with other countries. But it had not been successful in preventing Congress from taking matters into its own hands. The cheese amendment was still on the books, and there seemed to be a growing determination in some Congressional quarters to try to remove entirely the President's discretion under Section 22 unless he demonstrated a willingness to apply it with more vigor.

Beginning in 1953 a marked shift took place in the roles of the Executive and legislative branches with respect to agricultural import restrictions. The Executive branch retreated a considerable distance from its earlier opposition to agricultural restrictions that conflicted with trade agreements and began to apply Section 22 in a manner conforming to the demands for restrictive action being voiced in Congress. Congress, in turn, allowed Section 104 to expire and after 1953 refrained from further restrictive legislation in the agricultural field. The shift began with the Section 104 commodities. Following an investigation by the Tariff Commission ordered by President Eisenhower in April, 1953, the President proclaimed Section 22 quotas or fees on butter, dried milk products, cheese (including all types then subject to control under Section 104), peanuts, peanut oil, flaxseed, and linseed oil.[67] A few days later he revived the earlier commission report on filberts, which had been rejected by President Truman, and proclaimed an absolute import quota for the balance of the crop year. In October, 1953, following a commission recommendation for an import quota on oats,[68] the United States negotiated an arrangement with Canada under which Canada agreed to restrict Canadian exports of oats to the United States in lieu of Section 22 action. In March, 1954, Section 22 quotas were proclaimed for rye and its products.[69] In November, 1954, following a Tariff Commission recommendation for import quotas on tung oil and tung nuts,[70] the United States negotiated an understanding with Argentina and Paraguay under which these countries agreed to limit exports of tung oil and tung nuts to the United States in lieu of Section 22 quotas. In October, 1954,

67. U.S. Tariff Commission, *Specified Manufactured Dairy Products, Flaxseed and Linseed Oil, Peanuts and Peanut Oil, Tung Nuts and Tung Oil:* Report to the President Under Section 22, June, 1953. Section 22 action on these products was made conditional on the expiration of Section 104 of the Defense Production Act, which Congress permitted to lapse after it became clear that Section 22 restrictions would in fact be applied.

68. U.S. Tariff Commission, *Oats, Hulled or Unhulled, and Unhulled Ground Oats:* Report to the President Under Section 22, October, 1953.

69. U.S. Tariff Commission, *Rye and Rye Flour and Rye Meal:* Report to the President Under Section 22, March, 1954.

70. U.S. Tariff Commission, *Tung Nuts and Tung Oil:* Report to the President Under Section 22, September, 1954.

Section 22 quotas were proclaimed for barley and its products.[71] Earlier restrictions on imports of dairy products were broadened in 1957 when Section 22 quotas were imposed on butter substitutes, including butter oil, and on certain articles containing butterfat.[72]

Most of these limitations have continued in effect since their establishment, although for some of them the amounts originally fixed have been changed. The original undertakings by foreign governments to limit exports have been later replaced by formal Section 22 quotas. As a rule, the size of the absolute quotas, or of the tariff quotas subject to Section 22 fees, that were proclaimed by the President have been somewhat less restrictive of imports than the amounts recommended by the Tariff Commission. Those relating to dairy products, fats and oils, peanuts, etc., were less restrictive than the treatment required under Section 104, but were nevertheless heavily protective.[73]

By the end of 1955, a large number of the agricultural commodities for which domestic support programs were in effect had been made subject to import quotas or fees. An important exception was wool, which in many ways is of more significance to United States international trade policy than any other competitive agricultural import.[74] During 1953 both the Department of Agriculture and the Tariff Commission (although by a split vote of four to two) recommended Section 22 fees on wool, an action whose effects on trade relations with Australia, New Zealand, and South Africa might well have unraveled the network of United States trade-agreements commitments with the whole of the British Commonwealth. The proposal for raising the wool tariff was strongly opposed by the domestic wool-manufacturing industry. Normally inclined to favor high tariffs, the wool fabricators in this case objected to a higher tariff on raw wool because its price-raising effect on finished

71. U.S. Tariff Commission, *Barley, Hulled or Unhulled, Including Rolled Barley and Ground Barley, and Barley Malt:* Report to the President Under Section 22, September, 1954.

72. U.S. Tariff Commission, *Butter Substitutes, including Butter Oil, containing 45 percent or more of butterfat:* Report to the President Under Section 22, March, 1957; and U.S. Tariff Commission, *Certain Articles containing 45 percent or more of butterfat or of butterfat and other fat or oil:* Report to the President Under Section 22, July, 1957.

73. For a survey of the investigations made by the Tariff Commission and the actions taken by the President under Section 22, see U.S. Tariff Commission, *Investigations Under Section 22 of the Agricultural Adjustment Act,* Outcome or Current Status of all Investigations, 4th ed., May, 1958; and 5th ed., July, 1960.

74. Wool has great significance in United States trade policy because it is one of the largest dutiable imports—around $200 million annually; because it is one of the largest dollar earners for the Sterling Area and British Commonwealth; because the United States-Commonwealth understanding on trade policy could easily collapse under the strain of higher tariffs or quotas on United States imports of wool; and because this understanding provides the underpinning on which any wide international trade arrangement, such as GATT, must rest.

woolen goods would handicap them in the intensifying market battle with nylon, dacron, and other synthetic fibers.

Against this background the President turned down the idea of an import fee on wool and instead requested legislation from Congress, which would replace the earlier method of price supports by a system of direct payments to wool growers financed by earmarking customs revenue from the existing wool tariff. These recommendations were accepted by Congress, with some adjustments favoring the wool growers, and became incorporated in the National Wool Act of 1954. Thus, further restrictions on the wool trade and the consequent breaching of trade-agreements commitments on wool were avoided. The new arrangement also prevented the contraction of domestic consumption and the depressing effect on imports which would have followed from raising prices. Nevertheless, the National Wool Act of 1954 added substantially to the *net* protection against import competition previously afforded the domestic industry. For under the old system of price support the returns to growers could not be supported in excess of 90 per cent of parity; under the new system the maximum was boosted to 110 per cent, and ample funds for the purpose were provided. If enlarging the returns to domestic growers proves to be a determining factor in reversing the decline of the domestic wool industry, the National Wool Act of 1954 would seem to be more effective for the purpose than the earlier system.

THE GATT WAIVER

A modern writer on international trade theory has observed that because of the real or presumed benefits that national governments may anticipate from trade restrictions, and because of the political effectiveness of special interest groups, an international free-trade system has a natural tendency to disintegrate and must be enforced by some kind of international convention.[75] The judgment holds equally well for modest systems falling far short of free trade and would have been sound even in the absence of the author's premise that carefully designed trade restrictions can yield a net economic gain to the country imposing them (although admittedly at some other country's greater expense). In the postwar period the international convention devised for the purpose of preventing the disintegration of the movement toward freer trade has been the GATT. The extent to which it can accomplish this purpose is dependent not only on the substance of the "freer-trade" rules that it embodies but on the observance of those rules by member governments.

75. Tibor de Scitovszky, "A Reconsideration of the Theory of Tariffs," *The Review of Economic Studies,* IX (Summer, 1942), 89-110.

To be sure, no set of rules can be inflexible without various "escapes" and safety valves, or the convention would break under the strain imposed upon it by the divergent pulls of national governments responding to the urgencies of local situations. But neither can the rules be so elastic that they fit with comfort whatever nationalistic trade posture a government may choose to take, or the convention would be meaningless. In any case, the integrity of the convention requires that such rules as are agreed upon be observed in reasonable good faith, or be suitably changed. Weak rules that are observed, if not too weak to be useful, are a surer guarantee against disintegration than strong rules that are flouted.

It is obvious from what has been said elsewhere that beginning in 1951 the course of agricultural policy in the United States was such as to propel the United States government away from the GATT rules on agricultural trade. For a time this movement was not too serious. Even though the restrictions on dairy products were an abrupt departure from the GATT precepts, as well as damaging to foreign relations, this was frankly recognized by the Executive branch, and genuine efforts were made to remove them. But the series of Section 22 quotas and fees which made their appearance after 1952—this time seemingly endorsed by the Executive branch rather than being forced upon it by unconsidered acts of Congress—inevitably led the United States into an untenable position in the GATT society. Whatever rationalizations might be introduced to justify the ways of Section 22 to the ways of GATT, the sense of the GATT community was that the United States was not carrying out its commitments in good faith.

In these circumstances the choice facing the United States, if the integrity of the GATT arrangement was not to be seriously undermined, was either to modify the Section 22 actions it had taken or to try to regularize their legal position under GATT. The latter course was the one decided upon. During the general review of the GATT's provisions early in 1955, which was held in accordance with the desire of many member governments to re-examine their commitments in the light of postwar experience, the United States obtained a waiver from the GATT rules for any Section 22 actions that it had taken in the past or might have to take in the future.

The waiver was open-end: it did not require prior approval by the GATT members of future Section 22 actions that might contravene the GATT rules, nor was it subject to any time limit. It did, however, require that the United States afford to other interested member governments an opportunity to consult with it, and to make suitable representations, before taking further Section 22 actions; that it review existing ones upon request; and that it remove or modify restrictions where circumstances might make this possible. It also reserved the right of affected countries to take retaliatory action against the United States. In granting the waiver, the parties to the GATT declared their "regret that circumstances make it necessary for the United States to continue to apply import restrictions which, in certain cases, adversely affect the trade of a number of contracting parties, impair concessions granted by the United States and thus impede the attainment of the objectives of the General Agreement."[76]

The negotiation through which United States officials obtained the support of the great majority of the GATT members for the Section 22 waiver has been called a skillful one. But the skill lay rather in containing the potential spread of the Section 22 philosophy to many other countries than in securing a waiver for the United States. Given the economic power of the United States and its determination to apply Section 22 quotas and fees in any case, the granting of the waiver was perhaps a foregone conclusion. Other factors at work, to which some weight must be given, were that the magnitude of the farm surpluses burdening the United States attracted a degree of understanding from other governments that might have been missing a year or two earlier, and that by 1955 the new Administration could point to the fact that it had taken steps that promised to prevent further surplus accumulation by adjusting domestic price-support programs to more reasonable levels.

But some damage was done, the ultimate extent of which is not yet clear. At the time the waiver was granted to the United States for Section 22, certain waivers were also given to other governments, although these were made subject to stringent conditions not applicable to the United States.[77] The danger is not yet over that the precedent set by the United States for agricultural products may be followed by others, a development that might mean the eventual abandonment of the postwar attempt to apply an international code of behavior for agricultural trade.

SURPLUS DISPOSAL

Traditional international trade policy has always frowned more heavily on the practice of squeezing the other fellow out of some foreign

76. Decision of March 5, 1955. GATT, *Basic Instruments,* Third Supplement, June, 1955, p. 35.

77. A so-called "hard-core" waiver from the GATT's no-quota rules authorized the continuation of import restrictions beyond the time when they would be justified by balance-of-payments difficulties if their sudden removal would cause serious injury to a domestic industry; but each such restriction had to be approved by a majority of the GATT members in advance. See *ibid.,* pp. 38-41. This waiver has been used only by Belgium, exclusively for the purpose of protecting agricultural production.

market than on forcing him out of the domestic. Thus, preferences, discriminations, and bilateralism, by which the exports of one country can be favored over those of another, have been singled out for special condemnation. Import tariffs and quotas to protect the home market with an even hand against all foreign invasion have received wider tolerance.

The distinction between the home and foreign markets has been drawn not so much because of a nice calculation that it is measurably more "uneconomic" to fence off foreign markets than to curtail foreign access to the domestic market.[78] Rather the distinction has originated as a historical delineation of "rights" in the long moral and political struggle of sovereign governments to get along with each other. Out of this struggle there has grown the feeling that although there is an inherent right of each national government to reserve its home market for domestic producers—a right that can be controlled only by intergovernmental contract—it is an invasion of the rights of other sovereign governments, even though these rights may not be recorded anywhere, for one government to gain exclusive protection for its producers in the market of another country. A good, although perhaps extreme, illustration of this attitude can be found in the policy of the United States during the 1920's that insisted upon nondiscriminatory treatment for United States exports but asserted that the height of the United States tariff, as long as it was nondiscriminatory, was solely a matter of domestic concern.[79] It is this attitude, which, at bottom, accounts for the fact that the unconditional most-favored-nation (MFN) clause reached a high stage of development in international relations while national governments were as yet unwilling to make any serious or concerted attempt to reduce the protective walls with which they sheltered their domestic markets against all foreign competition as a whole.

Export bounties and subsidies and other kinds of "dumping" receive the same moral frown in the international trade community as discrimination and preference. Their effect is similar. By means of them the producers of the exporting country gain a special position in some foreign market at the expense of producers in a competing export country. A

78. To be sure, economists and officials have long pointed out that, in general, nondiscrimination is a policy to be preferred to discrimination on economic grounds alone. But this is a different thing from comparing the damage done by discrimination with that done by domestic protection. In making the latter comparison general principles alone are of little help, since account must be taken of the degree of discrimination, the height of protection, and the size of the markets affected by both. Attempts to formulate judgments of this kind—for example, that the United States protective system is better or worse economically than the Commonwealth preferential system—have been unconvincing.

79. See Chap. I, pp. 48-53.

United States export subsidy on, say, wheat to Japan, will evoke more bitterness in Canada than United States import quotas under Section 22 on, say, Canadian barley, oats, and rye.

The history of United States experience with export subsidies has been given earlier: they were applied to wheat and cotton with some plausible claim that they would not effect an invasion of foreign markets; but, even so, they were a source of trouble in United States foreign relations. And in the postwar trade negotiations resulting in GATT no effective rules limiting export subsidies could be agreed upon because of the nature of the United States agricultural program.

This hiatus in the trade rules began to be more serious in the 1950's when United States agricultural surpluses began again to assume large proportions and when producers and legislators began to look to foreign markets as the place to unload them. In this new search the technique of direct export subsidization with Section 32 funds began to be overshadowed by another device that had been learned in the experience of Lend-Lease and the Marshall Plan: the use of agricultural surpluses as a means of giving foreign aid. To be sure, Section 32 subsidies were used from time to time in the postwar period and were a subject of discussion at GATT meetings,[80] but from the viewpoint of foreign countries, the larger threat of United States dumping operations seemed to come from the new disposal-aid programs.

The American Farm Bureau Federation can perhaps be credited (or, from the viewpoints of some foreign countries, debited) for the disposal-aid method of moving surpluses into the world market. Building on the experience of the Marshall Plan with counterpart funds,[81] the Bureau suggested that the Mutual Security Program carry certain appropriations for aid in the form of agricultural surpluses, the recipient governments to contribute an equivalent value in local currencies that could be used for mutual security purposes. The result was the passage of Section 550 of the Mutual Security Act of 1953 directing the use of $100 to $250

80. United States export subsidies have been regularly reported to the GATT forum (as required by Article XVI) where they have often been the subject of complaint by other fruit-exporting countries.

81. Under the European Recovery Program each country receiving United States grant aid was required to contribute an equivalent amount in local currency to a counterpart fund that could then be used for retiring governmental debt, for local currency loans to producers, or for other purposes intended to further economic recovery in Europe. Except for small percentages reserved for payment of administative expenses of the United States govenment, counterpart funds were the property of the European government concerned, but could only be spent by agreement between that government and the United States. The counterpart idea was continued under the Marshall Plan's successor, the Mutual Security Program, although the use of the funds was more restricted.

million of program funds for exports of agricultural surpluses. This was not too different from the earlier practice of allocating certain Lend-Lease and ECA funds for United States agricultural products, except that in the earlier period the allocations were usually well below the amounts that would have been taken anyway and the justification for the Mutual Security Act appropriation appeared to rest more on the desire to get rid of surpluses than on the need for foreign aid.

The new program was quickly expanded. In 1954 Section 550 was continued (through Section 402 of the Mutual Security Act of 1954), and appropriations were increased to $350 million. But more important, Congress enacted separate surplus-disposal legislation in the Agricultural Trade Development and Assistance Act of 1954, better known as Public Law 480. Under this legislation some $700 million additional money was provided to promote the "sale of surplus agricultural commodities for foreign currencies" (Title I) and $300 million to transfer agricultural commodities to friendly countries in order "to meet famine or other urgent relief requirements" or "to friendly but needy populations without regard to the friendliness of their government" (Title II). In 1955 Title I appropriations were increased to $1,500 million; in 1956 another $1,500 million in sales authority was added. By June, 1957, the entire $3,000 million worth of surplus commodities had been contracted for and, in response to the President's request, the Congress authorized an additional $1 billion. In 1958 another $2,250 million was added; in 1959 another $3,000 million; and in 1961 another $2,000 million, making $11,250 million in all.[82] Mindful of the charges of export dumping that some friendly countries might level at the United States, the Act directs the President to "take reasonable precautions ... to assure that sales ... will not unduly disrupt world prices of agricultural commodities."

The device of selling United States agricultural surpluses for the local currency of the importing country, instead of for dollars or other convertible currencies, was intended to get around the obstacle of balance-of-payments restrictions against United States exports. It should be noted that, unlike the counterpart funds created under the Marshall Plan, the local currencies received for agricultural products exported under Title I of Public Law 480 become the property of the United States government. Still, large amounts of such currencies can hardly be used by the United States except for assistance purposes, that is, for grants or loans to foreign

82. The 14th Semiannual Report on Activities of The Food-for-Peace Program Carried on Under Public Law 480, 83rd Congress, as Amended, 87th Cong., 1st Sess., House Document No. 223, August 14, 1961, p. 1. Total authorizations under Title II are $1,400 million.

countries, without intensifying the balance-of-payments difficulties of the country concerned.[83]

Even if such currencies were used, for example, to purchase strategic materials for the United States military stockpile, such purchases would have to be over and above normal stockpile purchases of foreign materials; otherwise, the usual flow of dollars to foreign countries arising from stockpile operations would be diminished; and the net result of the entire transaction—export of agricultural surpluses and import of strategic materials—would be to place a strain on the foreign exchange reserves of the foreign country concerned.[84] It is best, therefore, to consider the programs under Title I primarily as a means of disposing of United States agricultural surpluses in such a way as to contribute to foreign aid.

In addition to the disposal-aid program under Title I of Public Law 480 and the disposal-relief program under Title II, Congress authorized the CCC to engage in international barter transactions (Title III). Under this authority agricultural surpluses are exchanged directly for strategic and certain other materials. By the end of fiscal 1957 some $900 million worth of agricultural commodities had been exported under barter contracts.[85] By mid-1961 another $500 million worth of contracts had been concluded, making $1,400 million in all.[86]

Public Law 480 was originally regarded as a temporary measure. It has been extended several times, and under the slogan "Food-for-Peace" it has virtually become permanent legislation. It has lifted United States export subsidization to a wholly different magnitude, one that to many countries has seemed to threaten the continued existence of a substantial portion of their export trade.

No one can object in principle to the good sense and humanitarianism

83. The law provides that local currencies received through programs under Title I of the Act may be used for (a) developing new markets for United States agricultural commodities; (b) buying strategic materials for the military stockpile; (c) buying military equipment, materials, facilities, and services for the common defense; (d) financing the purchase of goods or services for other friendly countries; (e) promoting balanced economic development and trade among nations; (f) paying United States obligations abroad; (g) making loans to promote multilateral trade and economic development; and (h) financing international educational exchange activities. Programs under Title II of the Act contemplate the transfer of agricultural products directly on a grant basis and do not require the creation of local currency deposits owned by the United States for which some further use must be found.

84. Foreseeing this need, Congress in the terms of the Act authorized the use of foreign currencies to build supplemental stockpiles. But this, too, is not free of difficulty; for presumably the United States already stockpiles all that it reasonably needs for military preparedness, and the building up of over-large stockpiles creates its own brand of nervousness in commodity markets.

85. Raymond F. Mikesell, *Agricultural Surpluses and Export Policy* (Washington, D.C.: American Enterprise Association, 1958), p. 13.

86. *14th Semiannual Report on the Food-For-Peace Program*, p. 2.

of giving to hungry people food that otherwise would go to waste. Once surpluses have been created, it seems far better to give them away than to destroy them, or even than to carry them in storage year after year at a very substantial cost.[87]   Moreover, if surpluses can be used to promote economic development abroad, an important objective of United States foreign policy can be furthered.   The problem is how can this be done without at the same time depriving of their livelihood people in other countries engaged in producing and selling the same commodities to the same hungry populations who are the recipients of United States generosity?   The only way in which large stocks can be given away rapidly without danger of this result is by simultaneously increasing, by an equal amount, total consumption of the commodities concerned in the aid-receiving countries.   This is no easy task.   There are often difficult problems of internal distribution and consumption habits within the aid-receiving countries.   There is also the temptation on the part of aid-receiving countries to reduce imports from other countries of commodities received as a gift from the United States in order to conserve scarce foreign exchange.   If these and similar difficulties are surmounted, then there can be no reasonable objection on the part of foreign countries to the disposal-aid operation, which becomes a trade-creating device rather than a trade-diverting one.   To the extent that they are not surmounted, then the disposal-aid program has the usual effects of an export subsidy and, as such, is properly a matter of foreign complaint.

But supposing the disposal-aid program is successful in avoiding the disruption of other countries' export markets, its success might not be an unmixed blessing.   It is often politically more attractive at home to deal with the farm problem by means that create surpluses than by means that gear agricultural production to demand.   And the fact that surpluses sometimes get too large even for politicians to explain is one of the few forces working toward more rational farm policies.   The suppression of the surpluses by creating subsidized outlets for them abroad, therefore, might simply delay for a time adjustments that will one day prove to be necessary, and make these adjustments harder both for the United States and for those foreign-consuming countries that have meanwhile become accustomed to receiving agricultural products on a subsidized or grant basis.   It would seem an unlikely conjuncture of events that the United States will wish permanently to give foreign aid to particular countries and also that the aid that those countries can regularly use will be in the form of just those agricultural commodities of which the United States produces persistent surpluses through its farm policies.

87. Annual storage costs attributable to government-held stocks have run as high as $1 billion annually.

CHAPTER V

The United Kingdom, the Commonwealth, the Common Market, and the United States

A prime objective of United States commercial policy before, during, and after World War II has been to end the British Commonwealth system of preferential trade, which was firmly established and extended in the Ottawa Agreements of 1932. In trade agreements with the United Kingdom and Canada during the 1930's, though the United States succeeded in reducing a few preferences, the principle of preferences was not breached. In the postwar General Agreement on Tariffs and Trade (GATT), preferences were not to be expanded, but existing ones were excepted from the most-favored-nation (MFN) clause. Some of these preferences were reduced or eliminated in GATT negotiations at Geneva in 1947 and subsequently, but many remain. If the United Kingdom should accede to the European Economic Community (EEC), it would lay to rest the system of Commonwealth preferences. The attraction of preferential trade with continental Europe will have succeeded in doing what the United States failed to accomplish during three decades of persistent efforts.

This chapter is concerned with the question of Britain's joining the EEC, the customs part of which is frequently referred to as the Common Market. It discusses (1) the general background of the EEC and the Commonwealth; (2) various factors involved in United Kingdom accession to the EEC; (3) the status of the negotiations for Britain's accession; (4) the relevance of United States trade legislation; and (5) some conclusions. It is not so directly related to United States commercial policy as the preceding chapters. It would be difficult, however, to overestimate the importance of these European developments for this policy and for other United States economic and political interests.*

* Editor's note: This chapter was written before the negotiations for United Kingdom accession to the European Economic Community broke down in January, 1963. As the volume goes to press, the prospect for the successful conclusion of these present negotiations is not promising. However, much of the chapter is relevant whether or not the United Kingdom ultimately joins the EEC.

1. GENERAL BACKGROUND

THE EEC

The European Economic Community or Common Market, established in 1958 by the Treaty of Rome, is a customs union of six nations—France, West Germany, Italy, and the three Benelux countries. Although the subject matter is economic, the EEC is prompted by the ultimate objective of political federation or confederation, and its decisions are political ones of far-reaching importance, not only to the rest of Europe but also to the Atlantic Community, the Commonwealth, and the rest of the world. In fact, the Soviet Bloc already shows signs of apprehension that this merger of sovereignty may succeed in creating a center of power in Western Europe that would confound the dogma of imperialistic rivalry between capitalistic states.

As an economic venture, the Treaty of Rome is far more than a customs union.[1] It provides for the free movement of capital, labor, and enterprise, as well as for free trade. The treaty also creates a Social Fund, a European Investment Bank, and an Overseas Development Fund. The Social Fund helps re-train workers; the European Investment Bank extends credit to less developed regions of the EEC and helps industries adjust to the new competition; and the Overseas Fund provides economic aid for the development of associated or dependent territories in Africa. The institutions of the EEC are similar to those of the European Coal and Steel Community (ECSC), which foreshadowed them. There is an intergovernmental Council of Ministers and an independent executive, the European Economic Commission. The same court and assembly now serve both the ECSC and the EEC.

THE COMMONWEALTH AND TRADE

The British Commonwealth today consists of some 730 million people, nearly one-quarter of the world's population. It is neither a political, nor geographical, nor racial bloc, but a fragile association of states that have evolved from the British Empire in the course of two centuries (see Table, p. 229). With the notable exception of Canada, the other Commonwealth nations are at least in some sense associated with the Sterling Bloc.[2] Thus, the concrete ties are currency and tariff prefer-

1. For more extensive treatment of the economic aspects of the EEC, see Isaiah Frank, *The European Common Market: An Analysis of Commercial Policy* (New York: Frederick A. Praeger, 1961); Emile Benoit, *Europe at Sixes and Sevens: The Common Market, The Free Trade Association, and the United States* (New York: Columbia University Press, 1961); and Bela Balassa, *The Theory of Economic Integration* (Homewood, Ill.: Richard D. Irwin, Inc., 1961).

2. For a statistical treatment of the tendency toward regionalization of trade in the sterling area, see Erik Thorbecke, *The Tendency towards Regionalization in International Trade, 1928-1956* (The Hague: Martinus Nijhoff, 1960).

ences, most of which are embodied in the Ottawa Agreements negotiated in 1932. The other ties are intangible and largely indefinable.

Though India and Pakistan, which are so desperately short of foreign exchange for their economic development plans, are naturally concerned, it is likely to be the Old Dominions—Canada, Australia, and New Zealand—which will protest if the United Kingdom does not succeed in protecting their special interests in its negotiations for membership in the Common Market. Ceylon, Ghana, Cyprus, and Malaya are largely indifferent or reconciled to the United Kingdom joining the EEC. Interestingly, the new African states of the Commonwealth, especially Nigeria, currently display some reservation and doubt with regard to associating themselves with the EEC.

BRITISH COMMONWEALTH OF NATIONS*

Aden	Ghana	Pitcairn
Antigua	Gibraltar	Qatar
Australia	Gilbert and Ellice Is.	St. Christopher-Nevis
Bahamas	Grenada	St. Helena
Bahrein Islands	Hong Kong	St. Lucia
Barbados	India	St. Vincent
Basutoland	Isle of Man	Sarawak
Bechuanaland	Jamaica	Seychelles
Bermuda	Kenya	Sierra Leone
British Guiana	Malaya	Singapore
British Honduras	Maldive Islands	Solomon Islands
British Virgin Islands	Malta	Southern Rhodesia
Brunei	Mauritius	Swaziland
Canada	Montserrat	Tanganyika
Cayman Islands	Nauru	Tonga
Ceylon	New Guinea	Trinidad and Tobago
Channel Islands	New Hebrides	Trucial Oman
Christmas Island	New Zealand	Turks and Caicos Is.
Cocos-Keeling Islands	Nigeria	Uganda
Cyprus	North Borneo	United Kingdom
Dominica	Northern Rhodesia	Western Samoa
Falkland Islands	Nyasaland	Zanzibar
Fiji	Pakistan	
Gambia	Papua	

* Although the Queen is a symbol of sorts to Commonwealth nations, various members do not acknowledge any formal allegiance.

The Irish Republic, although not a member of the Commonwealth, is not a "foreign" country. This distinction has had the incidental effect of continuing Anglo-Irish tariff preferences after the separation of Eire. The distinction creates some difficulty because other countries are loath to accept it.

Although Commonwealth nations account for one-quarter of all free world trade, their influence as a collective entity has diminished to the point where it is no longer very important. While its leading members are individually influential, the Commonwealth has no common policy. Without the bilateral arrangement of which Britain is the cornerstone, the system would have no economic coherence. The roughly $2.8 billion of trade in each direction between Commonwealth countries other than the United Kingdom is dominated by the exchange of goods that are not peculiarly Commonwealth in nature—Canadian and Australian grain, Indian and Ceylon tea, Pakistan jute, Malayan rubber, and Australian wool. Apart from a further increment of intra-Commonwealth trade that is dictated by geography (for example, the trade between Australia and New Zealand), the remainder "defies analysis and assessment because of its very unimportance."[3]

In the past five years, the Commonwealth's share of United Kingdom imports declined from 45 to 39 per cent, while the Commonwealth's share of United Kingdom exports declined from 47 to 41 per cent. Five years ago the Commonwealth overseas sold the United Kingdom 28 per cent of its exports and bought from the United Kingdom 26 per cent of its imports; the corresponding figures are now 25 and 22 per cent. This decline in the relative importance of Commonwealth trade started soon after Ottawa, was checked in the immediate postwar years, and accelerated in the late 1950's.

There are several reasons for the erosion of Commonwealth trade in addition to the deliberate reduction of tariff preferences by trade agreements. Because many preferential rates are in the form of specific duties, the degree of discrimination has fallen with the large rise of prices since the 1930's. Another factor is the natural change in the composition of trade. Demand for food grows less rapidly than the demand for other products of trade. Since the most important preferences granted by Britain were on food, the importance of British preferences has declined in relation to its total imports.

Trade agreements and rising prices have had similar effects on the preferences granted to the United Kingdom by the Commonwealth overseas. Another influence of great importance which is eroding Commonwealth trade is the growth of infant industries. At Ottawa, the overseas Commonwealth countries granted preferences on their imports of manufactures, especially consumer goods. Since that time, the more im-

3. Ann D. Monroe, "The British Dilemma: Commonwealth or Common Market?" *Current History*, XLIII (July, 1962), 11-15; see also The Economist Intelligence Unit, *The Commonwealth and Europe* (London: The Economist Intelligence Unit, Ltd., 1960).

portant countries have developed their own manufacturing industries with protective tariffs and restrictive quotas. Although the preferences granted to Britain are still on the books, they are largely ineffective.

The pattern of Commonwealth trade is also subject to two other influences. First, the United Kingdom market for Commonwealth exports is too limited to satisfy the growing needs of developing countries for foreign exchange. Second, Britain alone cannot meet the Commonwealth's need for capital imports. Initially the United States and now the EEC are looked to as sources of foreign economic assistance. German loans have been tied to German exports, and as a result of the persistent United States balance-of-payments deficit, the United States has adopted the same policy. But even without tied loans, foreign economic assistance is likely to continue to undermine the relative importance of Britain for Commonwealth trade.

In short, although United Kingdom preferences remain quite significant for some products, the overseas Commonwealth is outgrowing the British market. In addition, efforts to redirect British exports have already succeeded in making the United Kingdom a larger earner of dollars than the rest of the Sterling Area. The conclusion is inescapable: while British membership in the Common Market may precipitate a limited number of very awkward adjustments, especially for temperate foodstuffs and in particular for New Zealand, the broad effects will be only to speed up the established trend away from bilateral United Kingdom–Commonwealth trade.

BRITAIN AND EUROPEAN INTEGRATION

In the light of Churchill's 1940 offer of a full union with France and his 1948 declaration at the Hague Congress calling for "economic and political union," the history of Britain's attitude toward European integration before 1961 is a record of vacillation and missed opportunities.

The aborted European Defense Community would have served Britain's interest, so when the French Assembly defeated the treaty in September, 1954, Sir Anthony Eden hastily improvised the Western European Union.[4] "But the moment of British leadership was brief. Western European Union assumed no greater importance than the Council of Europe [which Britain had stymied]. . . . Indeed from 1955 until 1960 British diplomacy was back in the old groove. Unable to

4. See PEP, *European Organisations* (London: George Allen & Unwin Ltd., 1959) and A. H. Robertson, *European Institutions: Co-operation, Integration, Unification* (New York: Frederick A. Praeger, 1959).

understand that Germans and Frenchmen could really want to merge aspects of their national sovereignty. . . ."[5]

The British approach to the continent was negative in spirit. The Messina Conference of 1955, which led to the Treaty of Rome in 1957, seemed unrealistic to the pragmatic British. After France, West Germany, Italy, and the three Benelux countries had accepted the Spaak Report as a basis for negotiations, Britain declined their invitation to help draft the Treaty of Rome. The response that Britain mustered to the continental initiative was to follow the suggestion that the customs union of the six countries be surrounded by a larger free-trade area open to all member countries of the Organization for European Economic Cooperation (OEEC). In 1956 Selwyn Lloyd had put forward a so-called "Grand Design" for a single assembly to absorb the proliferation of assemblies, namely, the Council of Europe, Western Union, the NATO Parliamentarians, and if possible, the European Coal and Steel Community. To continental federalists, this seemed a move to drown European integration in the Atlantic, and subsequent negotiations for superimposing a larger free-trade area on the Common Market were cast under a cloud of suspicion.

The low-tariff Dutch saw in the proposal for a larger free-trade area a market for their exports, though their enthusiasm was tempered by Britain's exclusion of agriculture. Supported by business interests, German Economic Minister Erhard was also sympathetic, but Prime Minister Adenauer was content to rest by bridging the Rhine with France, while French political leadership did not welcome Britain on the continent. On the economic side, it was argued that the United Kingdom was not entitled to garner the benefits of free trade without the responsibility of full membership in the institutions of the EEC. The Belgians and Italians perhaps "took up less pronounced positions on this issue. M. Spaak was concerned with preserving the federalist character of the Community; Belgian business was less sure of its competitive position than the Dutch. Like the Italians, the Belgians were therefore reluctant to hurry France into acceptance of the British scheme."[6]

An earlier British initiative for creation of a free-trade area might have had a chance of success, but Britain came late to the continental party. Skepticism regarding Britain's posture toward political integration on the continent enabled France to scuttle the effort at *rapprochement* without a very serious effort to resolve the economic issues involved in surrounding the EEC with a larger free-trade area.

5. U. W. Kitzinger, *The Challenge of the Common Market* (Oxford: Basil Blackwell, 1961), p. 86.
6. *Ibid.*, p. 91.

Even after this failure at the end of 1958, when the EEC was already under way, Britain was still not prepared to burn traditional bridges and seek full partnership. It chose, instead, a defensive move and improvised an independent European Free Trade Association (EFTA) of seven countries. The other members are Norway, Sweden, Denmark, Austria, Switzerland, and Portugal (Finland is associated).[7] Although the dictates of geography strongly favor trade between the Inner Six (EEC) and the Outer Seven (EFTA), Europe has been divided into rival blocs, which discriminate against each other, as well as against the "Forgotten Five," which joined neither bloc.

Both a customs union and free-trade area involve zero tariffs on partner trade. The basic difference is that a customs union requires a common external tariff, while a free-trade area allows each member complete tariff autonomy on trade with the rest of the world. The United Kingdom strongly prefers a free-trade area because it allows retention of Commonwealth preferences. In addition, agriculture is substantially excluded from the EFTA. As regards the EEC, specifically, the institutions of the Treaty of Rome are expected to become more significant than the external tariff. By contrast, the Stockholm Convention of the EFTA was hastily drawn, is extremely simple, and has no political overtones.

The EFTA added a market of less than 40 million people to Britain's domestic market, while a free-trade area superimposed on the EEC would have added over 200 million. Since the Scandinavian tariffs are generally lower than the British, the northern partners gained rather more preference as well as the much larger British market.

As a bargaining device for gaining easier access to the Common Market, the EFTA failed.[8] In addition, Britain has acquired a measure of responsibility for the fate of its EFTA partners, should it abandon them to join the EEC.

Thus it was only after belated soul-searching that the growing momentum of the EEC led the United Kingdom to seek full membership and offer to subscribe to the Treaty of Rome. This decision had a chilling effect on Commonwealth relations, especially with Canada. Harsh words at a Commonwealth economic conference in Accra (September, 1961) led the London *Sunday Times* to observe that "nobody seems able to keep

7. For more extensive treatment of the EFTA, see F. V. Meyer, *The European Free-Trade Association: An Analysis of "The Outer Seven"* (New York: Frederick A. Praeger, 1960).

8. The EFTA venture seemed to annoy rather than coerce France. When the new EFTA inquired about establishing headquarters in Paris, De Gaulle is said to have replied, *"Mais Paris n'est pas un hotel."*

on good terms with the Canadians."[9]   The United Kingdom accounts for no more than one-sixth of Canada's trade, compared with more than half for Nigeria and more nearly one-third for Australia, India, and Ceylon.

2. FACTORS IN UNITED KINGDOM ACCESSION TO THE EEC

In attempting to evaluate United Kingdom accession to the EEC, a number of factors needs to be considered.   The economic gains and losses resulting from an extension of the EEC customs union is one.   Others include the effects of such accession on terms of trade, investment, the spirit of competition, agriculture, Commonwealth preferences, payments balances, exchange rates, and the like.

CUSTOMS UNION GAINS AND LOSSES

It can be demonstrated that a customs union has both positive and negative effects on the economic efficiency and welfare of the world.[10] The exporting partner will gain, the importing partner may gain or lose, and, at least initially, the outside world will lose as a result of preferential trade expansion between partners.   Perhaps the customs union problem may be clarified by an example.

Before the EEC.—Suppose that under conditions of rising costs of production, the same item delivered in London costs $70 when imported from either the United States or Germany but $100 when produced in the United Kingdom.   Protected by a specific duty of $30, United Kingdom producers are able to compete with imports.   But because of the constraint of rising long-run cost curves, the British market is shared by producers in all three countries.

After the EEC.—If Britain joins the Common Market, the duty on German supplies will be entirely eliminated, while the EEC external tariff will be applied to imports from the United States.   Assuming that the EEC external tariff is the same as the former United Kingdom tariff,

9. In view of the current Canadian demands on the United Kingdom in the name of Commonwealth loyalty, it should be recalled that the United Kingdom is technically free to eliminate Canadian preferences without the consent of Canada. The Ottawa pledges were abrogated in an exchange of letters of October, 1947. At that time, it was the United Kingdom that had been reluctant to waive Ottawa rights. This led Canada to seek a joint ending of these preferential obligations. See the exchange of letters, October 30, 1947, between L. D. Wilgress, Canada, and T. M. Snow, United Kingdom, in Great Britain, *Provisional Consolidated Text of the General Agreement on Tariffs and Trade and Texts of Related Documents,* Cmd. 8048, September, 1950, pp. 59-61.

10. A few paragraphs here are adapted from Don D. Humphrey, *The United States and the Common Market* (New York: Frederick A. Praeger, 1962), pp. 6-12. The partial equilibrium model can be found in Don D. Humphrey, "The Effects of a Customs Union in Western Europe," *The Southern Economic Journal,* XVII (April, 1961), 283-92.

two things will happen: partner trade will be created, and United States-United Kingdom trade will be partly destroyed.

First, German exports will displace United Kingdom production until rising marginal costs in Germany equal falling marginal costs in the United Kingdom at an equilibrium price of, say, $90.

Second, German exports to the United Kingdom will also displace United States exports to the United Kingdom to the point where falling marginal costs in the United States reduce costs by $10, an amount equal to the fall of United Kingdom costs. United States supplies costing $70 plus a $30 duty cannot compete with German supplies costing $90 free of duty. If any United States exports are to survive the discriminatory tax, they will have to sell for $90 including the tax.

To the extent that high-cost United Kingdom production is displaced by lower-cost partner imports, both partners benefit and the United States is not injured. Thus, trade creation, as measured by the production-contracting, consumption-expanding effects in the United Kingdom, will increase the economic efficiency and, under certain conditions, the welfare of the world. But to the extent that German supplies costing $90 displace United States supplies costing $70 (plus a discriminatory tax of $30), both the United Kingdom and the United States are injured. Thus, trade diversion decreases the economic efficiency and welfare of the world. It is worth remembering that the loss from trade diversion results from the lowering of partner tariffs, even though the initial duty on outside imports remains unchanged. Whether, in this example, the United Kingdom gains or loses, and whether world efficiency and welfare are increased or decreased, depends upon the balance of these trade-creating and trade-diverting effects.

The preceding example was based on increasing costs of production. Under these conditions, some part of the initial United Kingdom imports from the United States may survive the customs union, though only at less favorable terms of trade to the United States. (In the example, the United States supply price would have to fall by the difference between the tariff [$30] and the increase of Germany's supply price [$20] or by $10.)

Under conditions of constant costs, the effect of a customs union on the volume of trade with the outside world is more devastating. Constant costs or flat supply curves mean that no supply will be offered at lower prices. Thus, members of a customs union will substitute high-cost partner supply for the whole of low-cost imports from the outside world, because, unlike under increasing-cost conditions, no cost adjustments can be made in this outside supply to compensate for the tariff preference given the customs-union partner. However, creation of a customs union will substitute low-cost partner supply for all of high-cost home production of protected items not imported from the outside world. Again, to determine the net effect of the customs union, gains and losses have to be compared.

The classical gains from free trade are sufficiently familiar that we need only to indicate very roughly the order of their magnitude. With protective import duties of, say, 20 per cent on imports from the EEC, United Kingdom consumers now pay $120 for home production, which could be obtained in exchange for United Kingdom exports costing only $100. As duties are reduced, step by step, from 20 per cent to zero, the gain from each increment of trade creation will also fall from 20 per cent on the first to zero on the last. Following Meade,[11] we may say that the increase of welfare is someplace between 20 per cent and zero or, say, an average of 10 per cent on the additional trade created. The extra trade created by joining the EEC would have to reach gigantic proportions equal to one-fifth of United Kingdom national income in order to increase welfare by 2 per cent, i.e., 20 per cent of the average gain of 10 per cent on each unit of extra trade. More favorable terms on United Kingdom exports to the EEC are assumed to offset less favorable terms on United Kingdom imports.

The main purpose of the exercise is only to show that it would not be an economic disaster if the United Kingdom fails to join the EEC. An increase in the nation's economic welfare of 2 per cent is important; but it is not a matter of affluence or poverty.

Whatever the gains from trade creation between partners, they may be offset, in whole or in part, by losses from trade diversion with the rest of the world. In contrast to uniform tariff reduction, regional free trade replaces low-cost imports from outside the customs union with high-cost partner trade. Thus, if the external tariff of 15 per cent diverts United Kingdom demand from United States to German supplies, the United Kingdom will lose the whole of the difference in cost on each unit of trade diverted. Note that the loss to the United Kingdom per unit of trade diversion may equal the whole of the tariff, while the gain per unit of trade created is more likely to average half of the initial tariff, unless supply functions have peculiar shapes.

Since membership in the EEC may mean that the United Kingdom will have to tax Commonwealth supplies, many of which are now duty-free, the loss to the United Kingdom could be relatively severe. There is,

11. J. E. Meade, *The Theory of Customs Unions* (Amsterdam: North-Holland Publishing Company, 1955).

however, one mitigating condition: it appears that United Kingdom tariffs on manufactures average somewhat higher than those of the Six. The trade diversion effect will be reduced somewhat if Britain's initial tariffs are lowered as a result of membership in the EEC.

There is one reason for supposing that the trade created between partners in an enlarged Common Market may exceed trade diversion. An EEC, enlarged by the United Kingdom and other countries that seem likely to follow, will account for a very substantial fraction of the trade that has been suppressed by protective tariffs and that would be re-created by free trade between partners. Thus, a larger area of free trade is more likely to increase the economic welfare of its members than is the existing EEC. The implication for the rest of the world is just the opposite. An EEC comprising most of Western Europe is certain to increase the injury inflicted on the outside world, unless the EEC is persuaded to reduce the common external tariff.

Thus far, we have neglected the indirect effects of trade diversion. It will be clear that Germany, for example, may expand its exports to partners either by increasing production or by diverting supplies from Latin America. Now if United States exports are pushed out of the Common Market by German supplies formerly sold in Latin America, then the United States will be looking for customers while Latin America is looking for markets. Thus, secondary trade expansion between countries in the outside world may mitigate but not wholly offset the direct losses from trade diversion.

Owing to existing Commonwealth preferences, the indirect effects of United Kingdom membership in the EEC on trade between the United States and the overseas Commonwealth is a special case. An end of Commonwealth discrimination, without the new discrimination of the EEC, would produce positive benefits to the world. Since the United States starts with Commonwealth discrimination, the gain from secondary trade expansion associated with the end of one discrimination could more than offset the loss inflicted by the new discrimination of the EEC. In other words, just as the United Kingdom will have some special losses to deduct from its gains, the United States may have some special gains to deduct from its losses.

TERMS OF TRADE

Although no significant terms-of-trade effects can be assumed among partners in the EEC, this is not so for trade with the outside world. The general rule is that the customs union will turn the terms of trade in its own favor by restricting imports from outside countries, even though tariffs are not raised. Because of the discriminatory effect of the common external tariff of the EEC, demand for imports from the outside world will be restricted and those that survive will be available at more favorable terms of trade. While all members of an enlarged EEC may expect more favorable terms on dutiable imports from North and South America and Asia, the tendency for an improvement in Britain's terms of trade will be mitigated by loss of preferences in the overseas Commonwealth. Thus, if Canadian demand, which is now distorted by a handsome preference on British automobiles, is diverted to the United States, British cars are likely to fetch a lower price in Canada. For the same reason, the diversion of United Kingdom demand from the United States to partner trade will turn the terms on the surviving volume of United States exports in favor of the United Kingdom.

Just as there is likely to be secondary trade expansion (for example, between the United States and the overseas Commonwealth), so there will be secondary terms-of-trade effects that partially offset the primary effect. The diversion of Common Market exports away from the outside world as a result of free trade among partners will increase the demands of Latin America and Asia for United States goods and, so, tend to offset the direct terms-of-trade effect.

DIVERSION OF CAPITAL

The same force—tariff discrimination—that diverts outside trade away from the customs union may also divert capital to the customs union from third countries. United States companies, who see the threat to their exports, commit capital to the EEC, not only to participate in the large market but also to avoid tariff discrimination and to compete on an equal basis. There were reports of a similar diversion of British capital before Britain decided to seek admission. This is no more or less than the attraction of monopolistic protection for investment inside the EEC. Thus, capital is diverted from more to less productive employment, and the economic efficiency of the world is decreased by the capital that flows to the EEC as a means of avoiding tariff discrimination on exports that would otherwise be produced elsewhere.

Needless to say, this comes at a bad time for the United States balance of payments, which will be worsened both by trade diversion and, for the time being at least, by capital diversion.

In defending themselves, spokesmen for the EEC have sometimes said that the increase of imports into the EEC from outside the customs union shows that there has been no trade diversion. This is empiricism gone bankrupt, for there are several influences at work, and although the question is not currently important, it may become so in the future.

1. The growth of the six countries would have increased imports from the outside world in any case. It is only the extra growth associated with economic integration that can be credited with extra imports and counted as an offset to trade diversion.

2. As noted above, capital as well as trade is diverted. The diversion of United States capital from investment both at home and in third countries, as a result of tariff discrimination by the EEC, is a misuse of resources. But at the time of the capital outflow, direct foreign investment does stimulate United States exports to the Common Market. Thus, part of the increase of United States exports reflects a misdirection of investment in an effort to circumvent tariff discrimination. This part of the capital outflow, therefore, must be reckoned as an additional negative effect and not an offset to the negative effect of trade diversion.

3. The return of convertibility has encouraged both United States investment in Europe and European borrowing in the United States. Thus, a second part of the capital outflow also stimulates United States exports, but it cannot be counted as a negative effect that decreases economic efficiency in the world as a whole.

4. Government expenditures for military bases and troop support have increased significantly in recent years, with the lion's share going to Common Market countries. The increase of government expenditures in Europe would be expected to increase United States export trade, though by far less than the expenditures.

5. The rise of United States tourist expenditures in Europe in excess of those by Europeans in the United States would also be expected to increase United States exports.

For all these reasons, the simple fact of an increase in United States exports to the EEC cannot be regarded as serious evidence in regard to the issue of trade diversion. Nor, on the other hand, does a decline in the United States share of the EEC market necessarily indicate trade diversion. Trade creation between partners would naturally be expected to decrease the United States share of Common Market trade. Of course, trade diversion would decrease the United States share of the EEC market still further, but secondary trade expansion might be expected to increase the United States share of other world markets.[12]

12. Because of a cut in the EEC's external tariff pending tariff negotiations, it seems unlikely that significant trade diversion occurred before 1962. In the so-called Dillon round of tariff negotiations of 1960-1962, the United States claims to have got the better deal, in the limited sense that it received more concessions on its current exports than it gave on

The United States share of foreign markets has also been affected in recent years by the deterioration of its competitive position, probably reflecting a disequilibrium exchange rate. In 1961, this situation improved slightly, and the current outlook is for further improvement. Full employment and long-order books in Europe and relatively greater upward pressure on European wages and prices than on those in the United States, where unemployment and idle capacity persist, may easily lead to an increment of expansion in United States exports to Europe. But this would be no more than is dictated by an equilibrium exchange rate.

For some, strictures as to the complex of positive and negative effects of a customs union do not make the venture in European integration any the less exciting. The Common Market has ushered in an era of intellectual ferment and fresh initiative, as well as new competition. The hive of activity in Brussels (the temporary headquarters of the EEC) has had its impact on private life as well as on public policy. The Common Market "has triggered off all kinds of Community meetings between young people and University teachers, lawyers and designers, civil servants and trade unionists. . . . The spirit of passive resignation has fled from the centre of the continent. . . . The economic aspects we have outlined . . . matter. But what matters far more is the questing spirit that lies behind them, and which in their turn they foment."[13]

In any case, static analysis does not exhaust the economic effects of the Common Market, much less its implications as a venture in political economy for the twentieth century.

THE COMPETITIVE SPIRIT

The familiar benefits of free trade are derived from three sources: classical international specialization, economies of scale, and competition. Of these, the effect of the threat of import competition on the spirit of enterprise may be the most important: "The most successful institutions are likely to be imitated in the countries that do not yet have them; the better industrial and commercial practices are likely to displace the inferior ones; and the behaviour and habits of thought of the more ambitious, more imaginative, more pushing and more ruthless are likely to prevail and be adopted also by their more easy-going competitors."[14]

If opening the United Kingdom market to foreign competition re-

its imports. But since the implication of tariff reductions depends on the volume of trade that had been suppressed, rather than on the volume that survived the initial tariff, this is too tricky to warrant any predictions as to the net effect of reciprocal tariff concessions.

13. Kitzinger, *Challenge of the Common Market,* p. 47.

14. Tibor de Scitovszky, *Economic Theory and Western European Integration* (Stanford, Calif.: Stanford University Press, 1958), p. 23.

kindles the spirit of enterprise, there will be cost-reducing improvements in production, as well as the static effects of trade creation and diversion. The losses from trade diversion may be recouped in whole or in part if the extra growth of the EEC is sufficiently large.[15]

For countries with a small home market, the advantage of optimum-size plants may depend on international trade. For the United Kingdom, however, a home market of 52 million consumers, plus the demand of 40 million additional people in the EFTA, should be large enough to warrant optimum-size plants in most industries. But there are other industries (of which the airplane industry is a notable example) where a still larger market offers economies. Moreover, there are likely to be external economies as well as competitive advantages in having a larger number of optimum-size plants in a larger number of industries.

In view of Britain's history of dependence on protected Commonwealth markets, its relatively low postwar rate of growth, and the less than-aggressive competitive spirit sanctioned by private business and condoned by public policy, a competitive jolt, combined with a larger market, could restore the British economy. More effective competition in a larger free market also calls for modernization of internal transport and labor-saving innovations in manufacturing.

If a competitive jolt is the proper prescription for United Kingdom industry, as many believe, then there is no necessity for joining the continent in order to take the cure. Unilateral tariff cuts would suffice. The hitch is whether, given the easy option of selective tariff cutting, British manufacturers would still accept the kill or cure dosage that free trade may provide. It would be possible, if the balance of payments so dictate, to make the pill more palatable by coating it with an equilibrium exchange rate.[16]

Massive unilateral tariff cuts are not realistic, however, if for no other reason than that they are unnecessary. President Kennedy's trade program offers Britain a real alternative to partnership in the Common Market. If the United States, the United Kingdom, and the rest of the EFTA negotiated massive tariff cuts with the EEC, Britain could, per-

15. On the assumption that the growth of the existing EEC would be 90 per cent in twenty years, it has been estimated that the national income of the same countries would have to rise by at least 120 per cent, in order for the growth effect to exceed the negative effect of trade diversion. See Paul Erdman and Peter Rogge, *Die Europäische Wirtschaftsgemeinschaft und die Drittländer* (Basel: Kyklos-Verlag, 1960).

16. At the same time, we may note that Britain's competitive position may well have been weakened in the last decade by a slightly overvalued currency. It will be suggested later in this chapter that high interest rates, imposed for balance-of-payments reasons, have made it more difficult to get the kind of investment that would have made it possible to match wage increases with extra productivity.

haps, keep a small piece of her Commonwealth cake and eat competition too.

The first question is whether Britain would be losing benefits of vital importance by not sharing in the institutions of the Common Market. There seems little to suggest that this is the case, unless Britain obtains a commitment that an enlarged EEC will pool its gold and dollar reserves and allow the entire Sterling Area to draw on them. Such an eventuality would be of immense advantage to the United Kingdom.

But the institutions fashioned at Rome were not designed to succor the United Kingdom. Nor do the governments of Adenauer and De Gaulle seem disposed to make an accommodation for the United Kingdom equivalent to that given France by the treaty. The institutions of the Common Market were designed to finance the improvement of peasant agriculture and to dispose of farm surpluses, to give French Africa preferential treatment as well as capital for economic development, and to mitigate, if need be, the rigors of free trade. On the farm front, as will be explained, it is quite clear that the shift from United Kingdom direct subsidies to EEC import taxes would not only be a regressive step that would contract the European market for Commonwealth food, but one that would cost British consumers handsomely and might worsen the balance of payments besides.

AGRICULTURE

The farm policy of the EEC involves two distinct questions: the method by which farmers are protected and the degree of protection. In different ways, both the United Kingdom and the Commonwealth overseas will be affected by the answer to each of these questions.

As far as food policy is concerned, it is a clear disadvantage for Britain, though not for its farmers, to join the Common Market. When free trade within the EEC is achieved after the transitional period, farmers will be protected either by variable levies on imports or by ordinary duties. The revenue will be pooled and used to raise productivity in the less advanced regions of the EEC by better methods of farming and by investment in equipment. The revenue will also be available to subsidize the exporting of farm surpluses. This would benefit the efficient and relatively well-to-do farm regions.

Since the United Kingdom is by far the largest importer of foodstuffs in Europe, British consumers would be paying taxes to improve continental agriculture and to dispose of surpluses produced mainly by some continental countries. This is supranationalism at its worst, for Britain would be restricting Commonwealth imports by subsidizing high-cost production on the continent as well as at home, and the effect would have adverse implications for Britain's balance of payments.

The United Kingdom and existing members of the EEC presently employ quite different methods to protect their farmers. In contrast to the EEC, United Kingdom farmers are subsidized directly by the British Treasury at the cost of approximately $1 billion annually. The continental system is the more familiar one whereby consumers pay higher prices for domestic production, because imports are taxed. The British system of direct subsidy has the desired effect of stimulating home production without the undesirable effect of restricting consumption by higher prices. It is a great pity that the British system of protection cannot be adapted by the EEC (and the United States, for that matter) in preference to the continental system. To the extent that consumption is reduced by higher prices, the taxing of imports inflicts injury on producers in the outside world without a corresponding benefit to farmers in the Common Market.

The shift from direct subsidy to import taxes will inevitably raise the British cost of living. If this leads to stronger demands for higher money wages, it may worsen the British balance of payments by raising the money costs of production. The tax reduction made possible by elimination of the direct farm subsidy would only very partially offset the higher cost of food. It is estimated that adopting the continental approach to agricultural protection will raise the United Kingdom cost of living some 2.5 to 3 per cent. But the consensus of competent observers is that, while this would be serious, the cost is not sufficient to keep the United Kingdom out of the Common Market.

To British farmers, it makes little real difference whether protection takes the form of direct subsidies or indirect payment by consumers in the form of higher prices. While the EEC countries are agreed as to the broad shape of their agricultural policy, the degree of future protection is not yet firmly established.

What counts with farmers, including those in the United Kingdom, is the degree of protection, and on this, the various members of the EEC will have trouble reaching agreement. The basic issue is the extent to which demands of high-cost peasant agriculture, especially in Germany, prevail over the lower prices needed by more efficient producers in France. The fact that the United Kingdom would almost certainly oppose a Common Market price for cereals high enough to appease German farmers may be a minor reason for Adenauer's notable lack of enthusiasm for United Kingdom membership in the EEC.

Since the average price received by United Kingdom farmers is lower than that of EEC farmers, there is no reason to suppose that British agriculture as a whole will suffer. In fact, the more efficient sectors of British agriculture are likely to benefit, but free entry of truck crops and fruits from the continent is expected to deal high-cost British horticulture a hard blow.

While the United Kingdom has already accepted the financial principle of pooling the revenue collected on food imports, there is no valid reason why the EEC should not compromise with the present United Kingdom system of direct subsidies. This would provide lower food prices and less taxing of British consumers for the benefit of continental producers, and it would still be an advantage to the continent. It is small wonder, then, that France, the largest beneficiary of high prices, insisted on more specific commitments from the United Kingdom before agreeing to arrangements for imports of temperate foodstuffs from the Commonwealth. This became the final sticking point on which the negotiations for United Kingdom membership broke down in August, 1962, without reaching an agreement.

The Commonwealth overseas stands to lose from Britain's joining the Common Market. The only question is how severe the jolt will be, especially for food producers. Although British farmers are substantially protected, the United Kingdom remains a large importer and, in the main, food imports from the Commonwealth are free of duty. Thus, the Commonwealth exporter faces the prospect of a double jolt. First, he is likely to lose the preference he now has in the United Kingdom market, which would put him in the same competitive position as the United States. Second, the common external tariff, especially the variable levy on imports, is very likely to expand EEC production faster than consumption. Moreover, the danger of protection from a common EEC program is far greater than that from individual countries. Even though a nation protects its own farmers, it tends to buy its imports at world market prices. But the Common Market principle of community preference means that high-cost partner production will be stimulated and imported into food-deficit countries at the expense of low-cost imports from the outside world. Thus, although the degree of EEC protection is not firmly established, there are strong reasons for apprehension. Unlike the common external tariff on manufactures, which is the average of member-country tariffs, food imports are subject to variable levies. In opposing an EEC policy of relatively high market prices for foodstuffs, the United Kingdom would be supporting the interest of the United States, as well as that of Canada, Australia, and New Zealand. United States interests conflict, however, when the United Kingdom seeks special treatment for imports from the Commonwealth beyond a transitional period.

COMMONWEALTH PREFERENCE

Should Britain subscribe to the Rome Treaty as it stands, it would mean an end of Commonwealth preference, in respect to both exports and imports. These pose quite different problems. In return for giving up preferences that it receives in the overseas Commonwealth, Britain would gain free access to the more dynamic Common Market, where it now sells about one-seventh of its exports. Britain would also avoid the loss of some part of its share of the EEC market owing to the discrimination against outsiders by free trade between partners. This discriminatory effect operates even for a country like Germany, for example, whose initial tariffs will not be greatly changed by the common external tariff. A separate part of the negative effect of staying out of the EEC stems from the fact that the bulk of British exports to the existing EEC are sold to the low-tariff Benelux countries. By joining, Britain would avoid the higher Benelux duties that result from "averaging up" as the common external tariff is established. While the higher duties of France and Italy will be brought down at the same time, an outside country will face the disadvantage of competition with duty-free supplies from Germany and Benelux.

Although Britain's exports to the Commonwealth are three times the size of those to the Common Market, exports to the continent are growing while those to the Commonwealth have been stagnant. While it cannot be assumed that the Common Market will continue to grow at the dramatic rates of recent years, it seems safe to suppose that it will outstrip the growth of Commonwealth markets by a wide margin. Moreover, the preferential treatment Britain receives has not enabled it to hold its share of Commonwealth markets. As an economic calculation, it may be advantageous for Britain to sacrifice Commonwealth preferences, which are a wasting asset, in return for free access to the Common Market. But, however one may weigh Britain's larger stake in the Commonwealth against the more dynamic expansion of the Common Market, the advantage cannot be so great that the argument for joining leaves Britain no real alternative.

From the Commonwealth point of view, the loss of preferences in the British market poses more difficult questions. While Britain is only substituting one system for another, the overseas Commonwealth will be discriminated against by the Common Market. That is to say, the Commonwealth would move from positive to negative preferences.

Britain now grants preferences that average 8 to 10 per cent for almost half of its imports. Concretely, however, the formidable problems of substituting Common Market discrimination for Commonwealth preferences are not so extensive as they may seem in the abstract, because the two associations are substantially complementary rather than competitive. The issues arise: (1) where raw material imports from the Commonwealth are duty-free in Britain but taxed by the EEC; (2) where imports of tropical foodstuffs from the associated African states compete with the Commonwealth; (3) where the United Kingdom grants preferences on imports of manufactures; and (4) where the United Kingdom imports large quantities of temperate zone foodstuffs that are highly protected by the EEC.

Negotiation of British entry into the EEC is made easier by the fact that more than half of Commonwealth exports subject to preferential treatment is taxed by neither the United Kingdom nor the EEC. The more important exceptions are aluminum, newsprint, wood pulp, lead, and zinc. Thus, Australian wool, for example, would bear nil duty in an enlarged Common Market, but Britain would import aluminum from France free of duty while Canadian aluminum would be taxed. Where an enlarged EEC persists in protecting its primary processing industries, the Commonwealth will either lose its United Kingdom market or suffer less favorable terms of trade, unless special terms are expressly provided.

Tropical foodstuffs present a different problem in that they are not produced by either the United Kingdom or the EEC. Here we see an aspect of the survival of British and French colonial empires in the form of two competing preferential systems. Tropical foodstuffs account for one-sixth of Britain's preferential imports. Unless the former British territories are associated with the EEC on the same basis as former French and Belgian territories, the African states presently associated with the EEC will be able to expand sales in the British market at the expense of the Commonwealth. But if the enlarged EEC extends the same preferential treatment to the former territories of all members, then Latin America will find it exceedingly difficult to share in this growing market. The clear interest of the United States, in this case, lies in trying to eliminate tariffs all around, and the United States trade legislation of 1962 provides for this opportunity.

Preferential British imports of manufactures account for less than 10 per cent of the total, and they are about equally divided between those from low-wage and high-wage countries. These call for different treatment. It would be a miscarriage if imports from low-wage countries were treated less liberally as a result of Britain joining the Common

Market. So far, the United States has taken a disproportionate share of Asian exports of manufactures. By its liberal treatment of Indian textiles, Britain, too, has made a contribution, although this may be offset by its discrimination against Japan. The only solution consistent with the responsibility of rich, industrial countries is for the Common Market to liberalize its own treatment of low-wage manufactures rather than to force Britain in the opposite direction.

Only 4 per cent of Britain's preferential imports are manufactures from high-wage countries—mainly Canada. The loss of this preference would be of no more than marginal importance to Canada since these items account for less than 3 per cent of its exports, and it would gain some bargaining power from the closing out of British preferences in Canada. In the case of a few items—for example, motor cars, which Canada imports free of duty from Britain—the present discrimination is quite significant.

Although Britain's preferential imports of temperate foodstuffs are only slightly larger than those of tropical foods, they pose much more intractable problems, especially for New Zealand exports of meat, butter, and cheese, which are highly dependent on the United Kingdom market. Australia is also a supplier, while Canada has an important stake in both the United Kingdom and EEC markets.

Even where European countries individually restrict food imports, the farm policy of the EEC need not, but seems likely to, increase the self-sufficiency of the area. This is because of the express policy of giving Community preference. Where a country protects only its own farmers, it tends to import the balance of its food requirements from the cheapest source. However, free trade within the EEC will encourage imports of partner supplies and expansion of partner production at higher prices than prevail in world markets.

In creating free trade at uniform prices within the EEC, it will be most difficult to avoid stimulating the production of the more efficient farmers, especially in France, where grain prices are relatively low as compared with those in Germany. For obvious political reasons, French production is likely to be expanded more than German production is reduced, if it is reduced at all, and similar results seem likely as between the more and less efficient regions more generally.

It may be noted that, within limits, the discrimination against third-country imports, which is predicted for agriculture, is implicit in the principle of a customs union. Owing to the common external tariff, the importing partner in a customs union is always liable to have to pay more for supplies from partners than from third countries. The reason for fearing that the EEC will progressively exclude the farm products of third countries is political. Since farmers everywhere seem to have political power disproportionate to their numbers, it is more difficult to reduce the protection of farmers than that of manufacturers. The danger is that the EEC will have to suppress imports or reduce the existing protection of farmers in less efficient member countries.

BALANCE OF PAYMENTS

The Treaty of Rome may make it very difficult for a member to protect its balance of payments, at least within the EEC, by direct control of trade and payments. After the transitional period, a member's decision to restrict imports or the outflow of capital may be overridden by majority vote. While a temporary disequilibrium may be weathered by loans to the deficit country, this does not cure the deficit.

As long as national governments retain primary responsibility for wage policy, full employment, and growth, recurrent disorder in the balance of payments is predictable under a policy of fixed exchange rates. While members have an obligation to consult on a co-ordinate monetary policy, this is a weak instrument compared with direct controls. So far, the EEC countries have enjoyed a honeymoon balance of payments, supported by initial devaluation of the French franc, a persistent United States deficit, and a chronic weakness of the pound sterling. Correction of the disorder means a stronger dollar and pound, which implies weaker currencies for continental Europe.

The weak-currency problem is more likely to be exacerbated than abated by the free flow of capital. Foot-loose capital is prone to shift from deficit to surplus countries and make a bad payments situation worse. While free movement of labor may serve as a means of adjustment for the long pull, this is likely to be a one-way road from poorer to richer countries.[17] By helping to restrain wage increases, an in-movement of labor is, perhaps, more likely to help surplus countries avoid inflation than to improve the competitive position of the deficit country. In any event, labor is so much less mobile than capital that free trade and factor movements may imply the need for more frequent ad-

17. The possibility that trouble may be stored up in the provision for free movement of labor has received too little attention. One reason why Europe is relatively stable today is that existing countries are composed very largely of their own nationals. Although there are relatively large numbers of Italians working in Switzerland and elsewhere, these workers would be returned to their homeland in event of serious unemployment. But if foreign workers become permanently settled with their families, one can easily imagine the possibility of serious political disorder, unless one believes that the historical leopard on this issue will change his spots.

justment of exchange rates than has been sanctioned since the Second World War.

Suppose that after joining the EEC, the United Kingdom has a payments deficit with its partners because its prices are not fully competitive. The overvaluation of sterling tends to produce unemployment because Britain cannot export enough to balance its accounts. The surplus partners, on the other hand, are overexporting, and hence they have an excess of demand as compared with balanced trade. The surplus countries now reach full employment, and they employ high interest rates to hold down excess demand and avoid inflation. This attracts capital from the deficit country, where low interest rates prevail in an effort to stimulate domestic output. The balance-of-payments disequilibrium would be enlarged by the free flow of capital from the deficit country to the surplus countries, where it is not needed.

This dilemma has produced the prescription and practice of employing monetary policy to protect the foreign balance from wayward capital movements and fiscal policy to support domestic objectives. The prescription is logical as an expedient in that two conflicting objectives, expansion of domestic employment and protection of the foreign balance, may well require two independent instruments of policy. But if the medicine is given only to the deficit country, the policy of high interest rates and budgetary deficits may postpone a basic solution of the balance-of-payments problem. A symmetrical dosage would call on surplus countries to rely on budgetary surpluses to control inflation and lower interest rates to avoid creating perverse capital flows from deficit countries.

The United Kingdom has repeatedly employed high interest rates to shift the financing of trade to other financial centers and to attract footloose money. On two occasions, the Bank of England discount rate has been raised to 7 per cent. At the same time, we have witnessed sluggish long-term investment and growth rates in the British economy though, apparently, at full employment. Thus, while fiscal policy may be employed to support full employment, the risk of high interest costs is that long-term growth may be impaired. Full employment without the extra productivity, which depends on extra investment, supports upward pressure on wage rates. The result is all too likely to delay improvement in a country's competitive position.

Since there is a limit to how far the deficit country can manipulate the interest structure without restricting the kind of long-term investment that would satisfy wage demands with productivity gains, high interest rates may condemn a weak-currency country to sluggish growth rates and thus perpetuate its balance-of-payments dilemma. If monetary policy is to serve balance-of-payments objectives, then, the surplus countries should lower their interest rates in order to avoid attracting capital and should rely on budgetary surpluses to avoid inflation.

It is technically possible for deficit countries to solve the problem by either deflation or unemployment, but these are harsh measures. And if surplus countries employ high interest rates to restrict the excess demand that is implied by disequilibrium exchange rates, the deficit country may have to choose between direct controls and adjustment of the exchange rate, in order to avoid unemployment or secular stagnation.

It is reasonable to ask that countries avoid inflation. But if they do this, and if balance-of-payments disequilibria appear or persist for any reason, the surplus countries cannot in fairness employ high interest rates and exacerbate the situation by attracting unwanted capital from the deficit country. The doctrine that monetary policy should serve balance-of-payments objectives implies that surplus countries should adopt low interest rates as befit creditor nations. The only feasible alternative may be more frequent adjustment of the exchanges.

EXCHANGE RATES

If members of the EEC cannot resort to direct controls in the future, as in the past, a major policy issue is whether to insist that the exchange rates between national currencies should be pegged more rigidly or adjusted more readily.

On the one hand, it will be argued that fixed rates are a powerful instrument supporting the co-ordination of national monetary policies, which is essential for economic integration. We have already seen why fixed rates may condemn the deficit country to relative stagnation, however. The essential point is that the prescription of high interest rates for deficit countries may restrict the investment that is needed to improve their competitive position and, thus, to keep pace with the productivity gains of the surplus countries. Until the EEC succeeds with the substance of political integration, less reliance on direct controls may call for a more flexible exchange-rate policy.

The Rome Treaty obligates members to treat exchange-rate policy "as a matter of common interest."[18] It does not call for the maintenance of fixed rates. In fact, the Common Market venture was launched on depreciation of the French franc, while subsequent appreciation of the German mark and Dutch guilder is said to have been undertaken with-

18. If a member fails in this obligation and acts unilaterally, the other members are permitted to take special measures, for a limited period, to counter the distortion of competition.

out advance consultation with partners. Although neither the treaty nor the experience of the EEC militates very strongly against adjusting pegged exchange rates, Professor Meade is rightly concerned about the dangers of undue rigidity. He states that "those who have built the EEC have a definite prejudice in favour of fixed rates of exchange partly on orthodox financial grounds and partly on the grounds that this is a necessary first step towards a single European Currency—which perhaps more than anything else would be the symbol of real European Union."[19]

The postwar attitude of reluctant adjustment of pegged rates is compatible with the French type of inflation (before 1958), which makes recurrent depreciation obvious and inevitable. The greater danger lies in a modest disequilibrium that drags on year after year and that is bad enough to dampen the expansion of the domestic demand that is necessary to insure a high rate of growth, but not yet blatant enough to dictate action forthwith: "It could be rather like the economic consequences of [the United Kingdom] returning to the Gold Standard in 1925."[20]

The fragile character of the postwar key-currency system is apparent, and it has already attracted the attention of economists. The emergence of convertibility, the rapid progress of the EEC, and the prospect that it may be enlarged by the membership of Britain and others, all reinforce the existing need for a revision of the system.[21]

THE STERLING AREA[22]

The financial policy of the EEC is of particular importance to the United Kingdom because its responsibilities are broader than those of other European countries. Sterling is a reserve currency serving many countries overseas. Members of the area pool their gold and dollar reserves in London. In return they have an open door to the London capital market.[23] Britain gains dollars from this arrangement since the

19. James E. Meade, *UK, Commonwealth and Common Market* (London: Institute of Economic Affairs, 1962), p. 42.

20. *Ibid.*, p. 43.

21. See Fritz Machlup, *Plans for Reform of the International Monetary System*, Princeton University, International Finance Section, Special Papers in International Economics, No. 3 (August, 1962); and U.S. Congress, Joint Economic Committee, Subcommittee on International Exchange and Payments, *Factors Affecting the United States Balance of Payments*, Compilation of Studies, 87th Cong., 2nd Sess., 1962.

22. For a more extensive treatment of the Sterling Area, see F. V. Meyer, *Britain, the Sterling Area and Europe* (Cambridge: Bowes & Bowes, 1952); and A. R. Conan, ed., *The Rationale of the Sterling Area, Texts and Commentary* (London: Macmillan & Co. Ltd., 1961).

23. Britain has also invested significant sums in Canada. These were not of the same order as United States investments. But, unlike the United States, whose capital outflow finances an export surplus, Britain has a large trade deficit with Canada.

overseas Sterling Area earns more dollars than it spends. The advantage, however, entails considerable cost in terms of the outflow of British savings that might have been usefully invested in home industry. Moreover, while the Sterling Area still plays an important role, its usefulness seems to be modified by three developments.

1. Britain's own dollar earnings have grown steadily until they now exceed those of the rest of the area.

2. The strain of providing capital becomes more acute as the area's growing demand for external capital becomes more urgent.

3. The political independence of three main dollar-earning colonies, Malaya, Ghana, and Nigeria, may bring into question Whitehall's influence on their pattern of trade. While colonies could be persuaded to save dollars by conserving on their expenditures for dollar goods, independent countries may be less amenable. Compared with the United States, the United Kingdom's relative share of West African imports has been many times higher than that of India and of Pakistan. The question is whether African trade may not follow the pattern already evident in the Commonwealth countries of Asia, namely, a shift toward continental Europe and the United States.

In the past, Britain has maintained freedom of payments within the Sterling Area by restrictions on transactions with both continental Europe and the Dollar Area. If United Kingdom membership in the EEC is to mean that Britain can no longer resort to direct controls for balance-of-payments reasons, the consequences could be far-reaching. Although the Rome Treaty does not say so expressly, it seems to leave the door open for members to restrict trade or payments with outside countries, as provided by the GATT. But if the United Kingdom were obliged to impose restrictions on transactions with the Sterling Area, while maintaining free trade and capital movements with the EEC, the clear implication is that the outflow of British capital would be diverted from poor sterling countries to rich continental Europe.

Such a predicament could spell the doom of the Sterling Area, for overseas members would find sterling less attractive to hold and might progressively shift their sterling balances into dollars and other currencies. Even those who recognize that the character of the Sterling Area is changing and who would like to see it merged into a new system of world payments also recognize that this is the wrong way to proceed.[24] Since Britain's short-term sterling liabilities are very much larger than

24. See J. E. Meade, "The Future of International Trade and Payments," *The Three Banks Review*, No. 50 (June, 1961), 15-38.

her pool of gold and dollar assets, any large attempt to convert could precipitate a liquidity crisis of dramatic proportions.

The common external tariff of the EEC necessarily involves discrimination against imports from the Sterling Area (and all other outside countries) in favor of partner trade. The United Kingdom can scarcely afford to compound the discrimination by adding payments restrictions that discriminate against the Sterling Area in favor of Europe. As to the rest of the world, which accounts for only one-third of British imports, the restriction of imports from sources other than the EEC and the Sterling Area would have to discriminate in the extreme in order to be effective.

The foregoing has implicitly assumed that the combined balance of payments of all Common Market countries was in balance with the outside world. But suppose that the EEC as a whole were in a deficit position long enough that the choice was between simultaneous depreciation of all member-country currencies and a joint program for the restriction of trade and payments. It is likely to be very difficult for members to agree in this case; depreciation may favor some members, while direct controls would be more suitable for others. If import restrictions were employed, it is certain to be extremely difficult to reach joint agreement as to which products should be restricted and to allocate import licenses among partners. Such considerations also argue for a frame of mind that accepts adjustment of the exchanges.

Members of the EEC can economize on their monetary reserves and also take a preliminary step toward creation of a European currency by pooling their gold and dollar reserves. The pooling of reserves would enable the EEC to hold smaller idle balances than is prudent at present, when each country wants to hold enough reserves to weather a balance-of-payments deficit that may last for quite some time.

Existing members of the EEC would begin with a strong creditor position, which would enable them to draw on the pool in the future. On the other hand, Britain's weak reserve position would be greatly improved. The gross disparity between the net reserves of the United Kingdom and of existing members makes an awkward starting point for the pooling of reserves. In March, 1961, Britain held gold and dollar assets of $3 billion against sterling liabilities of $10.9 billion, a net negative position of $7.9 billion. By contrast, the existing members of the EEC held $16 billion of reserves against which they had only $2 billion of short-term liabilities, a positive position of $14 billion. There is nothing wrong with a key-currency country owing more than it holds as reserves. The trouble is that the gold and dollar reserves held in London to serve the entire Sterling Area are too slender for the liquid sterling liabilities that they support.

Since the existing members of the EEC would be making a large loan available to the United Kingdom, they would want to consider restricting the conditions under which it could draw on the pool. The real problem is that unless India, Australia, New Zealand, the new African states, and other members of the Sterling Area were quite free to convert their sterling balances now held in London by drawing on the EEC pool for what Britain owes them, the restriction of drawing rights would be incompatible with Britain's obligations to the overseas Sterling Area. Of course, the immense strengthening of the pound sterling by a European pool of gold and dollars would greatly improve the liquidity of the Sterling Area. But here again, as in matters of trade policy, a better solution would look toward a still broader resolution of this problem by all members of the International Monetary Fund or the Atlantic Community.

3. UNITED KINGDOM–EEC NEGOTIATIONS

Negotiations for United Kingdom accession to the EEC were conducted during the summer of 1962. Before they broke down in August, no accord was reached on the treatment of imports from the overseas Commonwealth by an enlarged EEC. However, a partial understanding was realized with respect to wide areas of Commonwealth trade in the event of British membership.

With regard to Africa and the Caribbean, it was agreed that independent countries of the Commonwealth (and those that will shortly become independent) will be eligible for associate membership under Part IV of the Treaty of Rome. The existing EEC is negotiating a new association convention, which is expected to take effect from January 1, 1963. With exceptions noted below, it is for the United Kingdom to indicate, after consultation, which Commonwealth countries are to become associate members on the same basis as existing associate members in Africa. If some of the eligible countries do not become associate members, there are to be further consultations between the United Kingdom and the EEC as to alternative economic arrangements. In particular, it was recognized that later discussions will be needed as to the Common Market's external tariffs on tropical foodstuffs and tropical products of interest to Commonwealth countries that do not become associate members of the EEC.

No agreement was reached, however, as to the type of association that the EEC would accept for the Federation of Rhodesia and Nyasaland.

The old problem of preferential treatment for Rhodesian tobacco, which the United States had to accept in negotiating the Anglo-American trade agreement of 1938, may still be a sore spot, complicated by the existing associate membership of Greece, a tobacco-exporting country.[25]

Enlargement of the EEC, whether by full or associate membership, creates extra discrimination against those who remain outside. This is apparent in the case of Caribbean countries. If the bananas of associated African states are to enjoy free entry into an enlarged Common Market, then the Caribbean Commonwealth must also be associated in order to avoid injury. But if the West Indies enjoy free entry to the European market, then their exports of cheap manufactures will be stimulated to the disadvantage of Asian producers. The understanding resolves this issue by including the Caribbean but excluding the Commonwealth countries of Asia. The EEC agreed, however, to work out with the United Kingdom a policy for the treatment of imports from Hong Kong.

Since Singapore, Sarawak, North Borneo, and Brunei may become members of a Greater Malaysian Federation, which is under discussion, the position of these territories was left for later consideration. Basutoland, Bechuanaland Protectorate, and Swaziland present technical problems owing to the existing customs union with South Africa. These problems also are to be given later consideration.

A significant area of understanding was reached with respect to treatment of imports from India, Pakistan, and Ceylon. As regards tea, the existing common external tariff of 18 per cent would be reduced to zero by an enlarged EEC. The common external duty on cotton textiles (mainly 18 per cent) would be applied by the United Kingdom in four stages: 3.5 per cent on accession to the EEC, 7 per cent eighteen months later, 12.5 per cent one year thereafter, and the full external duty when it applies throughout the Community.

The enlarged EEC would seek to negotiate trade agreements with India, Pakistan, and Ceylon by the end of 1966 at the latest. The objective of the agreements would be to maintain and increase the foreign currency earnings of these countries and in general to facilitate their economic development. It was recognized that tariffs, quotas, and measures to promote private investment and to provide technical assistance may be involved.

Until the above trade agreements are concluded, it was agreed that

25. The Federation of Rhodesia and Nyasaland represents Britain's most difficult and dangerous "colonial" problem today. Nyasaland is a self-governing protectorate with an African legislature, while Southern Rhodesia is a fully self-governing colony, whose government is controlled by white men. Copper-rich Northern Rhodesia is a protectorate expecting to elect its first legislature in the fall of 1962.

immediate steps would be taken to restore trade if imports into the enlarged Community declined from the average tonnage of 1959 and 1960. In the meantime, the United Kingdom would restrict imports from India and Pakistan to about their present level.

The United Kingdom is to apply quotas on jute goods, which increase by seven hundred tons annually, until abolished on January 1, 1970. (Certain heavy jute goods from East India are to be considered later.) As for "Other Manufactures and Processed Foods," the common external tariff is to be reduced to zero on sports goods, cashew nuts, and handloom products (the latter subject to an agreement on definition). The remainder of the products under this heading are subject to a substantial delay in the timetable for application of the external tariff, which would become fully effective on January 1, 1970.

As expected, temperate foodstuffs of Canada, Australia, and New Zealand offered the greater difficulty. Nonetheless, a substantial area of agreement was found, and it seems clear that the broad shape of EEC policy, if there is to be a final accord, has been established. The outstanding issues are to reduce broad language to more specific terms.

The existing EEC has expressly agreed that the enlarged Community would offer "reasonable opportunities" in its markets for the sale of temperate foodstuffs. It was recognized that the Community's future price policy would largely determine the market for exporting countries, and the agreement is to define this policy as soon as possible.

All seven governments had previously agreed, in the context of an enlarged EEC, to take an early initiative to seek world-wide agreements for leading agricultural products. Agreement would be sought on price and production policies of both importing and exporting countries, the maximum and minimum quantities to enter international trade, stockpiling policy, and the special aspects of trade with developing countries. Such world-wide agreements would be subject to revision every three years. Should the objective of world-wide agreements fail, the EEC would conclude agreements for the same purpose with those countries who wished to do so and, in particular, with Commonwealth countries.

As regards the transition period, the EEC agreed that the principle of Community preference would be applied in a manner that would avoid abrupt breaks in the pattern of trade. It further agreed that cereals now enjoying preferential treatment by the United Kingdom should benefit from an agreed application of the principle of Community preference. This important understanding implies that United States exports of grain may be subject to double discrimination, i.e., discrimination in favor of Common Market producers plus some remnant of Commonwealth preference.

The EEC recognized the unusual position of New Zealand owing to its heavy dependence on United Kingdom markets, and it agreed to consider special measures for dealing with New Zealand trade.

4. UNITED STATES TRADE LEGISLATION

The reason the United States Trade Expansion Act of 1962 has been justly applauded both abroad and at home is that it makes possible a solution of problems, which "might until recently have been considered so utopian as not to merit serious consideration."[26]

The provision of the legislation permitting free trade is limited to those three-digit Standard International Trade Classification (SITC) manufacturing industries for which the United States and the EEC, as it may be enlarged, account for 80 per cent of free-world exports. Tariff concessions under this heading would be extended to all members of the GATT. Extensive use of this provision would be a big step toward avoiding trade diversion and expanding mutually beneficial trade.

A second provision allows free entry of tropical products. It represents an attempt to open up the Common Market to all producers of coffee, cocoa, etc., rather than to continue the existing preferential arrangement for African states. The economies of associated African states have been built up on a basis of preference, and merely to cut the umbilical cord and stop there might deal them a serious blow. But to perpetuate this "dependence" indefinitely is out of joint with the times. If, in the past, Washington has at times been strident with the British about preference, its posture about perpetuating dependent African nations is salutary.

It is the authority to cut duties by 50 per cent which is of most interest to the Commonwealth. A 50 per cent step toward multilateral free trade on a broad front, by the United States, EEC, EFTA, the Commonwealth, and Japan, would greatly extend the gains from trade creation and probably would avoid most of the injury from trade diversion by the EEC. As a general rule, it is not necessary for a customs union to reduce its external tariff to zero in order to avoid trade diversion.

Of course, massive use of both the 100 per cent EEC authority and the much broader 50 per cent authority would open the sluice gates still wider, and therefore it is preferable. Extension to third countries of nil tariffs, under the 100 per cent authority, would help to compensate Canada and Australia for the loss of British preferences. While some

26. Meade, *UK, Commonwealth and Common Market*, p. 36.

may feel, and rightly, that this would be paying them for giving up sin, the fact remains that Commonwealth preferences are an old sin tolerated by the GATT. Nonetheless, bold as these provisions may have seemed to Washington when the Administration position was being formulated, they suffer from two drawbacks.

First, they do not satisfy well-informed Canadian experts who believe that their secondary manufacturing could not survive a 50 per cent tariff reduction. They believe, however, that free trade would allow Canada the opportunity to specialize and achieve economies of scale in some lines. Thus, Canadian experts hold that nil tariffs for some industries would be more acceptable to Canada than a 50 per cent cut in tariffs. The trouble is that the 100 per cent authority of the United States legislation does not include any of the manufactures in which Canada is interested, even if the EEC is enlarged by the membership of the United Kingdom and other European countries.

Second, and more important, the 100 per cent provision is significant only if the United Kingdom joins the EEC. The United States and the existing EEC account for 80 per cent of free world trade in two industries only—aircraft and margarine and shortenings. It is a miscarriage of the great effort that has gone into the trade expansion legislation of 1962 that the nil tariff provision will be aborted if the United Kingdom fails to join the EEC.[27]

Although the 100 per cent authority appears to have been drawn with a view to encouraging United Kingdom admission to the EEC, the 50 per cent authority provides a constructive alternative. The GATT approach would offer some opportunity for reciprocal concessions to the overseas Commonwealth for giving up United Kingdom preferences and would still enable the United Kingdom to take the prescription of a competitive jolt.

In strict economic terms, there may not be a decisive difference between the United Kingdom going to free trade with the continent and an all-out multilateral approach via the GATT. This assumes, of course, that the United Kingdom would be prepared for massive across-the-board tariff cutting in the GATT. The multilateral approach avoids the loss of trade diversion. Also, the first 50 per cent cut of effective duties provides much larger gains than the second. On the other side, there is the important fact that zero tariffs avoid a great deal of customs nuisance, which remains to haunt us even under quite nominal duties.

The very success and momentum of the Common Market is an attrac-

27. For other limitations on the use of the 1962 trade legislation, see Chap. II, pp. 114-23.

tion. The United Kingdom can share in this market about as well from the outside as from the inside, provided it takes the competitive cure at the GATT. There is little reason to suppose that the existing EEC would either wish or be able to resist massive reciprocal tariff reduction if such a program were pushed boldly by the United States, the EFTA, and the Commonwealth.

While the GATT approach may enable the United Kingdom to make the best of both worlds economically, it could leave it isolated from the continent politically. We may conclude that the choice of joining or not joining the continent should be resolved in terms of its political, rather than its economic implications. Here the question is whether, as a member, the United Kingdom would widen the horizon of the EEC, without sapping its vitality. The view that Britain sees world problems more often in Atlantic than in continental terms, argues that United States interests may be better served by Britain inside than outside the EEC. Such, at least, has been the assessment from Washington. However, press reports regarding first steps toward a political federation or confederation of the existing six members of the EEC indicate that both Adenauer and De Gaulle would prefer to start the process of political integration without the United Kingdom.

5. CONCLUSIONS

From a cosmopolitan point of view, the interest of the Free World would be served by the integration of an enlarged European Community that is liberal-minded, outward-looking, and concerned with building a bridge between East and West, between developed countries and undeveloped countries, and between free enterprise and socialism.

In reference to his own countrymen, Professor Meade writes:

. . . we must fight against our tiresome fault of self-satisfied priggishness; for there are many very liberal men and women actively engaged in the construction of the new European institutions on the continent of Europe and many illiberal and narrow-minded persons exercising influence in the UK. Nevertheless, there are two facts in UK political life which could enable us to make a significant contribution to the political structure of Europe.

First, while we are bad at many things, we are good at Habeas Corpus, parliamentary democracy, one-man-one-vote, and freedom of speech. This set of Gladstonian virtues may be old-fashioned; but the recent history of Europe makes one realise how foolish it would be to belittle them. Moreover, the Scandinavians and the Swiss—our present partners in the European Free Trade Association (EFTA)—are also good at these same things. If our entry into the EEC brought them in as members or as associates, these liberal forces in Europe would be further strengthened.

Second, both the development of the British Empire into a loose Commonwealth covering all races, all continents, all creeds, all stages of economic development, and most types of economic system and also the use of sterling as a world currency mean that we in the UK have necessarily a habit of looking outward over the world which is less ingrained in most of the continental Europeans.[28]

The United States has been an ardent champion of the EEC, despite the customs union effect, which threatens to expand partner trade at the expense of trade with the outside world. Enlargement of the EEC by the membership of the United Kingdom and others would extend the injury, unless the Community's external tariff is reduced.

From a cosmopolitan point of view the GATT approach is preferable on strictly economic grounds. From a Commonwealth point of view it is certainly preferable. The United States interest lies not so much in having the United Kingdom as a member of the continental club as in having every effort exerted to liberalize the EEC. In sum, it appears that one should not try to put too fine a point on the economic effects of United Kingdom membership in the EEC as compared with a more or less equivalent dose of competition under the GATT. In political terms, however, the integration of Western Europe could make all the difference.

The architects of the EEC are committed to the political unification of Europe, and for this reason the United States has supported the venture. For such a breath-taking accomplishment, the implied economic injury to non-members would be but a small price to pay. But, there can be no guarantee of ultimate success in that undertaking, and in the meantime the progressive integration of only six countries in the heart of Europe runs the risk of dividing, rather than uniting, all of Western Europe.

Once the existing EEC gained momentum and strength, it was but natural for the United States to support British membership, for its ultimate goal is a united Europe based on an expanding world economy. In addition to the reasons for British membership stated so eloquently by Meade, there may also be the particular consideration that "while nurturing her trade with Commonwealth countries and financial ties with the sterling bloc, the British have usually viewed postwar political issues through an Atlantic window."[29]

Whether the United Kingdom will benefit from partnership with the

28. Meade, *UK, Commonwealth and Common Market*, p. 10.
29. Humphrey, *United States and the Common Market*, p. 173.

continent depends not only on the express terms of the Treaty of Rome
but also on the more specific understandings reached during the negotiations for admission. We must recognize, moreover, that the power and
influence of the EEC will assume new proportions with the United
Kingdom as a member. If, as seems likely, Norway, Denmark, and
Ireland follow Britain into the EEC, the Community would then represent 10 per cent more people than the Soviet Union and 25 per cent more
people than the United States. Such an enlarged EEC would produce
more coal and steel than the United States and account for roughly 40
per cent of free-world trade. An economic unit of this magnitude implies
world responsibilities far beyond those of the individual member countries.

The criticism of Britain's vacillation before seeking full membership
is not for acting cautiously but for failing to assess correctly the implications of a successful Common Market with the United Kingdom on the
outside. A venture of such vast import for the future needs the support
of more than a bare majority. In order to succeed, it needs a large
consensus at many levels of private and public life.

The negotiations on United Kingdom membership are complex and
arduous. Many difficult problems must be expressly resolved, and much
also depends on the frame of mind in which Britain enters and is received
into closer association with the continent. Unless there is a substantial
meeting of the minds as well as *pro forma* agreement, British partnership
might stall the momentum of economic integration and, more importantly, of political federation among Germany, France, Benelux, and Italy.
On the other hand, Britain may bring experience and stability to the
partnership that would serve to counterbalance any inward-looking am-
bitions for power that may appear from time to time on the continent.
The problem is how to enlarge and liberalize the EEC without sapping
its vitality and momentum.

Blessed with prosperity and good luck, executives of the EEC have
seized every opportunity to accelerate the established timetable. Although the Common Market has already achieved such momentum that
nations are queuing up to get in or be associated, it "cannot be expected
to sustain its meteoric rise unhindered by the pull of gravity from historic
centers of power, both inside and outside Europe. But, in matters of
such grave moment as the forging of new institutions of government . . .
appropriate to the technology of the Twentieth Century . . . [we are right
to believe] in success until the contrary is demonstrated. . . . It is hard
to know which baggage should be jettisoned first: the unattainable aims

of those who remember nothing of the past or the skepticism of those who see nothing *but* the past."[30]

Should Britain join the Common Market? The question admits of no unqualified answer either from a British or a world point of view. It depends on whether the Community develops the habit of looking out on the world or of resolving its own inner conflicts at the expense of the outside world. And in the end, the decision must be made on a basis of probabilities, rather than certainties.

30. William L. Clayton, assisted by Don D. Humphrey, "U.S. Trade and the Common Market," *Headline Series*, No. 154 (July-August, 1962), p. 8.